A History of the Guards Armoured Formations 1941–1945

A History of the Guards Armoured Formations 1941–1945

Charles Richard Trumpess

Pen & Sword
MILITARY

First published in Great Britain in 2024 by
Pen & Sword Military
An imprint of Pen & Sword Books Limited
Yorkshire – Philadelphia

Copyright © Charles Richard Trumpess 2024

ISBN 978 1 03610 788 8

The right of Charles Richard Trumpess to be identified as
Author of this Work has been asserted by him in accordance
with the Copyright, Designs and Patents Act 1988.

A CIP catalogue record for this book is
available from the British Library

All rights reserved. No part of this book may be reproduced or
transmitted in any form or by any means, electronic or mechanical
including photocopying, recording or by any information storage and
retrieval system, without permission from the Publisher in writing.

Typeset by Mac Style
Printed in the UK by CPI Group (UK) Ltd, Croydon, CR0 4YY.

Pen & Sword Books Limited incorporates the imprints of After
the Battle, Atlas, Archaeology, Aviation, Discovery, Family History,
Fiction, History, Maritime, Military, Military Classics, Politics,
Select, Transport, True Crime, Air World, Frontline Publishing, Leo
Cooper, Remember When, Seaforth Publishing, The Praetorian Press,
Wharncliffe Local History, Wharncliffe Transport, Wharncliffe True
Crime and White Owl.

For a complete list of Pen & Sword titles please contact

PEN & SWORD BOOKS LIMITED
47 Church Street, Barnsley, South Yorkshire, S70 2AS, England
E-mail: enquiries@pen-and-sword.co.uk
Website: www.pen-and-sword.co.uk
or
PEN AND SWORD BOOKS
1950 Lawrence Rd, Havertown, PA 19083, USA
E-mail: uspen-and-sword@casematepublishers.com
Website: www.penandswordbooks.com

Contents

Abbreviations	viii
Acknowledgements	xi
Introduction	xii
Operation GOODWOOD	xvi
Operation BLUECOAT	xvii
Operation MARKET GARDEN	xvii
Operation VERITABLE	xviii
Primary Sources	xviii
Section One: Formation and Training	1
Chapter 1 Armoured Doctrine and the Inter-War Years	3
Plan 1919	4
The Evolution of the Armoured Division	5
Chapter 2 Formation of the Guards Armoured Division	7
Chapter 3 Resistance to Putting Guardsmen into Tanks	9
Was the Conversion to Armour Detrimental to the Infantry?	10
Chapter 4 Early Organisation and Training	14
Battle School, Battle Drill	15
The Imber Incident	16
Battle Drill and Training Deficiencies	17
Lessons Learned and Forgotten	19
Training Ground and Equipment Deficiencies	21
Exercises in Futility?	22
Chapter 5 6th Guards (Armoured/Tank) Brigade	25
Trial by Fire	29

| Chapter 6 | Allan Adair's Fitness to Command | 31 |

Chapter 7	The Guards Ethos	35
Guardsmen Basic Training		35
Recruitment, Selection and Social Elitism		39
The Guards Manpower Crisis		44

Chapter 8	Tanks: Covenanter to the Sherman	46
The M4 Sherman		46
New Equipment, Same Tactics		48
The Churchill Infantry Tank		50

Section Two: Into Battle and Lessons Learned — 53

Chapter 9	Operation GOODWOOD	55
Normandy		55
OVERLORD		55
Prelude to GOODWOOD		56
The Operational Challenges of GOODWOOD		56
The Guards at GOODWOOD		57
Assessment and Legacy of GOODWOOD		59
GOODWOOD Lessons Learned		61

Chapter 10	Learning to Fight in the Bocage	64
A Summary of Lessons Learned		65
A Failure of Application		67

Chapter 11	Operation BLUECOAT	68
Battle of Caumont		70
Lessons Learned by the 6th Guards		75
Post-BLUECOAT Criticism		75

Chapter 12	Tank Casualties and Loss of Confidence	77
Sherman Pros and Cons		78
Survivability		79
The Perception and Reality Gap		81
The Churchill Tank: Overcoming Obstacles		83

Chapter 13	The Liberation of Brussels	86
Operation MARKET GARDEN		86
A Brief Historiography		88
MARKET GARDEN Lessons Learned		89

Operational Character	91
The Failure to Relieve Arnhem	93
Confidence or Conceit?	99
Chapter 14 Operation AINTREE	101
A Guardsman's Testimony	104
A Cuckoo in the Nest	106
Chapter 15 Operation VERITABLE	107
The 6th Guards and the Rhineland Battles	107
Operation BLOCKBUSTER	110
Lessons Learned from VERITABLE	111
An Infantry Battle for an Armoured Division	112
The Application of Lessons Learned in Training	112
Chapter 16 The Division as Learning Organisation	115
Mad Night Dash	117
Artillery, Rockets and Tanks	118
Action at Ems Bridge	119
Chapter 17 6th Guards (Armoured) Brigade: From the Rhine to Münster	121
The Grenadier Guards and British Airborne	124
The Final Push	125
The End of the Guards Armoured Experiment	126
Conclusions	132
Political Effectiveness	132
Strategic Effectiveness	133
Operational Effectiveness	136
Tactical Effectiveness	139
Final Assessment	142
Postscript	146
They Were Not Divided	146
The Book Dispute	148
Rosse and Verney	149
Rosse and Hill	156
A Bridge Too Far	164
Notes	168
Bibliography	190

Abbreviations

AFV	Armoured Fighting Vehicle
AP	Armour-piercing shell
BN	Battalion
BAOR	British Army of the Rhine
CG	Coldstream Guards
CL	Centre line (main axis of advance)
CO	Commanding Officer
COY	Company
DSD	Director of Staff Duties
GAD	Guards Armoured Division
GG	Grenadier Guards
GOC	General Officer Commanding
HC	Hollow charge (explosive warhead designed to penetrate tank armour)
HCR/HHCR	Household Cavalry Regiment
HE	High-explosive shell
IG	Irish Guards
NBA	Net Book Agreement
NCO	Non-commissioned officer
POW	Prisoner of War
RAC	Royal Armoured Corps
RAF	Royal Air Force
RCAF	Royal Canadian Air Force
RE	Royal Engineers
SG	Scots Guards
SHAEF	Supreme Headquarters Allied Expeditionary Force
SQDN	Squadron
TCL	Troop-carrying lorry
TP	Troop
TRG	Training
TEWT	Tactical exercise without troops
WG	Welsh Guards

Second World War British Armoured Divisions

Composition

250 TANKS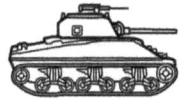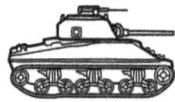

15000 TROOPS

3400 VEHICLES

18%

Tank crew & armoured reconnaissance

25%

Rifle battalions

57%

Support services: artillery, engineers, signals, transport, supply & medical units

Guards Armoured Division

Main Combat Elements

5th Guards (Armoured) Brigade

- 2nd (Armoured) Battalion Grenadier Guards
- 1st (Armoured) Battalion Coldstream Guards
- 2nd (Armoured) Battalion Irish Guards
- 1st (Motor) Battalion Grenadier Guards

32nd (Infantry) Brigade

- Brigade HQ
- Three Rifle Battalions
- Machine-Gun Battalion

Service Arms

- Armoured Car Regiment
- Armoured Recce Regiment
- Anti-Tank Regiment Royal Artillery
- Anti-Aircraft Regiment
- Field Regiments Royal Artillery
- Field Squadrons Royal Engineers

Battlegroups – November 1944 – May 1945

5th Guards (Armoured) Brigade)

Grenadier Guards Battlegroup

2nd (Armoured) Battalion Grenadier Guards
- Battalion HQ
- 1 Recce Squadron
- 1 Maintenance Troop

1st (Motor) Rifle Battalion Grenadier Guards
- Battalion HQ
- 1 Support Company

Irish Guards Battlegroup

2nd (Armoured) Battalion, Irish Guards
- Battalion HQ
- 1 Recce Squadron
- 1 Maintenance Troop

3rd Irish Guards Infantry Battalion
- Battalion HQ
- 1 Support Company

32nd (Infantry) Brigade

Coldstream Guards Battlegroup

1st (Armoured) Battalion Coldstream Guards
- Battalion HQ
- 1 Recce Squadron
- 1 Maintenance Troop

5th Coldstream Guards Infantry Battalion
- Battalion HQ
- 1 Support Company

Welsh Guards Battlegroup

2nd (Armoured) Battalion Welsh Guards (Armoured Recce Regiment)
- Regimental Head Quarters
- 1 Recce Squadron

1st Welsh Guards Infantry Battalion, replaced by 2nd Battalion Scots Guards from March 1945
- Battalion HQ
- 1 Support Company

2nd Household Cavalry Regiment, Divisional Armoured Car Regiment attached from Corps

6th Guards (Tank) Brigade

Main Combat Elements

4th Tank Battalion Grenadier Guards
- Battalion HQ
- 1 Recce Troop
- 1 Maintenance Troop

4th Tank Battalion Coldstream Guards
- Battalion HQ
- 1 Recce Troop
- 1 Maintenance Troop

3rd Tank Battalion Scots Guards
- Battalion HQ
- 1 Recce Troop
- 1 Maintenance Troop

Acknowledgements

I would like to express my thanks to the people who made this book possible. I am indebted to Margaret Hensey for diligently conducting research of the Rosse Papers, Birr Castle Archives. Similarly, I must thank Lisa Shortall, archivist, Offaly Archives, for her kind assistance in accessing the Birr Castle Archives. My appreciation also goes to Lord and Lady Rosse for allowing us access to the Rosse Papers.

I am extremely grateful to Colonel (Retd) Tom Bonas, Regimental Adjutant, Regimental Headquarters Welsh Guards; Christopher Enraght-Moony, Regimental Archivist, Welsh Guards; and Major (Retd) Robert Cazenove, Regimental Headquarters Coldstream Guards, Wellington Barracks, London, for their kind assistance with my research.

I would like to thank my good friend and graphic designer David Busbridge, BrightBulb, who created the series of maps that help to illustrate the historical narrative of this book. I would also like to thank the members of the 6th Guards Tank Brigade Facebook Group for their help and support in researching this book, especially Bernie Hudson and Philip Goodfellow for sharing the stories of their relatives who served with the Brigade.

Finally, I must extend my thanks to the staff of the National Archives, Kew, London, Imperial War Museum, London; Templer Study Centre, National Army Museum, London; The Liddell Hart Centre for Military Archives, King's College London; Churchill Archives Centre, Cambridge; University of Buckingham Library; and The Second World War Experience Centre, West Yorkshire.

Introduction

This book is about the Guards Armoured Division and its sister formation, the 6th Guards (Tank) Brigade. Although the two formations shared a common origin, they went on to forge very different operational records. One unit's record would be tarnished by failures while the other would be applauded for its successes. In 1945, with the war in Europe won, they would be reunited on a bleak German airfield to say farewell. During the intervening years, they faced criticism, public ridicule, the threat of disbandment, and many other challenges. Nevertheless, these armoured Guardsmen would ultimately prevail on the battlefield.

History is dynamic, not static. The historian must examine and interpret the available evidence to arrive at the best estimate of the facts. However, a complete, perfect picture of the past will forever elude us. Certainly, in researching and writing this book I have attempted to piece together the facts from a jigsaw of primary and secondary sources. Nevertheless, at various junctures in the writing of this book, I have had to hypothesise about certain events and the motivations of key actors. Perhaps you will agree with my assessments and conclusions. Perhaps not. Conceivably, tomorrow another historian will discover some long-forgotten document that casts a whole new light on this story, but for today, let us proceed.

In response to the threat of German invasion, the Guards Armoured Division formed in the spring of 1941. The Guards Armoured was one of eleven armoured divisions raised by the British Army during the Second World War.[1] Initially, the Division consisted of two armoured brigades, each of three armoured battalions, a motor battalion, and a support group, mainly of artillery.[2] As the name suggests, the Guards Armoured Division consisted of battalions of Foot Guards and a contingent of Household Cavalry. The organisation of the Division would change several times over the years to improve balance and ensure greater armoured and infantry co-operation.

But why convert the Foot Guards, considered by many to be first-class infantry, into an armoured formation?[3] Newspaper articles including one in the *Daily Herald* asked sceptically if 'spit-and-polish' Guardsmen could ever adapt to a new armoured role.[4] As the threat of invasion receded, the Guards Armoured

Division and 6th Guards (Tank) Brigade embarked on years of training while the war raged elsewhere.

This book examines the decision to form the Guards Armoured Division and then keep it at home for an extended period of training once the threat of invasion had passed. We will consider whether the Guards battalions would have been better employed earlier overseas in an infantry role. Once deployed to Normandy, the fighting quickly revealed shortcomings in the Division's training and equipment. The Division would have to adopt new operational and tactical procedures. In contrast, the 6th Guards (Tank) Brigade's first action during Operation BLUECOAT was both a success and an affirmation of its training with the 15th (Scottish) Division.

The primary focus of my research has been to examine whether the expedient of transforming battalions of Foot Guards into an armoured division was successful or should the Guards have been retained in their infantry role? This introduction summarises the relevant historiography on the subject and raises several questions about forming the Guards Armoured Division, training, ethos, and combat effectiveness.

A great deal has been written about the campaign for north-west Europe. However, since 1955 only three books have been published on the history of the Guards Armoured Division. The remaining titles on the subject can be categorised thematically by memoir and biography, unit, formation, operation, campaign history and strategic analysis.

The first of these titles, written by Major General G.L. Verney, was published in 1955, *The Guards Armoured Division, A Short History*.[5] The official divisional history was released the following year, entitled *The Story of the Guards Armoured Division*, by Captain the Earl of Rosse and Colonel E.R. Hill.[6] Both books are largely amalgamations of regimental war diaries. The third title, published in 1979, is the *British Guards Armoured Division* by John Sandars and Michael Chappell.[7] In this book, the whole history of the Division is condensed into forty pages. Additionally, in 1946, the *6th Guards Tank Brigade: The Story of Guardsmen in Churchill Tanks* by Patrick Forbes was published.[8]

A question to be examined in this book is why the Guards Armoured Division's extensive training failed to prepare it adequately for operations in Normandy. Rosse and Hill, for example, dedicate just fourteen pages to the formation, training, and reorganisation of the Division between the spring of 1941 and June 1944. Similarly, Verney covers the same period and subject matter in sixteen pages. Additionally, there is some variance of opinion on precisely who suggested raising a Guards Armoured Division in the first place.

The Guards Armoured Division was formed from battalions of the Grenadier, Coldstream, Scots, Irish, Welsh Guards and 2nd Household Cavalry Regiment.

Between 1946 and 1956, the following series of official Guards and Household Cavalry regimental histories were published that cover the Second World War: *Welsh Guards at War* (1946) by Major L.F. Ellis,[9] *The Grenadier Guards in the War of 1939–1945: The Campaigns in North-West Europe* (1949) by Patrick Forbes,[10] *History of the Irish Guards in the Second World War* (1949) by Major D.J.L. Fitzgerald,[11] *The Coldstream Guards: 1920–1946* (1951) by Michael Howard and John Sparrow,[12] *The Household Cavalry at War: Second Household Cavalry Regiment* (1953) by Roden Orde[13] and *The Scots Guards: 1919–1955* (1956) by David Erskine.[14] Each of these books follows a similar expository style, format and chronology. Each book covers the formation, organisation, and training of the Guards Armoured Division in similarly brief, prosaic narratives. They mainly offer uncritical, subjective interpretations of events.

An online search of *The Guards Magazine* archive returned 200 results based on the term 'Guards Armoured Division'.[15] The majority of search results were death notices, obituaries, anniversaries and the like. Of the 200 results, twenty-three articles and book reviews mentioned the Guards Armoured Division. Overall, these articles contribute little new information to help answer the questions this book poses. However, one piece did offer some interesting insights. An article by General Sir Michael Gow, Scots Guards, entitled 'Churchill and the Foot Guards in World War Two', examines how the prime minister, Winston Churchill, resisted attempts to reduce or disband Guards formations due to manpower shortages within the army.[16] This piece helps illustrate the unique position the Guards occupied within the army and the British establishment. It also touches on the question of whether the Guards Armoured Division should have remained an armoured formation or reverted to an infantry role.

Although not specifically about the Guards armoured formations, a series of secondary sources discuss British armoured doctrine, organisation, training, equipment, and leadership. Timothy Harrison Place's *Military Training in the British Army* is of particular interest.[17] Harrison Place maintains that Britain's failure to develop a uniform doctrine of armoured warfare across the British Army during the 1920s and 1930s had severe consequences during the Second World War. According to Harrison Place, the British Army was poorly trained, ill-equipped, and badly led throughout the campaign in north-west Europe. If Harrison Place is correct, then the Guards Armoured Division was a product of this dysfunctional training system and destined to fail. However, Harrison Place is also critical of how the 6th Guards (Tank) Brigade prepared for war. My research contradicts his assertion that the 6th Guards training was equally deficient to that of its sister formation. This book examines the gap between training theory and operational practice and what that meant for the Guards.

Why the War Office felt the need to rush new armoured divisions into service in 1941 requires an understanding of British armoured doctrine during the 1920s and 1930s. Books such as *Men, Ideas and Tanks* by J.P. Harris,[18] *To Change an Army* by Harold R. Winton,[19] and *Raising Churchill's Army* by David French help explain the disorganised mechanisation process during the inter-war years and the lack of a coherent armoured doctrine in 1939.[20] However, for all its deficiencies, the army was able to recover the situation by 1942 and steadily improve its performance. French argues that a uniform concept of doctrine, strategy and tactics coalesced around the forceful, egocentric personality of Field Marshal Montgomery (promoted September 1944). As the 21st Army Group commander, he created a master plan for his campaigns in north-west Europe.

In John Buckley's two books, *Monty's Men*[21] and *British Armour in the Normandy Campaign 1944*,[22] he comes to the same conclusions as Harrison Place and David French on doctrine. Buckley argues that the British Army had no coherent armoured doctrine in 1939 and misinterpreted the German successes of 1940, mistakenly seeing the tank as the primary weapon on the battlefield. In both books, Buckley provides only brief descriptions of the formation and operations of the Guards Armoured Division and 6th Guards (Tank) Brigade. In *British Armour in the Normandy Campaign 1944* he argues that after a faltering start, British armoured formations learned to adapt to changing situations on the battlefield better than the Germans. In this book, I will examine the performance of the Guards armoured formations as learning organisations and how they translated lessons learned into operational and tactical improvements.

In his book *The Sharp End: The Fighting Man in World War II* John Ellis examines the experiences of soldiers from induction and training to combat.[23] Based mainly on veterans' testimonies, he explains why the Guards Armoured Division was considered an exemplar of close infantry and armoured co-operation because units of the same regiment were brigaded together and had trained and operated jointly for a long period.

Browned Off and Bloody-Minded by Alan Allport examines how Churchill's army was raised, trained, and fought the Second World War.[24] The book touches on the reasons for the formation of new armoured divisions in 1941. Interestingly, Allport argues that little thought was given to transforming Guards battalions into an armoured division and suggests the decision was a mistake. However, he only uses the testimony of Lord Carrington, who was a junior officer in the Grenadier Guards at the time, as evidence for his conclusions.[25] There is a consensus between David French, Buckley, and Ellis that British armoured formations did adapt successfully to fighting in Normandy despite deficiencies in doctrine, training, and equipment. However, when it comes to the Guards Armoured Division, opinions diverge. Alan Allport argues that the transformation to armour was a mistake and waste of good infantry.

In contrast, John Ellis believed the brigading together of infantry and armour from the same regiments was advantageous. Lord Carrington was not alone in his criticism of taking trained infantrymen and converting them to armour. However, he also believed that his division became a skilled armoured formation once the conversion was complete. In his memoir, Lord Carrington mentions the success achieved by brigading men of the same regiments together.[26] This book examines this dichotomy of transforming infantry to armour and assesses the outcomes.

The lack of literature that focuses exclusively on the Guards Armoured Division and 6th Guards (Tank) Brigade is somewhat offset by the numerous titles that examine many aspects of its operational history. The most noteworthy of these operations include Operations GOODWOOD, SPRING, GROUSE, MARKET GARDEN, VERITABLE and PLUNDER. It was not within the scope of my research to attempt to examine the history of every operation undertaken by the Guards. Instead, I have focused on four operational case studies: GOODWOOD, BLUECOAT, MARKET GARDEN and VERITABLE to help provide the necessary context to answer the questions posed in this book.

Operation GOODWOOD

Operation GOODWOOD continues to generate a good deal of historical debate and controversy. Subsequently, it has become a popular subject for academics, historians, and military theorists. However, this book will confine itself to discussing the performance of the Guards Armoured Division during GOODWOOD and its aftermath.

Ian Daglish's book *Operation GOODWOOD*[27] starts with a quote from *The Story of the Guards Armoured Division* for 18 July 1944, which describes the nature of the fighting as extremely confused.[28] The author describes the Guards as full of enthusiasm before their first engagement but poorly prepared for the coming battle. He argues that the Guards pre-invasion training had focused mainly on weapons proficiency rather than battlefield tactics and that infantry and armour had never worked together. Overall, Daglish's assessment of the Division is a negative one. He sees the Guards as a highly disciplined but inflexible organisation, led by arrogant, aristocratic officers unwilling or unable to learn the all-arms tactics required to fight in Normandy. However, immediately after GOODWOOD, the Guards and 11th Armoured Divisions would take the lessons learned and reorganise their formations to improve infantry and armoured co-operation down to the company and squadron level.

This book examines the Guards' ethos and unique position within the army and the British establishment.

In his article 'The Test of Command: McNaughton and Exercise "Spartan"', John Nelson Rickard examines General A.G.L. McNaughton's removal from command of the 1st Canadian Army following exercise SPARTAN in March 1943.[29] During this exercise, the Guards Armoured Division, minus its infantry, was hurled against a well-prepared defensive line equipped with anti-tank guns and repulsed with heavy casualties. The following year, the Division found itself in a remarkably similar situation during Operation GOODWOOD. As Daglish suggested, the Guards appeared to have learned little from their training at home.

Operation BLUECOAT

Designed to alleviate pressure on the American breakout across the Cotentin Peninsula at the end of July 1944, Operation BLUECOAT was the 6th Guards (Tank) Brigade's first battle. It was also the only occasion when elements of both Guards armoured formations operated together. Ian Daglish's book *Operation Bluecoat* examines the campaign in great detail. He dedicates a chapter to the break-in operation conducted by the 15th (Scottish) and the 6th Guards (Tank) Brigade that secured vital high ground south of Caumont on Sunday, 30 July. Daglish also observes how British armoured formations had started restructuring to improve co-ordination between tanks and infantry.[30] Major J.J. How's *Normandy: The British Breakout* contends that 1 August 1944 was the day the battle for Normandy was decided, and it was Operation BLUECOAT that triggered the eventual collapse of German forces in France. However, his book only contains passing references to the Guards' operational role during BLUECOAT.[31] John Buckley takes a more critical view of the operation in his book *Monty's Men: The British Army and the Liberation of Europe.*[32] The operation cost 2nd Army a heavy toll in casualties that it could not afford to pay. Subsequently, several senior commanders were sacked by Montgomery for unsatisfactory performance. As a reward for its success during Operation BLUECOAT, the 6th Guards (Tank) Brigade lost Brigadier Gerald Lloyd-Verney, who replaced Major General Erskine as commander of the 7th Armoured Division, the famous Desert Rats.

Operation MARKET GARDEN

The failure of Operation MARKET GARDEN continues to excite historical debate. However, this book only focuses on the operational role and combat performance of the Guards Armoured Divisions during MARKET GARDEN.

Several common themes emerge from the secondary literature on MARKET GARDEN and the role of the Guards Armoured Division. In *Operation MARKET GARDEN*, edited by John Buckley and Peter Preston-Hough, John Peaty questions whether elite forces such as the Guards Armoured Division and 1st Airborne Division would not have contributed more to the war effort as line infantry.[33] Peaty concludes that on balance, neither the Guards nor Airborne made a sufficient contribution to the war effort to justify their elite status. This special or elite status afforded the Guards is something we will examine. In William F. Buckingham's *Arnhem 1944*[34] and Antony Beevor's *Arnhem*,[35] both authors are critical of the Guards' sluggish performance and rigid observance of military conventions.

Operation VERITABLE

Operation VERITABLE cleared German forces between the River Maas and Rhine in conjunction with the American Operation GRENADE. The intention had been for the Canadian 1st Army to breach the German lines, after which the Guards Armoured Division would exploit the gap created. However, poor weather, topography, and the destruction of the Roer dams turned the battlefield into a quagmire. Instead of the quick armoured thrust anticipated, the 5th Guards (Armoured) Brigade was held in reserve for much of the battle. VERITABLE would be the Guards' last major battle of the war. Books such as W.D. and S. Whitaker's *Rhineland*[36] and R.W. Thompson's *The Battle for the Rhineland*[37] provide detailed accounts of Operation VERITABLE and the role played predominantly by the 32nd Guards (Infantry) Brigade. However, these secondary sources are written in an expository style, presenting the known facts with little analysis or opinion. The 6th Guards (Tank) Brigade operated in Brigade Groups, first under the command of the 15th (Scottish) Division and then the 3rd British Division during VERITABLE. Although the 6th Guards was redesignated an armoured brigade in early February, they would remain in an infantry support role throughout the operation. In books such as *Monty's Iron Sides: From the Normandy Beaches to Bremen with the 3rd Division*[38] by Patrick Delaforce and *The Iron Division: The History of the 3rd Division 1809–1989*[39] by Robin McNish, the 6th Guards are acknowledged for their steadfast support of the infantry during weeks of bitter fighting.

Primary Sources

In his memoir, *A Guards' General*, Major General Sir Allan Adair describes the formation of the Guards Armoured Division.[40] In September 1942, Adair replaced Oliver Leese as division commander. He briefly describes the long period of training before deployment to Normandy. He recalled how this period of command of the Division was most difficult for him. Critics repeatedly told him that Guards' discipline and training were too reminiscent of the parade ground and would stifle the initiative required for armoured warfare. In his memoir, Adair focuses on recounting various operations rather than reprise the entire campaign for north-west Europe. He is also rather selective in his reminiscences. He never mentions that Montgomery wanted him removed from command.

There is a range of published primary source material from veterans of the Guards Armoured Division. *Esprit de Corps* by W.A. Elliott is the wartime diary of a junior officer in the 2nd Battalion, Scots Guards, who served in Italy and later with the Division.[41] In Lord Carrington's memoirs, *Reflect on Things Past*, he briefly describes his time with the Guards Armoured Division and recollects major operations such as GOODWOOD, the liberation of Brussels and MARKET GARDEN.[42] Although Lord Carrington thought the Guards Armoured had done what was expected of them during the war, he questioned the wisdom of forming the Division. In William Eager's self-published book, *Beyond the Rhine – The Sacrificial Lamb*, he briefly recounts his time in the 2nd (Armoured) Battalion, Irish Guards.[43] Robert Boscawen's *Armoured Guardsmen* is the author's wartime diary, later augmented with a series of factual corrections.[44] The book mainly focuses on the author's experiences in north-west Europe until he was wounded on Easter Day 1945. B.D. Wilson served as a junior officer with the 3rd Battalion, Irish Guards. His book, *The Ever Open Eye*, describes training and operations across north-west Europe until he was severely wounded in Holland.[45] Although subjective, his book is very critical of the Division's training and the abilities of senior commanders. In the memoirs of General Sir David Fraser, entitled *Wars and Shadows*, he goes into some detail about the pros and cons of raising the Guards Armoured Division.[46] He also discusses the lack of coherent armoured doctrine, minimal all-arms training, and command and tactical planning weaknesses. *The Times of My Life* by Sir John Gorman repeats many of Fraser's criticisms about a lack of armoured doctrine and all-arms training.[47] Gorman says that he could not understand why it took the Division so long to form Regimental Battlegroups, which did not happen until the end of August 1944. *The Whitelaw Memoirs* by William Whitelaw, 3rd Battalion, Scots Guards, only gives a brief description of his wartime experiences serving with the 6th Guards (Tank) Brigade.[48] However, Charles Farrell, Scots Guards, gives a much more in-depth analysis of the 6th Guards (Tank) Brigade's wartime performance in his book, *Reflections 1939–1945: A Scots Guards Officer in Training and War*.[49]

The primary focus of my research was to examine whether converting battalions of Foot Guards and elements of the Household Cavalry into armoured formations was successful. As the war progressed, the British Army had an abundance of armour and a chronic shortage of trained infantrymen. This lack of infantrymen inevitably raises a series of secondary research questions.

First, would the Guards Armoured Division have contributed more to the war effort if its battalions had remained infantrymen? Second, after nearly three years at home, why did the Division's training programmes fail to prepare it adequately for combat? Third, how did the Brigade of Guards' ethos, based on centuries of tradition, a culture of elitism, rigid discipline, and adherence to its own set of standards, positively or negatively influence the formation, leadership, training and operational efficiency of the Division and the 6th Guards (Tank) Brigade? Finally, the Guards Armoured Division repeatedly reorganised to improve the balance of its teeth or fighting arms and support services to meet its operational responsibilities. To what extent can we describe the Division as a learning organisation? How successful was it at assimilating new information and experiences to improve military effectiveness?

Section One

Formation and Training

Chapter One

Armoured Doctrine and the Inter-War Years

Before we look specifically at the raising of the Guards Armoured Division, it is important to understand the development of armoured doctrine within the British Army during the inter-war period.

The tank first saw combat at the Battle of Flers-Courcelette on 15 September 1916 during the First World War.[1] A British invention, the tank was hoped to break the stalemate of the Western Front. Instead, British artillery, aircraft and improved infantry weapons and tactics contributed more to the Allied victory of 1918 than the tank. Nevertheless, the tank had shown promise. After the war, the British Army entered a period of experimentation in tank design and development and armoured formations' strategic and tactical employment. However, the economic crash of 1929 and the subsequent Great Depression severely curtailed British military spending on tank development. It can be argued that the British did not design and build a first-rate tank until Centurion, which entered service in 1945 but did not see action.[2]

The Infantry Tank Mark II, commonly known as the Matilda, performed well for the British Army between 1940 and 1943. However, as a thickly armoured Infantry tank, the Matilda was slow and required a good deal of preventive maintenance. While not initially a problem, the Matilda's 2-pounder (40mm) main gun was soon outclassed by improved German tank guns and new medium and heavy tanks like the Panther and Tiger. The Matilda's gun fired armour-piercing (AP) rounds and did not have a reliable high-explosive (HE) capability. High-explosive ammunition was available, but it was rarely issued to Matilda crews and mainly proved ineffective against anti-tank guns and dug-in infantry.[3]

Dating back to the 1930s, the British Army had adopted a dual approach to tank development and employment. The British settled on a heavily armoured but slow Infantry tank, or 'I' tank, which could support foot soldiers in the attack, and a lightly armoured, faster Cruiser tank capable of independent action.

To understand why the War Office felt the need to rush new armoured divisions such as the Guards Armoured into service in 1941 requires an understanding of British armoured doctrine during the 1920s and 1930s. The British Army of the inter-war years had to meet its operational objectives on an extremely tight financial budget. Reduced in size and with limited resources after the First

World War, the army focused on immediate priorities such as policing the British Empire instead of preparing for another European conflict. Safeguarding the interests of the Empire required motor transport and armoured cars; vehicles capable of moving troops quickly to potential hotspots of civil unrest.[4] Some inside the British military and political establishments saw the development and maintenance of armoured formations as an expensive and unnecessary luxury. In 1919, Major General Sir Louis Jackson told an audience of the Royal United Services Institution that the tank was a freak only called into creation due to the unique circumstances of trench warfare on the Western Front.[5] Nevertheless, there was a general acceptance of the need for mechanisation across the British Army but differences of opinion about the employment of tanks.

As well as its critics, the tank had its champions both inside and outside the army, including J.F.C. Fuller, George Lindsay, Charles Broad, Percy Hobart, Frederick Pile and Basil Liddell Hart. Colonels J.F.C. Fuller and George Lindsay favoured tanks and armoured car formations with a minor role for infantry.[6]

Plan 1919

In the summer of 1918, Colonel J.F.C. Fuller was one of several British Army officers formulating theories about how tanks, aircraft and mechanised troops might be deployed to break the stalemate of trench warfare on the Western Front and achieve an Allied victory in 1919. However, Fuller's plans were overtaken by events and the defeat of Germany in November 1918.

What became known as Fuller's Plan 1919 did not evolve in isolation. For example, Major General Sir John Capper produced a paper entitled 'Proposals for the Use of Tanks in the Campaign of 1919' dated 21 January 1918. Fuller prepared his paper, 'The Tactics of the Attack as Affected by the Speed and Circuit of the Medium D Tank', in May 1918.[7] In turn, Fuller's paper was followed by another from Capper in July 1918.

Fuller's proposal envisaged the use of around 5,000 tanks, motorised infantry, and new ground-attack aircraft. In addition, Fuller's theory incorporated the use of a new kind of tank, the Medium D, which was faster and more manoeuvrable than anything previously available. Fuller's plan required the new medium tanks to exploit a breach in the enemy lines and then attack its headquarters, effectively removing the snake's head. However, Plan 1919 was less an operational plan and more an expression of a new operational idea to harness mechanical power and new technologies to gain a strategic, possibly war-winning advantage over the enemy.

Fuller's Plan 1919 would be published on several occasions during the inter-war period, including his memoirs in 1936. Captain Basil Liddell Hart, another armoured warfare advocate and theorist, subsequently promoted some of Fuller's ideas.

The theories in Plan 1919 contributed to the eventual dual approach to armoured doctrine adopted by the British that required role-specific vehicles. First, a heavily armoured but slow Infantry tank, designed to break through the enemy lines. Next, a fast-moving, lightly armoured Cruiser tank to exploit the breach. The Cruiser tanks would cut enemy lines of communications and disrupt command and control, performing a similar role to traditional horse cavalry. However, the eventual settling of the dual approach to armoured doctrine was not the logical consequence of a carefully considered plan.[8]

The Evolution of the Armoured Division

On 1 May 1927, the Experimental Mechanical Force was officially formed under Brigadier R.J. Collins. It consisted of a battalion of medium tanks, a battalion of armoured cars and tankettes, a motorised machine gun battalion, artillery, and engineers. The Experimental Mechanised Force developed many of the elements that would later be incorporated into British armoured divisions' organisational structure.[9]

In the 1930s, the army did progress with mechanisation and equipping units with tanks. However, too many types of tank formations emerged with infantry, medium and light tanks. Before the Second World War, the medium tank programme was abandoned due to technical and financial reasons. J.P. Harris explains, 'A general dissatisfaction with the underpowered medium tank prototypes of the mid-1930s led to the bifurcation of British medium tank development.'[10]

The failure of the medium tank project resulted in two types of tanks allocated to distinct formations. The slow, heavily armoured Infantry support tanks would be assigned to independent tank brigades that operated outside of divisional control. The faster, more manoeuvrable Cruiser tanks would form the basis of armoured divisions, initially of two armoured brigades with limited infantry and artillery support. Consequently, two types of armoured formation developed separate doctrines and operating procedures, which made achieving all-arms co-operation difficult. Historian and author Jonathan Fennell suggests that the British Army recognised the need for all-arms action, but its own organisational structure constantly prevented it from fulfilling this aim.[11] Williamson Murray, an American historian and author, suggests that part of the problem was how the army approached training. There was nothing to frame or unify the numerous decentralised training programmes. The British Army possessed no commonly understood battle doctrine.

As a result of the lack of a common battle doctrine, the army's various combat arms and supporting services tended to train in isolation, giving little thought or consideration to how their sister arms and services operated.[12] The compartmentalising of Infantry and Cruiser tanks was probably more detrimental than supportive in achieving all-arms co-operation. Specialisation tended to encourage what Murray calls the 'We-They' syndrome, whereby combat arms and services were often more suspicious, competitive, or antagonistic than collaborative in their relations with one another.[13]

Like its cavalry predecessors, the armoured division was designed to exploit the breakthrough and disrupt an enemy's communication and supply lines. The Cruiser tank became the principal armoured fighting vehicle (AFV) of the armoured division, but the right balance of forces was initially hampered by a lack of available tanks and an under-appreciation of the role of infantry and support services. Experience from North Africa in 1941 demonstrated that armoured brigades required more infantry than a motor battalion and more firepower with field artillery and anti-tank guns as part of the Support Group.[14]

Armoured divisions were not designed or equipped to attack fortified defensive positions. Nevertheless, they were mishandled in Normandy, most notably during Operation GOODWOOD, where airpower was supposed to breach the enemy line.[15] We will examine Operation GOODWOOD in more detail later.

The dual approach to armoured doctrine was fine in theory and during peacetime exercises but proved a failure on the battlefield. It soon became apparent that getting the right type of tank in the correct place at the exact time was seldom possible during wartime. Instead, the tank on the spot had to be able to deal with whatever the situation demanded. It was only towards the end of the war that the British adopted the idea of a universal or multi-role tank, the first being the Centurion.[16] Lieutenant General Martel, head of the Royal Armoured Corps (RAC), remained steadfast in his belief that the dual approach of Infantry and Cruiser tanks was the correct one. He strongly disagreed with General, later Field Marshal, Montgomery, who advocated the idea of equipping armoured forces with a single, multi-role tank.[17]

The British Army's failure to formulate and establish an explicit doctrine of armoured warfare during the 1920s and 1930s had many causes. The British Army ranked second in spending priorities for most of the inter-war period. The Royal Navy received most of the money for home defence, followed by the army. However, most of the army's spending went on mechanisation and policing the Empire. Prolonged underinvestment in the Royal Tank Corps, coupled with a political unwillingness to rearm from the mid-1930s, contributed greatly to Britain's lack of preparation for war.[18]

Chapter Two

Formation of the Guards Armoured Division

The Guards Armoured Division formed in the spring of 1941 in response to the continued threat of German invasion of the British Isles. Precisely where the original idea came from to convert battalions of Foot Guards and regiments from the Household Cavalry into an armoured division remains obscure and inconclusive. However, I do suggest a likely hypothesis.

In *The Guards Armoured Division, A Short History* by Major General G.L. Verney, he states that the government decided on a large increase in armoured formations, which subsequently gave rise to the formation of the Division.[1] In the official division history, *The Story of the Guards Armoured Division*, Rosse and Hill suggest that the idea of raising a Guards Armoured Division came from the Commander-in-Chief, Home Forces, General Sir Alan Brooke (later Field Marshal, 1st Viscount Alanbrooke).[2] However, Brooke's diaries make no mention of the Guards Armoured Division until 26 May 1941,[3] while Patrick Forbes, who co-authored the regimental history of the Grenadier Guards during the Second World War and wrote a history of the 6th Guards (Tank) Brigade, says the idea came from the Army Council.[4]

In his memoir, General Sir David Fraser contends that converting Guards battalions to an armoured role had a distinctly political element.[5] The defeat of France and evacuation of the British Expeditionary Force (BEF) from Dunkirk in 1940 had left the British Army's reputation tarnished as old-fashioned, backwards looking and ill-equipped to fight a modern, mechanised war. Fraser suggests that 'the conversion of those pillars of tradition, the Guards, to an eminently twentieth-century role would provide additional evidence of determined modernity'.[6] Fraser's assertion that politics and army public relations played a part in the Guards formation of an armoured division might be correct. However, Guards units were stationed around London during the spring of 1941, making them a convenient choice for armour conversion.[7]

Rowland Ryder's biography of Oliver Leese perhaps gets closest to the truth about the origin of the Guards Armoured Division. Ryder suggests the Division was the brainchild of General Alan Brooke, C-in-C Home Forces at the time.[8] After all, Brooke commanded the experimental Mobile Division in 1937, which would become the 1st Armoured Division. Brooke's cousin, Sir Bertram Sergison-

Brooke, was Major General commanding the Brigade of Guards and General Officer Commanding (GOC) London District until 1942. According to Ryder, it was Sergison-Brooke who recommended Leese as Division commander of the new formation. In a farewell letter to the Brigade of Guards circulated in Battalion Orders, dated 1 June 1942, Sergison-Brooke wrote, 'It was without hesitation that I recommended a year ago that an armoured division should be formed from the resources of the Brigade.'[9]

It is clear from General Alan Brooke's diaries that he and his cousin were close and socialised frequently. On 1 May 1941, Brooke attended a 1st Armoured Division exercise, and on 5 May, he took part in a Tank Parliament at 10 Downing Street, where tank production and expansion were discussed. On 26 May 1941, Brooke writes that his cousin 'Bertie' (Sergison-Brooke) is sailing ahead with the Division's composition after overcoming opposition.[10] From the available evidence, it seems likely that the idea to raise a Guards Armoured Division was a joint enterprise between the two cousins. General Brooke was a proponent of armoured forces, and his cousin was responsible for both the defence of London and promoting the interests of the Brigade of Guards.

In his book *Our Armoured Forces*, Lieutenant General Martel explains that in April 1941 the Royal Armoured Corps was ready to expand beyond its five armoured divisions and three tank brigades. He says that having decided to convert infantry formations wholesale to armour, 'The first decision arrived at was to form a Guards armoured division, but it was not reached without a good deal of trouble.' The War Office wanted Guardsmen to leave the Guards and join the Royal Armoured Corps. The Royal Armoured Corps, and probably the Brigade of Guards, resisted the idea of a new Guards division becoming 'part and parcel' of the Royal Armoured Corps. Eventually, the War Office relented and sanctioned the raising of a Guards armoured division, 'which would always be supplied and manned by Guardsmen'. Martel provides no explanation as to why the War Office was so adamant about transferring Guardsmen into the Royal Armoured Corps. The Guards possessed a great deal of autonomy within the British Army, recruiting and training its own men, for example. Perhaps the War Office predicted administrative, manpower, and resourcing problems ahead.[11]

Without fanfare, the formation of the Guards Armoured Division took place in a house in Weybridge, Surrey, on 19 June 1941 when a skeleton headquarters was inaugurated. Brigadier, acting Major General, Oliver Leese was telephoned by Lieutenant General Sir Bertram 'Boy' Brook, then General Officer Commanding (GOC) London District, informing him that he had been selected to command the new division.[12]

Chapter Three

Resistance to Putting Guardsmen into Tanks

In 1941, the formation of the Guards Armoured Division did not pass without controversy. The main question about the Division's formation was why waste highly trained infantrymen by converting them to armour? This question was buttressed by a series of subsidiary concerns about Guardsmen's physical, intellectual, and psychological suitability for tank warfare. Patrick Forbes suggests that 'it was a far-sighted and an extremely bold decision: far-sighted because, besides ensuring that the Army would have more armour to resist invasion, it created a formidable striking force for future offensive operations; bold because the Brigade of Guards had had no previous experience of armoured warfare. But bolder still because there were many responsible persons who predicted that Guardsmen, on account of their height and of their discipline and training, would never be successful in tanks.'[1] Hindsight, not foresight, seems to have prompted Forbes to write with such hyperbolic sentiment.

As we have seen, the Guards Armoured Division was raised in response to the German threat of invasion. Nevertheless, it can be argued that the Division was founded on a false assumption or misunderstanding by the British Army and War Office that the tank was the pre-eminent weapon on the battlefield. After France's defeat in 1940, new British armoured formations were raised on a misguided belief that the tank was a war-winning weapon. It was actually the speed, flexibility and all-arms capabilities demonstrated by German panzer divisions that made them such formidable opponents.[2] The initial organisational structure of the Guards Armoured Division, composed of two armoured brigades, each of three armoured regiments and just one motor battalion of infantry, underlines the point. It can also be argued that the British misjudged the relative importance of the German panzer divisions in their swift victory of May 1940. Author of the *History of the Irish Guards in the Second World War*, Desmond Fitzgerald wrote, 'According to the popular military theory at this time the infantry was already an obsolete arm. The Germans had won the Battle of France with unsupported armoured divisions, and the only answer to them was more armoured divisions.'[3]

In June 1940, a committee was hastily organised to review the Dunkirk debacle, chaired by General Sir William Bartholomew. Less than a month later, the committee published its findings and lessons learned from Dunkirk in the Bartholomew Report.[4] The report was critical of the defensive posture adopted by the BEF and its allies, suggesting it blunted the troops' offensive spirit. It recommended closer co-operation between the army and Royal Air Force. The report also advised the army to increase the number of tanks and anti-tank guns as a matter of urgency.[5] Military historian and author Martin Samuels suggests that senior officers came back from Dunkirk convinced little was wrong with the army's organisational structure and procedures. Instead, they preferred to believe that the defeat was due to a lack of aggression in British troops, the weakness of Britain's allies, and Germany's numerical and technical superiority.[6] Perhaps asking the army to examine, diagnose and remedy its own failings immediately after a major defeat was unrealistic.

Lord Peter Carrington, a former Grenadier Guards officer, and later a British Conservative politician, was convinced that forming the Guards Armoured Division was a mistake. He thought the idea that armour was pre-eminent on the battlefield and infantry obsolete was wrong.[7] Even in 1941, he also believed that a coming shortage of high-class infantry was entirely predictable. General Sir David Fraser, who served with Lord Carrington, also questioned the wisdom of converting highly trained infantry battalions to armour. He believed the ethos that made the Foot Guards such steady infantrymen did not translate into the efficient, imaginative training armoured troops required.[8]

The Guards Armoured Division's hurried formation in 1941 certainly raised more than a few eyebrows within the army and the broader British establishment. Nevertheless, the Guards' conversion to armour took place when the 9th, 11th, 42nd and 79th Armoured Divisions were being raised. In November 1941, for example, the 42nd Infantry Division also converted to armour, but this occurred without comment or criticism.[9] At least some of the later controversy about the Guards' conversion to armour was a consequence of the manpower shortage of 1944, questions over Allan Adair's suitability to command, and the Division's perceived battlefield performance. We will examine these matters in more detail later.

Was the Conversion to Armour Detrimental to the Infantry?

One of the objections raised at the Guards Armoured Division's formation was that it denied access to a reserve of highly trained infantrymen who could have been better used elsewhere. However, was the creation of the Division the drain on resources it first appeared? Along with the rest of the British Army, the Brigade of Guards expanded significantly between 1939 and 1945. The intake and outflow statistics for the Coldstream Guards is representative of the five regiments of Foot Guards. On 3 September 1939, there were 2,603 Coldstream Guardsmen. By July 1945, the Coldstream had recruited 11,593 Guardsmen, excluding officers. The outflow over the same period, including battle casualties, totalled 5,743.[10] The Grenadier Guards reported 15,000 recruits and 750 officers passing through their Training Battalion during the war.[11] By the end of September 1944, the five regiments of Foot Guards numbered twenty-one fighting battalions and 38,827 men. However, while 28,750 Guardsmen were retained in an infantry role, almost half were in training or holding battalions at home instead of being deployed overseas.[12]

On formation, the Guards Armoured Division consisted of six armoured and three infantry battalions plus support. In 1942, the Division was rebalanced by exchanging the 6th Guards (Armoured) Brigade (later 6th Guards (Tank) Brigade) for the 32nd Guards Brigade. The change in role from infantry to armoured battalions required a reduction in manpower. An infantry battalion numbered 961 all ranks while an armoured battalion comprised just 637 men. On conversion from infantry to armour, the six Guards battalions released 1,944 Guardsmen to be retained as infantrymen or assigned to other duties.[13]

A British Armoured Division consisted of approximately 250 tanks, 15,000 troops and 3,400 vehicles.[14] However, what is immediately apparent is the diminutive size of the tank force. Of the 15,000 officers and other ranks who constituted an armoured division, only 2,664 (17.76%) were tank crew or armoured reconnaissance. The infantry battalions contributed 3,763 troops (25%). The remaining 8,573 soldiers (57.24%) were support services such as artillery, engineers, signals, transport, supply, and medical units. An armoured division could perhaps more accurately be called an all-arms division.

There was a certain amount of scepticism about putting 'spit-and-polish' Guardsmen into tanks and whether their ethos or outlook would prove counterproductive in a new technical role.[15] In a *Daily Herald* report about the Guards Armoured Division's formation, the writer suggests that 'tank crews are not as a rule spit-and-polish men. They are rather like fighter pilots in their discipline. They are fighting mechanics who pride themselves on their grimy overalls.'[16]

In the spring of 1941, several Guards battalions stationed in London and the South-East of England were committed to home defence against the threat of invasion. However, the Guards' conversion to an armoured role did not preclude them from performing their primary task of defending London and the south coast. In a memorandum on the reorganisation of the 1st Battalion, Coldstream Guards to its new armoured role, it stated that no actual change of organisation, reduction of personnel or adjustment of ranks would take place until the end of September 1941. Although various training courses for officers and men were to begin immediately, the document was clear that the battalion must be able to reform as a rifle battalion in case of invasion. The memorandum also stated that training courses within the battalion would mainly consist of subjects necessary both for personnel of the future armoured battalion and those who would eventually go back to rifle battalions.[17]

In the summer of 1941, battalions selected for conversion to armour were put through a series of intelligence and aptitude tests to establish their suitability for training as drivers, mechanics, gunners, wireless operators and tank commanders. In a second memorandum about battalion reorganisation issued in September 1941, it stated that every Guardsman must volunteer for service in an armoured battalion, and that due consideration must be given to intelligence, initiative, mechanical aptitude, and reliability in the selection process. The document emphasised that tank commanders and crewmen must be able to cope with the many complexities of their individual roles and be able to work as part of an integrated team. The document went on to warn battalion commanders that 'any N.C.O. or man who is mentally not up to the job, no matter how good a soldier he is in barracks, will be a danger to his comrades in action'. Finally, the memorandum explained that the intelligence tests conducted in June should be used to classify men suitable for the various roles within an armoured battalion. Men found unsuitable for the conversion to armour were either retained by rifle battalions or assigned elsewhere.[18]

On formation, the Guards Armoured Division released nearly 2,000 Guardsmen to rifle battalions or other duties. Although often criticised for not cross-posting their troops like the rest of the British Army, this convention meant the Guards maintained their forces' integrity and strength. Later, the Guards' expansion easily offset the professed loss of infantrymen in 1941. Finally, tank crews were one of the smallest constituents of a British armoured division. It is unlikely that converting 2,664 officers and other ranks from infantry to armour made any significant difference to the war's prosecution or outcome. The fact that thousands of Guardsmen were available to the British Army when it was desperate for infantry replacements during the manpower crisis of 1944 is another question altogether.[19]

We can refute the objections raised against the formation of a Guards Armoured Division for four reasons. First, Guardsmen and NCOs proved quite capable of making the transition from infantry to an armoured role. The Coldstream Guards, for example, tackled the initial conversion to armour by selecting officers and men from the entire regiment for training. Less mechanically minded men could state a preference to transfer to another rifle battalion. In total, the 1st Battalion lost around 300 men who transferred out to be replaced by volunteers from other battalions. One reason for the influx of recruits to the armoured battalion might have been the opportunity for advancement. About half the new armoured battalion jobs were classed as tradesmen, such as fitters and electricians, which carried better pay than a Guardsman in a rifle battalion. Whatever their motivation, of fifty-three NCOs who attended the first instructors' courses, only six failed to achieve a first- or second-class qualification.[20] Second, the formation of the Guards Armoured Division might have created a perception of the loss of six infantry battalions. However, armoured battalions were smaller than infantry battalions, and so nearly 2,000 Guardsmen were retained as infantry. Third, the Guards battalions selected for conversion to armour were stationed at home in anticipation of a German invasion. The conversion to armour did not stop the Guards from performing their primary function of defending London and the south coast. Fourth, although not known at the time, the Guards would expand to twenty-one fighting battalions, most of them infantry. The subsequent growth of infantry battalions rapidly offset any perceived loss of six battalions to armour. By the autumn of 1944, there were 28,750 Guardsmen available to the rifle battalions.[21]

Chapter Four

Early Organisation and Training

Major General Oliver Leese was appointed divisional commander of the newly formed Guards Armoured Division. Leese had commanded a battalion of the Coldstream Guards before the war. Leese, described as a traditional Guards officer and straight as a die, set about the new Division's administrative organisation.[1] For the first six months of the Division's existence, officers and other ranks were sent away on various training courses such as driving, vehicle maintenance, wireless operations, and gunnery. During this period, Guardsmen acquired the necessary practical skills required to maintain and operate tanks. However, even the training basics were often hard to achieve as equipment, vehicles, most notably tanks, ammunition, and fuel were in short supply.[2] Initially, the Guards were issued with second-hand and well-worn Covenanter tanks and later Crusaders. These tanks had many deficiencies, including being mechanically unreliable, thinly armoured and under-gunned. Eventually, in 1943 the Guards would receive American M4 Sherman tanks, which would remain the principal armoured fighting vehicle of the Division for the remainder of the war. Towards the end of 1942, the 6th Guards (Armoured) Brigade was notified of its reclassification to an independent tank brigade, equipped with Churchill Infantry tanks.[3]

Within a year of his appointment as (GOC), Oliver Leese was reassigned to North Africa. His replacement was Major General Allan Adair. Adair formerly commanded the 6th Guards (Armoured) Brigade within the Division. In turn, Brigadier G.L. Verney assumed command of 6th Guards (Armoured) Brigade on 23 September 1942.[4] Adair would oversee the Division's long period of training in the Home Army and remain its commander for the rest of the war. In his memoirs, Adair explained how the new Division set about learning the practical basics of operating and maintaining tanks. He described frequent visits to other armoured units to gain knowledge and experience. The Division also brought in General Staff Officer (GSO1) Derek Schreiber, 11th Hussars, who was an experienced armoured officer, to help with organisation and training. However, Schreiber's contribution seems to have been limited.[5] He was the author of a series of training instructions and directives during 1941, but the Guards persisted with outdated and ill-advised cavalry-style charges into 1943.[6]

In his study of military training in the British Army, Harrison Place compares the Guards and 11th Armoured Division during their years of training in the UK. Even after the outbreak of war, individual regiments tended to adopt their own training methods and tactics. Harrison Place argues that the Guards' training was retarded by Major General Adair's reluctance to impose training instructions on his subordinate commanders. They continued to train their units how they saw fit.[7] Harrison Place's assessment seems correct. Murray suggests that part of the reason the British Army was unable to uniformly and quickly assimilate lessons learned was the numerous decentralised training programmes and lack of a commonly accepted battle doctrine.[8] In the Guards Armoured, there was a reluctance by senior commanders to impose anything like a uniformed doctrine on training. For example, Training Directive No. 1. Detailed Notes on Individual and Crew Training for Armoured Brigades, 21 August 1941, states:

> There is no desire at Divisional H.Q. to interfere with Brigade and Unit Commanders' responsibilities in the training and preparations of their commands for war.[9]

Battle School, Battle Drill

The severe shortages of equipment, vehicles, suitable training areas, and experienced instructors hampered the Guards' training between 1941 and 1942. Another problem was that much of the British Army's training lacked realism. Because of the equipment and vehicle shortages, military exercises often resembled pantomimes with flags used to represent tanks and rattles to signify machine gun fire.

In 1942, General Sir Bernard Paget set out his basic principles for army training. He argued that all training must be realistic to prepare all ranks physically and emotionally for the shock of battle. He also determined that all ranks, but especially junior leaders, be kept as fully informed as possible of the tactical situation on the ground. In this way, junior officers and NCOs could use their initiative and training to respond to changing situations and circumstances on the battlefield.[10]

The idea of training soldiers in small unit tactics under simulated battlefield conditions or battle drill was the brainchild of Major General Harold Alexander, Irish Guards. In 1940, Alexander wrote a paper on battle drill and set up a training school while in command of the 1st Division. In August 1941, after visiting the Battle School of the 47th (London) Division, Paget saw its potential, and quickly became a champion of the idea.

Paget ordered a battle school to be established in every division. To train instructors, Paget set up a central battle school, at Barnard Castle, County Durham. Paget appointed Major Lionel Wigram, a Territorial officer of the Royal Fusiliers, as chief instructor.[11] In March 1942, Paget invited a group of newspaper editors to the GHQ Battle School at Barnard Castle to demonstrate the new training methods being adopted by the army.[12]

In April, *The Scotsman* reported how the new battle schools were replacing the old barrack square, route march and target practice with realistic training that conveyed all the sound and fury of modern warfare. The reporter described a military exercise where the RAF strafed ground targets with live shells, bombs, and machine guns to give the ground troops a realistic impression of what it was like to be under fire.[13] Sergeant Charles Murrell, 1st Battalion, Welsh Guards mentions in his diary that several Guardsmen had returned from a battle school with wounds, and one had a piece of shrapnel embedded in his thigh. Murrell described the battle school experience as exhausting and dangerous, but good for morale and physical fitness, except for the occasional wound.[14]

The Imber Incident

The battle school concept was designed to inject a greater sense of realism into army training. However, on 13 April 1942 at Imber training ground, Salisbury Plain, the inherent dangers of using live ammunition and explosives in training was revealed. During a tactical demonstration of aircraft in their ground-attack role, twenty-five people were accidentally killed and seventy-one wounded. The training exercise, attended by a mixture of military and civilian dignitaries, had been organised as a dress rehearsal for a forthcoming visit by Prime Minister Winston Churchill three days later. A spectators' area was set aside for the demonstration and should have been marked by white chalk to identify it as a safe zone to the attacking aircraft, thus preventing a friendly-fire incident. However, there was some confusion between the army and RAF about whose responsibility it was to mark the area and it was never done.

Six RAF Spitfires and nine Hawker Hurricanes took part in the demonstration. The weather was reported as fine but hazy, making visibility poor. Sergeant William McLachlan, flying Hurricane BE417, mistook the crowd of spectators for dummy troops and launched his attack. Unfortunately, two other aircraft followed McLachlan's lead and strafed the spectators as well.

Later, a court of inquiry called to investigate the Imber Incident found that while Sergeant McLachlan was directly responsible, he had been insufficiently briefed. Additionally, McLachlan and his fellow pilots had not had an opportunity to fly a reconnaissance over the area beforehand. On 28 June 1942 Sergeant

McLachlan was shot down and killed during a night sortie against enemy shipping near Cherbourg.[15]

A tank commander in the 1st (Armoured) Battalion, Coldstream Guards, George Ernest Teal witnessed the Imber Incident first-hand. However, when interviewed for the Imperial War Museum's oral history project, he told a rather lurid, wildly inaccurate tale of a Nazi conspiracy to kill an Allied general who was attending the demonstration. Teal claimed that a Polish pilot, blackmailed by the Nazis, was at the controls of the Hurricane. Teal believed the Polish pilot was subsequently shot down attempting to make good his escape across the Channel, leaving a death toll of 120 victims. Apparently, a cover story was manufactured at the time that blamed the incident on Polish ground crew mistakenly loading live ammunition rather than blanks into the aircraft. Perhaps this cover story was the basis of Teal's erroneous memory of events.[16]

The *Daily Mirror*,[17] *Daily Mail*,[18] and *the Coventry Evening Telegraph* newspapers published stories about the Imber Incident in the days immediately after the tragic event. Clearly, the story did not justify a D-Notice (Defence Notice) by the official censor. In a rather brusque statement, the War Office and Air Ministry brushed aside the loss of life and simply emphasised the importance of the new training techniques:

> Under a recent War Office order, battle exercises are now given realism by the use of live ammunition in order to accustom the troops to actual war conditions. This was an exceedingly important part of the training.[19]

Sardonically, the war diary for the 1st Battalion, Coldstream Guards, merely records the Imber Incident thus:

> A demonstration of fighter aircraft attacking ground targets took place at Imber. Spectators from the battalion attended. A more realistic demonstration could not be wished for.[20]

Battle Drill and Training Deficiencies

According to Harrison Place, battle school and battle drills were initially viewed with a certain amount of scepticism by the War Office. Nevertheless, by 1944 the War Office had accepted them as a proven fact. Harrison Place also argued that the battle drill concept came at just the right time. By 1941 the army was vastly bigger than its pre-war establishment and was largely filled with civilians pressed into military service. The battle schools helped transform somewhat reluctant civilians in uniform into fighting soldiers. It also helped raise the morale of the Home Army, which was at a low point in 1942. This assessment seems correct, as the wartime diary of Sergeant Charles Murrell verifies that the physically demanding and realistic nature of the training proved a boon to morale, if somewhat hazardous to life and limb.[21]

The battle school movement might have improved British Army training in small unit tactics from 1942 onwards. Nevertheless, the Guards Armoured Division continued to struggle to develop a coherent training doctrine or create the necessary infrastructure to conduct all-arms training, particularly infantry and armoured co-operation. Additionally, the Guards Armoured often appeared unable to assimilate valuable lessons learned during training or transform tactical and operational workarounds into standard operating procedures. Instead, they would have to relearn some of the lessons of the training ground on the battlefield.

In a brief, five-page assessment of the organisation and training of the 2nd Battalion, Welsh Guards, between 1941 and 1943 several deficiencies were emphasised. In the summary section of the document, the author concludes that the battalion's first obstacle to proper organisation and training was a lack of equipment until late 1942. Next was an ignorance about what to train for and how to do it. Earlier in the document, the author explained how the newly appointed Major General Allan Adair appeared to abdicate his command responsibility to ensure his soldiers were properly trained:

> No training directives were issued to the battalion other than somewhat sketchy ones issued by G.H.Q. Home Forces every reached us. The Divisional Commander when pressed, took refuge behind a charming smile and an adroit evasion of the facts. So, we fell back upon our own resources and trial and error methods.[22]

Charles Farrell, 3rd Battalion, Scots Guards, recalled how he was assigned to the Guards Armoured Division tactical school with no combat experience or proper training. Farrell also believed it was a mistake not to have rotated officers from the Home Army with those on active service. In this way, units at home would have gained valuable lessons from officers with first-hand combat experience.[23]

Harrison Place argues that the 11th Armoured Division benefited greatly from Major General 'Pip' Roberts' appointment at the end of 1943. A North Africa veteran, Roberts was considered an expert in armoured warfare. In contrast, the Guards Armoured Division had a very limited reservoir of talent from which to draw a commander. Tradition and regimental parochialism dictated that Guards officers could only command Guards formations. Major General Allan Adair was a Grenadier Guards officer without any operational armoured experience.[24]

Early Organisation and Training

The introduction of infantry battle schools had improved Guards training somewhat from the previous year, but the Division's approach to armoured warfare remained outdated. In May 1942, the war diary of 2nd (Armoured) Battalion, Irish Guards, notes how they led the brigade in a massed formation charge during an exercise on Salisbury Plain. The war diary entry concludes:

> Tactically, the whole thing was a nightmare; but in its real purpose of practising leaders at all grades in the close control of their units, this 'Balaclava Charge' idea is certainly useful.[25]

A month later, Lieutenant Colonel C.K. Finlay became Commanding Officer of 2nd (Armoured) Battalion, Irish Guards. The war diary states:

> Among other things, he announced the long-awaited death of the 'massed tank charge' idea in our tactical training. It had served its purpose giving commanders of all grades experience in close control of sub-units. But it had survived so long and is so obviously suicidal that everyone was delighted to hear it was right 'out'.[26]

According to Martel, it was quite clear that the all-armoured idea was quite dead by the start of 1942. Nevertheless, the Guards persisted in practising outdated armoured tactics into 1943.[27]

Lessons Learned and Forgotten

The 2nd (Armoured) Battalion, Irish Guards, were only too aware of their training deficiencies. In October 1942, the war diary described a mock tank attack on some woods during an exercise. According to the battalion diarist, this exercise raised more questions than it answered. The diarists explained how the battalion's tanks had arrived onto their objective in advance of the infantry, but the trees proved an impenetrable barrier, which begged the question what should they do next: circle the wood until the infantry arrived to clear it of enemy troops? This would leave the battalion's tanks vulnerable to any anti-tank guns left operational after the wood had been subjected to an initial artillery barrage. The diarist suggests one possible solution was for the tanks to remain hull-down and provide fire support to the infantry. Another significant problem raised during the exercise was how to co-ordinate the arrival of tanks and motorised infantry onto an objective at the same time. The battalion diarist suggested that the infantry should ride on the tanks until within one hundred yards of an objective and then dismount.

Having settled on the idea of tank riders being the best solution to co-ordinate a joint infantry and armoured attack, the battalion diarist posed a new series of questions such as how many Guardsmen should each tank carry? How might carrying troops impede a tank's performance such as the traverse of its gun? The battalion diarist raised a string of reasonable questions and offered some practical solutions. However, outside of the motorised infantry, the battalion appears to have only run exercises with other armoured units and support services rather than any other infantry battalions within the Division.[28] In fact, it would be another year, and following an armoured attack debacle during Exercise SPARTAN, that 2nd (Armoured) Battalion, Irish Guards, and the 3rd (Infantry) Battalion, Irish Guards, would get an opportunity to practise tank and infantry co-operation. During a week's training, the two battalions formed combat groups consisting of one squadron of tanks and one company of infantry. According to the war diary of 3rd Battalion, Irish Guards, several joint exercises were held, and many lessons learned. The diarist concluded:

This had been a particularly valuable week's training for both battalions, and incidentally a very good opportunity for old friends to meet.[29]

Between September 1941 and June 1944, the Guards Armoured Division would progress from basic, competency-based training of armoured squadrons and infantry companies to full-scale divisional exercises including artillery, engineers, field workshops and medical units. Nevertheless, the Division's training was seriously deficient regarding infantry and tank co-operation.

Sir John Gorman, a former Irish Guards officer, explained that the Guards infantry battalions and armoured battalions seldom, if ever, trained together. Gorman also described how Guards officers often had contradictory viewpoints on how troops under their command should be trained, which only confused the men and wasted time, effort, and resources. Gorman's commanding officer, Lieutenant Colonel Kim Finlay, believed the armour would fight over the plains of France, Belgium and Germany with little assistance from the infantry.[30] In contrast to Finlay's *'masse de manoeuvre'*, the 3rd Battalion's commanding officer, Colonel J.O.E. Vandeleur, insisted on all-arms co-operation down to the smallest unit levels with tanks and infantry operating together.[31] The irony is that of all the regiments in the British Army, the five regiments of Foot Guards and two of Household Cavalry (Royal Horse Guards and Life Guards) should have had a natural advantage when training and operating in concert.

Similarly, former Guards officer Robert Boscawen said that in retrospect it seemed extraordinary how little training the 1st (Armoured) Battalion, Coldstream Guards, did in close co-operation with the infantry of the 32nd

Guards Brigade.[32] Brian Wilson joined the 3rd Battalion, Irish Guards, as a subaltern at the start of August 1944. In September 1944, during the fighting around Helchteren, Wilson's platoon was 'married up' with tanks for the first time. On reflection, he thought it surprising that as infantry in an armoured division, they had never received any training in Britain on operating with tanks.[33]

Most veteran testimonies examined for this book illustrate that, overall, the Guards Armoured Division's training regime lacked uniformity and sufficient realism to prepare troops adequately for battle. The training was largely, but not entirely, deficient in the application of infantry and armoured co-operation. Testimonies from William Griffiths,[34] Welsh Guards, and Stephen Simpson,[35] Coldstream Guards, further demonstrate the inconsistency with which training was applied. Both men believed the training they received did prepare them adequately for battle. Stephen Simpson also said that his battalion did train together with tanks on Salisbury Plain.

Training Ground and Equipment Deficiencies

A lack of equipment and adequate training areas caused difficulties for many armoured units, not just the Guards, preparing for the Normandy campaign. Farmland was at a premium throughout the war, limiting available space for large-scale training areas and exercises. However, there was also a great tendency by many units to conduct training by the book. The training was often too formulaic and lacked realism. Training exercises were frequently cancelled due to inclement weather, for example.[36]

Because of deficiencies in training, tank crews went to war with little tactical awareness. Harrison Place contends that the Infantry tank and Cruiser tank dichotomy negatively impacted training. Units tended to train for one type of tank or the other. The British Army's structure and disagreements over doctrine meant that tank brigades and armoured divisions did not adequately train for the job they would have to do, and infantry and tank co-operation in training was often lacking.[37]

The prevalence of anti-tank guns on the battlefield revealed more than failings in armoured doctrine and training. The British-manufactured A15 Crusader tank series, for example, was armed with a 2-pounder (40mm) main gun. This was replaced with the more potent 6-pounder (57mm) on later models. These guns were designed primarily to fire armour-piercing (AP) shells for engaging enemy tanks. British tanks lacked a suitable dual-purpose main gun that could fire both AP and the high-explosive (HE) shells needed to tackle soft targets such as anti-tank guns, soft-skinned vehicles, and infantry concentrations.

Only with the arrival of the American M4 Sherman tank in 1943 was this problem solved.[38]

British military historian and author Richard Doherty argues that by 1943, the army had assimilated many of the lessons learned from the fighting in North Africa. He points out that the basic divisional order of battle went through a series of changes from May 1942 onwards. An infantry brigade replaced the second armoured brigade within the armoured division structure to create a more balanced formation.[39] Alongside changes in the form of an armoured division, the War Office updated training manuals, replacing documents such as Army Training Instructions No. 3, Handling of an Armoured Division, 1941, with Military Training Pamphlet (MTP) No. 41, The Tactical Handling of the Armoured Division and its Components, February 1943, and MTP No. 63, The Co-operation of Tanks with Infantry Divisions. Although these later training pamphlets emphasised the importance of close infantry and armoured co-operation, their lessons were not always adopted uniformly by the Guards.

Exercises in Futility?

By the start of 1943 enough equipment, vehicles and training areas had become available for the Home Army to start holding large-scale military exercises such as SPARTAN in the spring and BLACKCOCK in the autumn. However, the utility of these exercises was questioned by officers and Guardsmen. In a report on the organisation and training of the 2nd Battalion, Welsh Guards, between 1941 and 1943, the author wrote that large-scale exercises like SPARTAN proved of little tactical use to the lower ranks.[40]

During Exercise SPARTAN, the Guards Armoured Division was under the command of 2nd Canadian Corps, 2nd Army. On 11 March 1943, the Canadian 5th Armoured Brigade and 5th Guards Armoured Brigade, both under the command of GOC Guards Armoured Division, fought a mock battle, which resulted in around 50 per cent casualties according to the umpires.[41]

The war diary of the 2nd Battalion, Welsh Guards, records that the tank attack first encountered minefields and then a strong force of enemy anti-tank guns.[42] The diarist of the 2nd (Armoured) Battalion, Irish Guards, briefly and rather caustically described what happened:

> At about 11.30am we are ordered to concentrate in what later proved to be the enemy pivot, with disastrous results. More than 50% of the 5th Guards Armd Brigade was wiped out that morning. So this was the encounter which everyone had been waiting for![43]

According to the war diary of 5 Guards Armoured Brigade, the failed armoured attack during Exercise SPARTAN was the result of poor intelligence:

> Intelligence is having a considerable boosting as a result of the experience of SPARTAN when lack of information led to theoretical disaster.[44]

Failed intelligence might have contributed to the Guards disastrous tank attack during SPARTAN. Nevertheless, at least some of the responsibility for what happened to the two armoured brigades must reside with the man commanding the operation, Major General Adair. Reading Adair's memoir, one would believe that Exercise SPARTAN was a great success, which the Division ended with a tank gallop through the best of hunting country near Towcester, rather than a disaster.[45] The mishandling of the Guards Armoured Division during SPARTAN raises concerns about the Division's ability to learn appropriate lessons from training exercises. The following year, the Guards Armoured Division would find itself in a remarkably similar position during Operation GOODWOOD in Normandy and suffer a similar fate for real.[46]

Following Exercise SPARTAN, Sergeant Murrell, 1st Battalion, Welsh Guards reflected on his belief that most Guardsmen prided themselves on being professional soldiers. He also believed that Guardsmen generally resented their time and talents being wasted on bull (army slang for senseless activities such as the excessive cleaning of kit, especially boots) and outdated training methods. In his diary, Sergeant Murrell wrote:

> The men of the Battalion are now fundamentally well-trained professional soldiers, and though they would never admit it have developed a pride in arms that makes them want to prove their worth against a worthy opponent on the battlefield. It is not the STUNTS (Army parlance for military exercises) and battle-drill and assault courses and shooting that men moan about – it is the shirking, the drilling and the bull and the futile and negative weapons training with rifle and bayonet, when we feel that the time could be more profitably employed in learning to use more extraordinary weapons.[47]

At the end of September, the sixth day of Exercise BLACKCOCK, Sergeant Murrell wrote in his diary about how long, dreary, and exhausting large-scale exercises like BLACKCOCK were, and how he saw little value in them from a Guardsman's point of view:

It is the battalion and company exercises that demand physical effort (at least from the Rifle companies). The bigger the stunt the greater the monotony and boredom and the physical demands made upon us.[48]

In 1943, the War Office published Military Training Pamphlet No. 41, which focused on the tactical handling of an armoured division and its components. The pamphlet recommended the development of battle drills to ensure uniformity of action in response to likely combat situations. The pamphlet also repeatedly stressed the need for all-arms co-operation to achieve operational objectives.[49] It remains unclear to what use, if any, training aids such as Pamphlet No. 41 were put by the Guards armoured battalions. However, the various decentralised training regimes across the Division were exposing and resolving many operational and tactical problems it would later encounter on the battlefield. In 1942, as we have seen, the Irish Guards recognised the utility of tank riders to deliver close infantry support onto an objective. In 1943, they found that creating tank squadron and infantry company battlegroups was an effective establishment for close infantry and armoured co-operation, especially when the battalions came from the same regiment.

Nevertheless, the Guards Armoured Division seems to have suffered from a form of corporate amnesia, whereby many of the valuable lessons learned in training and noted in war diaries were never collated, distilled into new training procedures, and disseminated across the organisation. The Division would not reorganise into Regimental battlegroups, for example, until the end of August 1944.[50] This failure to carry lessons learned during training forward onto the battlefield must be partly attributed to the senior leadership and administration of the Division. One certainly cannot imagine an energetic, focused leader such as Oliver Leese evading questions from his subordinates about how division training was to be conducted. Inevitably, we must ask the question was Major General Allan Adair fit to command the Guards Armoured Division?

Chapter Five

6th Guards (Armoured/Tank) Brigade

Before we examine Major General Allan Adair's fitness to command the Guards Armoured Division, we need to take a step back and look at the early years of the 6th Guards (Armoured) Brigade. The Brigade started life as part of the Guards Armoured Division under the command of Allan Adair, then a brigadier. In 1942, it was decided to reorganise British armoured divisions, which at that time consisted of two armoured brigades and a motor battalion of infantry. The new establishment of an armoured division replaced one of the armoured brigades with an infantry brigade, thus creating a more balanced formation. In November 1942, the 6th Brigade of the Guards Armoured Division was reassigned to the 15th (Scottish) Division, although six months would elapse before the two joined forces. The 32nd Guards (Infantry) Brigade replaced the 6th Brigade. Brigadier G.L. Verney, Grenadier Guards and Irish Guards, then assumed command of the re-christened 6th Guards (Tank) Brigade. The Brigade's establishment consisted of a Headquarters, the 4th (Tank) Battalion Grenadier Guards, 4th (Tank) Battalion Coldstream Guards, and 3rd (Tank) Battalion Scots Guards. Additionally, the signals squadron, brigade workshop, and RASC (Royal Army Service Corps) company all remained with the brigade.

Perhaps unsurprisingly, as an armoured division of two armoured brigades and just a motor battalion of infantry, the Guards Armoured Division practised rather crude massed armoured assault tactics during training. The war diary for the Headquarters, 6th Guards (Armoured) Brigade, Appendix B, sets out details of Exercise CRUISER on 5–6 June 1942. The exercise was carefully choreographed, even stating the time the enemy was scheduled to withdraw after being attacked. The exercise instructions required the Guards to perform a mass tank attack supported by artillery. Next, consolidation of the objective by the infantry of the Coldstream Guards Motor Battalion and a battery of anti-tank guns. Once the infantry was on the objective, the tanks retired to a reserve position. Although the attack was co-ordinated between the tanks, artillery, and infantry, it was not an integrated or co-operative effort. However, the fighting in North Africa had already shown that simply throwing tanks forward, *en masse*, albeit under an artillery barrage, was often a recipe for disaster when they met the enemy's anti-tank gun screen and tanks. Right up until November 1942, just before the Brigade was notified it would leave the Guards Armoured Division to join the 15th (Scottish) Division, it continued to practise this type of massed armoured assault. However, we see a marked change in the training regime of the Brigade shortly after its reassignment.[1]

The renamed 6th Guards (Tank) Brigade started joint training with the 15th (Scottish) Division in January 1943. According to the 15th (Scottish) Division's history, a special emphasis was placed on the practical co-operation of infantry and tanks. However, most officers and other ranks lacked battle experience. As a result, the lessons from the battles of North Africa were carefully studied for guidance. The Division's history also states that the friendships and understanding forged between the Guardsmen and Scottish infantry bred mutual confidence in each other and knowledge of each other's methods, which later proved invaluable in battle.[2]

In January 1943, the 15th (Scottish) Division was a mixed formation consisting of two infantry brigades and one armoured brigade. On joining the 15th (Scottish) Division, the role of the 6th Guards Brigade changed from one of fast-moving armoured exploitation following a successful breach of the enemy lines to one of infantry support during an attack. As a result of the change from an armoured to a tank brigade, the 6th Guards received British-built Churchill Infantry tanks, which were slow moving but heavily armoured.

Harrison Place argues that the 6th Guards (Tank) Brigade's training did not keep pace with the latest thinking or relevant War Office training pamphlets. Tanks were still advancing without infantry support during training exercises. He also contends that there was a lack of originality and tactical flexibility. Instead, the training was prescriptive. However, the available evidence of the joint training between the infantry battalions of the 15th (Scottish) Division and the 6th Guards (Tank) Brigade tells a different story.[3]

The war diaries of the 2nd Battalion, Glasgow Highlanders and the 6th Battalion, King's Own Scottish Borderers (KOSB), contain detailed descriptions of the training undertaken with the 6th Guards (Tank) Brigade between May and July 1943. Spread over an intensive two-week period, the joint infantry and tank training included films, lectures, demonstrations, TEWTs, and numerous field exercises. Each infantry company was affiliated with a tank squadron for the training period. Tank familiarisation demonstrations were held, followed by lessons on the practical carrying of infantry on tanks.

During 1943, the British Army lacked a purpose-built armoured personnel carrier capable of ferrying infantry forward alongside tanks within the battlespace. As a result of this deficit in troop-carrying capability, the 6th Guards (Tank) Brigade was quick to realise that the most expedient method of ensuring infantry and tanks crossed the start line together and arrived as close to the objective as practicable was to mount their infantry affiliates on the tanks. In contrast, the Guards Armoured Division failed to appreciate the value of tank-mounted infantry or 'tank riders' until after the failure of Operation GOODWOOD. In 1943, the Irish Guards appear to have been the only element of the Guards Armoured Division to have experimented with tank riders during a brief two-week window of training, but the lessons they learned were quickly forgotten.[4]

Over the next couple of weeks of training, the Scottish infantry and Guards tanks learned to form up, move to the start line, cross the start line, and advance together to an objective by day and night. Three types of attacks were practised during the training. First, the set-piece attack with a timed programme of artillery support was practised (described as inflexible and offering no room for manoeuvre). Next, the fluid battle was practised, which was hastily organised upon meeting heavy enemy opposition. Observed artillery support, firing on targets of opportunity, was provided rather than a timed plan of suppressive fire. The fluid battle scenario was described in the training instructions as offering greater flexibility and room for manoeuvre. Finally, the companies, squadrons, specialists, and support troops rehearsed the vanguard attack.[5]

On 14 and 15 June 1943, the 3rd (Tank) Battalion, Scots Guards took part in Exercise CENTAUR II. The intention of the exercise was to practise forming a mixed infantry and armoured vanguard before advancing to contact an enemy's rearguard. The vanguard mainly consisted of elements of the 6th Battalion KOSB including one section of the carrier platoon, one troop of tanks carrying one platoon of infantry, a detachment of 3-inch mortars, a pioneer platoon, an intelligence section, two snipers, an anti-tank gun platoon, and a machine-gun platoon.[6]

As the training progressed, the specialist infantry units such as the mortar platoons and anti-tank batteries were integrated into the training exercises along with support elements from the artillery and engineers. The troops also practised scenarios such as what to do when the infantry was advancing using heavy cover such as high hedges and ditches, which made it difficult for the supporting tanks to maintain visual contact. To help build rapport between the affiliated infantry and tank crews, joint drill parades, church services, football matches, and concerts were held. Additionally, the troops ate their meals together during field exercises.

As well as conducting a uniformed programme of training with the various infantry battalions of the 15th (Scottish) Division, the 6th Guards also took part in a series of brigade and divisional exercises such as ALEXANDER and BLACKCOCK. During these large-scale exercises everything from march discipline, supply procedures, refuelling of vehicles, harbouring of tanks and wireless communications to the breaching of minefields and full-scale attacks were practised.[7] A report following Exercise BLACKCOCK describes how the tanks of the Scots Guards carried various infantry units close to their objectives before supporting them in an attack. On one occasion, the report describes how following the prosecution of a 'fierce attack' the Scots Guards were then used in an armoured role. The Guards carried elements of the 7th Seaforth Highlanders forward for about a mile, dropped them off and then continued to advance to contact. The report does not explain who took the initiative to switch from providing close infantry support for the break-in attack to exploiting the breach, which was the role of an armoured brigade, not a tank brigade, according to doctrine. Nevertheless, the exercise demonstrates that the 6th Guards (Tank) Brigade was developing tactical flexibility and confidence in its abilities.[8]

Kenneth Banks Ohlson was an officer with the 531st Battery, 190 Field Regiment, Royal Artillery, 15th (Scottish) Division. Interviewed in 2013, Banks Ohlson recalled participating in a series of large-scale divisional exercises during 1943 and early 1944, mainly supporting the 7th Seaforth Highlanders. During his interview, Banks Ohlson expressed his belief in the importance of these large-scale exercises in preparing troops for the fighting they would face in Normandy. He also emphasised the importance of units getting to know each other and building rapport. Later, in Normandy, his battery frequently supported the 7th Seaforth Highlanders and Guards (Tank) Brigade. He occasionally operated as a FOO (Forward Observation Officer) from Guards' tanks. Thinking back, Banks Ohlson believed that some successful actions fought in Normandy were exactly like those they had practised on exercise in the UK.[9]

Many factors from a lack of resources and availability of training areas to War Office directives probably helped to stifle experimentation and innovation in the operational and tactical training of the 6th Guards (Tank) Brigade. Nevertheless, experiments were conducted to try to improve both training methods and tactics. In March 1943, the war diary of the 4th (Tank) Battalion, Coldstream Guards, records that during training several Churchill tanks were fired upon by a 2-pounder gun to give the crews an idea of what it was like to be under fire (battle inoculation). This activity resulted in two Guardsmen being wounded in the legs, although not seriously injured.[10]

Gordon Thomas Calthrop Campbell, Baron Campbell of Croy, served as an officer with the 131st Field Regiment, Royal Artillery, 15th (Scottish) Division, in the UK and north-west Europe. Interviewed for the Imperial War Museum's oral history Project in 1991, Lord Campbell recalled that he was attached to the Battle School, Barnard Castle, in 1943. During his time there, Lord Campbell took part in a series of experiments to support Churchill tanks with artillery fire. The tanks would advance directly under an artillery barrage during the experiments and onto their objective. Although the tanks used in the experiments suffered some superficial damage and occasional casualties from the bombardment, the tactic enabled heavily armoured Churchill tanks to hold an objective when unsupported by infantry. Lord Campbell believed that the rather unorthodox tactic of bringing down artillery fire right on top of Churchill tanks was used occasionally in Normandy. Lord Campbell's recollections serve to emphasise the importance of artillery firepower in supporting tanks while conserving infantry lives through the innovative use of shot and shell.[11]

Trial by Fire

In July 1943, a report by the Army Operational Research Group (A.O.R.G.) explained that a new method of infantry–tank attack had been proposed by the School of Infantry and tried out at Larkhill. It involved Churchill tanks advancing into a 25-pounder artillery concentration. The reasoning behind the trials was that in certain circumstances it was better to shell the enemy's anti-tank gunners vigorously and risk losing a few Churchills to friendly fire than allow the enemy to fire on the tanks, which would most likely result in much higher casualties.

The trials revealed that 25-pounder shell strikes to a Churchill tank's side armour, turret, and the plating over the driver and co-driver positions caused no damage. However, hits to the tracks, suspension, road wheels, glacis plate, turret ring, hatches, guns, periscope, and rear armour all caused some damage, albeit much of it superficial and repairable.

The projected number of hits to tanks during an artillery concentration was calculated using a simple mathematic formula. Calculate the area of a single Churchill tank, divided it by the total area in which shells would be landing, and multiply that by the number of shells fired. The total number of hits projected was the function multiplied by the total number of tanks in the area. Consideration was also given to the angle of falling shells. For example, thirty-six Churchill tanks advance through an area 600 by 200 yards. This area was being covered by an artillery battery of a) thirty-two guns or b) sixty-four guns, each firing 5 rounds per minute. The guns firing at a range of 5,000 yards, second charge (type of propellant), and a 20-degree angle of descent. Based on this information, the following probability table could be calculated:

No. Hits on Tanks	32 Guns	64 Guns
Tanks not hit	24	16
Tanks hit once	9	12
Tanks hit twice or more	3	8
Not hit in a vulnerable area	29	23
Hit once in a vulnerable area	6	10
Hit twice or more in a vulnerable area	1	3

The report pointed out that although a tank might be hit once or more in a vulnerable area, it did not necessarily follow that it would be knocked out. The report also suggested that this type of infantry–tank attack would be particularly suited to the use of airburst HE shells, which were more lethal against dug-in enemy troops and would do no damage to a Churchill tank.[12]

In June 1943, the army put theory into practice and conducted a series of trials to establish the feasibility of Churchill tanks advancing directly under an artillery concentration. Fifteen Churchill Mark IV tanks advanced into an area 300 yards wide by 400 yards deep. The area was covered by thirty-six guns, firing two rounds per minute from a range of 4,000 yards. The concentration lasted eight minutes, but the full number of tanks were only in the area for six minutes. According to projected figures, 76 per cent of tanks would not be hit, 20 per cent would be hit once, and 4 per cent would be hit twice or more. In the actual trial, just two tanks suffered direct hits, but one tank was hit twice. The second trial, which exposed the same number of tanks to a higher rate of fire but for a shorter duration, produced a similar result as the first trial. Overall, the trials at Larkhill found that theory and practice agreed reasonably well. The trials demonstrated that Churchill tanks could advance directly under an artillery concentration onto an objective with few casualties, if required to do so. Interestingly, the report only mentions tank casualties. The report does not calculate the likely risk to the tank crews or record if anyone was wounded or killed during the trials.[13] As we will see, the ability of Churchill tanks to operate without close infantry support for limited periods but under a curtain of suppressive artillery fire would prove tactically advantageous on the battlefield.

Chapter Six

Allan Adair's Fitness to Command

As we have seen, Major General Allan Adair replaced Oliver Leese as GOC Guards Armoured Division in September 1942. Adair had previously commanded the 6th Guards (Armoured) Brigade. Allan Adair had few qualifications that made him a suitable candidate to command an armoured division. He had no previous operational armoured experience. He had joined the Grenadier Guards straight from Harrow in 1916. In 1940, Adair was Second-in-Command, 3rd Battalion, Grenadier Guards, who fought several rearguard actions on the retreat to Dunkirk.

In Gregory Blaxland's book *Destination Dunkirk*, he describes a meeting between Major General H.E. Franklyn, 1st Division, and two new battalion commanders: Major Adair, Grenadier Guards, and Lieutenant Colonel Butterworth, North Staffords. Apparently, Franklyn was struck by the contrast between the two men. Butterworth was a quiet, reserved man while Adair was gay and light-hearted, inclined almost to giggle, which Franklyn found worrying. Blaxland suggests that Franklyn's anxieties about Adair's demeanour were unfounded solely based on his appointment as a division commander later in the war.[1] Similarly, Richard Collier remarked on Adair's curious behaviour during the defence of the Ypres–Comines Canal line. Collier repeatedly describes Adair's demeanour as courtly. He recounts an incident during the height of the fighting, when a Lieutenant Edward Ford, the carrier officer, returned to Battalion Headquarters to collect a supply of ammunition and deposit some wounded. Adair reportedly greeted the junior officer cheerfully and asked him if he had time for tea, seemingly oblivious to the unfolding crisis of the collapsing Dunkirk parameter.[2]

In October 1940, Adair was promoted to command the 30th Guards Brigade, defending the eastern approaches to London. At the end of May 1941, the Guards Armoured Division's establishment was announced during a conference at Headquarters, London District. In his memoirs, Adair freely admits, 'None of us knew anything about tanks, and we left the room feeling slightly dazed.'[3]

As GOC of the Guards Armoured Division, Major General Adair was ultimately responsible for the formation's training and preparations for battle. Nevertheless, Adair seemed blind to the Division's training deficiencies, such as allowing the armoured battalions to continue practising outdated, cavalry-styled massed charges with tanks.

An unfortunate side effect of the British Army's regimental system was a tendency for senior officers to abdicate responsibility for the training of battalions to subordinates. In August 1941, a training directive was circulated to the brigade and battalion staff of the Division. The second paragraph of the training directive amply illustrates the Division's lack of clear leadership or any uniform programme of training:

> There is no desire at Divisional H.Q. to interfere with the Brigade and Unit Commanders' responsibilities in the training and preparation of their commands for war.[4]

Adair appears to have accepted the precedent that battalions should be left to organise and run their own training. As we have already seen, when the 2nd Battalion, Welsh Guards, turned to Adair for help with their armoured training, he completely shirked his responsibilities. Instead, he chose to hide behind a curtain of charm and evasion, leaving the Welsh Guards to fall back on their own limited resources and trial-and-error training methods.[5]

In February 1944, Montgomery, now commander of 21st Army Group, wanted Adair removed because of a perceived lack of drive.[6] Montgomery wanted Lieutenant General Sir Richard O'Connor to make an unfavourable report about Adair, which he refused to do. Montgomery's intended replacement for Adair is unknown.[7] Of course, his choice would have been limited by the convention that dictated a Guards officer must command a Guards formation. In 1971, O'Connor wrote the following short appraisal of Adair:

> I thought he was considerably better than Monty thought him, and was continually fighting battles on his behalf. Bimbo Dempsey, I think, agreed with me.
>
> He was not an outstanding leader, but I had heard earlier in his service he had done well against a German attack. He had rather a silly laugh which annoyed some people. But I think he did the Guards Armd. Div. well.[8]

However, in 1975, O'Connor appeared to have changed his opinion of Adair somewhat and described him as 'not being a flyer'.[9] Similarly, the British 2nd Army commander, Miles 'Bimbo' Dempsey, regarded Adair as 'sticky'. He, Adair, did not have an outstanding reputation within the 21st Army Group.[10]

In a short, handwritten appraisal of General Adair and the Guards Armoured Division, Major J.K. Nairne recalled:

I only came across him once during his army service. He was the inspecting officer at the passing out parade at my O.C.T.U. in 1945. I was one of the very few who had any medal ribbons, and I think for this reason, when he came to me, he stopped and asked me who I had served with. When I rather emphatically replied, '51st (Highland) Division', he smiled and walked on. It was rather nice to be singled out, and in his speech to those who were 'passing out' he made an amusing remark connected with discipline, when he said he heard the Jocks shouting to his Guardsmen in their tanks at the Rhine crossing – 'Mind you don't scratch the paint'! In some ways I feel this remark rather characterized the Guards Armoured Division and its commander. Certainly as far as the jocks in the 51 (H) Division were concerned, there was really only one armoured division they thought highly of in the N.W. Europe campaign and that was the 11th Armoured Division. The one they had no use for was the 7th Armoured Division. The general feeling about the Guards Armoured Division was that they were methodical but slow.

I would think General Adair was a rather reserved and shy man. His only son was killed in action in Italy in 1943 which might have affected his ability in 1944/45.[11]

Major General Adair was one of just two divisional commanders who remained in post for an extended period during the Second World War. The tenure of divisional commanders during the war was typically short for one of two reasons. First, poor performance quickly got commanders sacked. Second, successful commanders were rapidly promoted.[12] The first GOC of the Guards Armoured Division was Major General Sir Oliver Leese, who remained in the post for just fifteen months before being promoted to Corps commander in the Middle East. We know that Montgomery tried and failed to have Adair removed from command. It appears that Adair was neither considered suitable for promotion by his superiors nor his current post as GOC Guards Armoured.

Allan Adair was a commander who inspired great affection and loyalty from his subordinates. He was quietly spoken, charming and could remain calm under pressure. General Sir David Fraser described him as 'much loved'.[13] Montgomery himself applauded Adair in a speech during the Farewell to Armour ceremony on 9 June 1945. Of course, it is impossible to know if Montgomery's praise was genuine.[14]

In his memoir, Adair conveniently omits the episode when Montgomery tried to sack him. Instead, he describes the months before D-Day as being difficult for him. The Division's training was criticised as being too reminiscent of the barrack square and lacked the dash required of armoured warfare. He also recounts an episode when Major Jock Askew, former Grenadier Guards, visited Montgomery many years after the war. When asked to voice his opinion of Adair, Montgomery is reported to have said, 'Oh, General Allan, he was the only one I knew I could never sack. My job was to fight the Germans. I wasn't prepared to fight the whole Brigade of Guards as well.'[15] Montgomery's glib comments about Adair and the Brigade of Guards' political power probably come closest to the truth of the situation.

Allan Adair was not the best candidate to command an armoured division in battle. He possessed no operational experience of armour and projected an image of the 'Gentleman Amateur'.[16] The Gentleman Amateur was a literary construct of the Victorian and Edwardian eras. It suggested that social class rather than education or professional training equipped young English gentlemen for leadership roles.[17]

Having failed to sack Adair, Montgomery was astute enough to know that he would need a legitimate reason to try to sack him a second time. Montgomery would also need a replacement officer who was acceptable to the Brigade of Guards. In Adair's defence, he never allowed Montgomery to question his command of the Guards Armoured Division. On balance, Adair's command of the Division, once committed to battle, appeared competent. Nevertheless, Adair seemed to have been a man who often used charm to obfuscate his own shortcomings as a commander. At times, he also appeared strangely detached from the realities of the situations faced by the units under his command. It is impossible to know with any certainty if Adair's sometimes curious demeanour and behaviour was a carefully constructed façade intended to portray the imperturbable 'Guards officer', genuine eccentricity, battle stress or grief over the loss of his son.

Chapter Seven

The Guards Ethos

The Household Cavalry and five regiments of Foot Guards serve the royal household and protect the British monarch. The first Royal Regiment of Guards was raised by King Charles II while in exile in 1656 and comprised 400 of the monarch's most loyal supporters. Since 1656 the Guards have carved a long and illustrious military history from the restoration of the monarchy in 1660 through numerous conflicts and two world wars to the present.[1] On the battlefield, the Foot Guards were regarded as steadfast infantrymen who could be relied upon to fulfil the most arduous tasks. Over time, each Guards regiment formed its own unique identity and military traditions while collectively the Guards devolved into a semi-autonomous subgroup of the British Army.

The British aristocracy has been a significant source of Guards officers because of the long and intimate association with the monarchy. Similarly, service in the Guards was often regarded as a prerequisite to accede to high office within the British establishment. In his memoirs, Major General Sir Allan Adair recites a litany of Guards officers who became senior clerics, politicians, civil servants, diplomats, and industrialists in later life.[2] In many ways, the Guards were a microcosm of the British class system of the nineteenth and early twentieth centuries. Membership of the Guards was something of a socially exclusive club.[3] In his memoir, former Coldstream Guards officer and military historian Michael Howard recalled his parents' delight when he joined his regiment because of the social cachet it brought to the family. Michael's father wrote that it was a great thing to have a son in the Brigade. Similarly, his mother took to wearing a Coldstream star on her hat or in her lapel as a fashion accessory.[4]

Guardsmen Basic Training

Stephen Simpson had repeatedly tried to join the army after the outbreak of war but had been rejected because he was underage and in a reserved occupation. Nevertheless, he was eventually offered a chance to join the Coldstream Guards. He had misgivings about joining the Guards as he knew they had a reputation for toughness and discipline:

The difference between the infantry and the Guards was that the Guardsman was supposed to be the elite, and had really hard and tough training, whereas the Light Infantryman was reputed to be more of an etiquette soldier.[5]

During the Second World War, recruits first went to the Guards Depot, Caterham, for basic training and then to Pirbright Depot for continuation training before joining a battalion. From 1877, Caterham was the establishment that transformed raw recruits into Guardsmen through a harsh regime of parade ground drill, physical fitness training, constant kit inspections and punishments for the slightest of rule infractions. Michael Howard recalled how he 'lost his name' for committing some minor infraction during his training, which resulted in him being confined to barracks for the weekend and forced to scrub floors as his punishment.[6] Over sixteen weeks, recruits were taught to be meticulous about every aspect of their new lives, from dress to personal hygiene. Trainee Guardsmen were taught and continually tested on regimental history to help foster a sense of esprit de corps.[7] According to Keith Briant, a former Irish Guards officer, there were six essential qualities Caterham sought to instil in every recruit: cleanliness, smartness, fitness, efficiency, pride in the Regiment and personal fulfilment. Briant explained that while these six fundamental principles are a common requirement of any soldier, the Brigade of Guards performed its own peculiar alchemy, which made Guardsmen feel that they could beat the world.[8]

At the end of basic training, newly qualified Guardsmen would be instructed to visit the regimental tailor, who would alter the standard army cap into a 'cheesecutter' where the peak no longer jutted out but went straight down over the nose. This tradition of transforming the army peaked cap served three small but essential purposes. First, it signified the transformation from civilian to Guardsman. Next, the cheesecutter instantly differentiated Guardsmen from other soldiers. Finally, the cheesecutter physically forced a Guardsman to maintain his military bearing. He had to keep his head up and posture erect to see where he was going.[9]

Today, partly due to their ceremonial role and modern media, the five regiments of Foot Guards and two regiments of Horse Guards are some of the world's most renowned and recognisable military units. However, during the Second World War, the Brigade of Guards was largely a closed book to anyone outside of the organisation. In April 1941, an article appeared in the *Ballymena Weekly Telegraph* entitled, 'An Irish Guardsman tells how the Army's No. 1 fighting man is made'. The article reported in rather jingoistic tones an interview with an unnamed Guardsman, who explained that it was forbidden for any member of the five Guards regiments to ever claim that his regiment was better than any of the others. The reason advanced by the Guardsman was that all Guardsmen belonged first, irrespective of their regiment, to the 'Brotherhood of the Brigade of Guards'. The article goes on to say that discipline in the Guards was regarded as either fearsome or wonderful, depending on your point of view. The correspondent concluded that Guardsmen took great pride in the fact that theirs was the most severe physical and military training in the world, and being a Guardsman was tantamount to being a paragon of all military virtues.[10]

In 1940, the novelist Gerald Kersh joined the Coldstream Guards as a Guardsman. He transformed his experiences of basic training at Caterham into a best-selling novel, *They Die with Their Boots Clean*, which was first published in December 1941. In the first few pages of the book, Kersh captures some of the fear and trepidation of the newly arrived recruits:

'You're in the Guards. It's like being in jail, only there's one difference.'
'What's that?'
'In jail you sometimes get a bit of time to yourself.'
'Oh, blimey. Do they give you hell?'
'Hell,' said the glum man, 'Hell. If they gave you hell, it wouldn't be so bad. Hell is paradise to what they give you here.'[11]

In 1939, Lord Carrington joined the 2nd Battalion, Grenadier Guards, at Wellington Barracks. He thought the Brigade of Guards had an unhealthy obsession with drill, dress and cleanliness while neglecting many precepts of basic military training. He suggested:

There was, despite all the fun, the loyalty, the pride of Regiment, a certain complacent lethargy, a view that life must continue according to some manifestly outdated guidelines, coming war or no coming war. To take a broader interest in any aspect of the military profession (I am not suggesting that I did) was regarded as insufferably bad form.[12]

Lord Carrington believed that the Guards' training regime needed significant modernisation, which did not happen. In his memoir, Michael Howard explained how the Brigade of Guards was officered by a social elite, who attended the same public schools, such as Eton, and were frequently interrelated across generations. According to Howard, when not fighting, Guards officers were expected to hunt, shoot, gamble and get drunk. However, professional soldiering or anyone hoping to make a career in the army was generally regarded with derision.[13]

Sir John Gorman recalled having reservations about applying to join the Irish Guards. Guards' officers were expected to fund themselves adequately for dress uniforms, mess bills and expensive conventions such as never travelling by bus, only by taxi, first class by train, and frequenting the most sought-after clubs, bars, and restaurants.[14]

As a Guardsman in the 2nd Battalion, Coldstream Guards, John Elliott felt that the Guards wasted too much time on ceremonial duties instead of training for the realities of modern warfare. He was also resentful that social class rather than leadership skills and ability determined which NCOs were recommended for officer training. He observed that 'the powers to be seemed to believe that leaders of men were automatically poured out of the public school system'. Elliott bemoaned what he saw as the inequity of the Guards system, where an NCO from a working-class background could never become an officer.[15]

Sergeant Charles Murrell, Welsh Guards, was a keen observer of and commentator on the traditions and cultural norms that constituted the Guards ethos. In his diary entry for 19 November 1942, he recounts a conversation between himself and a visiting medical officer:

> He confides in me almost as though I was (like himself) an outsider to the Brigade of Guards, and except that he is a commissioned officer and I am not, I suspect that we both come from a similar background. Like me he is, socially in between the 2 extremes, the Guards officers and the rankers. He is amusingly, and bitingly satirical about our excessive discipline, the excessive foot slamming on the square – and about the savage way we are broken in at the Depot – a system that shocks his medical code for the ill effects it could have upon the human body.[16]

In respect to his chosen profession and branch of service, Sergeant Murrell was not blind to the faults of the army and the Guards. A dedicated diarist, he meticulously documented, praised, and criticised how the Brigade of Guards operated. In his diaries, he repeatedly questioned the veracity of a system that relied almost exclusively on selecting its officers from the British aristocracy. In May 1944, General Eisenhower (affectionately known to Allied troops and the public as Ike) visited the Welsh Guards and gave a speech about the coming invasion of Europe. However, it was the Guards reaction to Eisenhower's speech rather than its content that drew Murrell's ire:

> Something happened that I've never seen before, when Ike had finished the men broke out into a spontaneous burst of hand clapping and they would have cheered lustily had anyone set them off. But, of course, Ike, like Monty,

is not of the Brigade of Guards. So, there was no official cheering for the General. It's time they got wise to themselves, these Guards' officers and took a peek outside the narrow, selfish world in which they live. Pampered Popinjays! They make one want to spew at times![17]

Recruitment, Selection and Social Elitism

Traditionally, the Guards recruited its officer cadets only from the most exclusive of private schools and the ranks of the British aristocracy. However, the war created recruitment challenges for the whole of the British Army and highlighted weaknesses in a selection process that relied heavily on a system of patronage and class bias to identify candidates with leadership potential. In early 1941, the Royal Armoured Corps found that it was not recruiting sufficiently good officers into its ranks. As part of its response to identifying and developing new officers, the Royal Armoured Corps created officer training units that consisted of one third public school boys, one third secondary comprehensive school boys and one third of older men, up to thirty, whose life experience had a positive and levelling effect on the group. In contrast, Guards armoured units recruited entirely from public schools, which General Martel believed was a mistake. The Royal Armoured Corps found that although public school boys tended to be more self-reliant, having lived away from home, often confined in stern institutions most of their young lives, they were often less capable than their secondary school counterparts.[18]

By 1941, it was clear that the army's system of Command Interview Boards set up to identify potential officers was not working. Around half the candidates recommended for officer training failed to meet the required standards. The three-man boards made their selections based on little more than personal preference, and the process was open to abuse and discrimination. In early 1942, new War Office Selection Boards (WOSB) were introduced to scientifically evaluate potential leaders. Candidates spent two or three days undergoing a series of tests and interviews to measure intelligence, initiative, and personal authority. By year's end, the quality of candidates going forward for officer training had increased significantly. Additionally, the social pool from which officer candidates were selected had also broadened. One in four new officers had not even completed secondary education.[19]

An effective mechanism for maintaining the Guards' exclusive status was a system of punitively high mess bills and expenses, making it impossible for an officer without independent means to pay his way.[20] In 1940, at the behest of his father, who had served with the Coldstream Guards during the First World War, Christopher Bulteel joined the regiment. Although he attended

Wellington College and Oxford University, albeit briefly, his family was not wealthy. On arrival at Sandhurst for officer training, he quickly discovered that life in the Brigade of Guards was ruinously expensive. After six months as a Guards officer, he found himself in severe financial trouble, and questioned his choice of regiment:

> My life was fast becoming impossible, not only because I knew, clearly, that I was in the wrong place and in the wrong social class (these padded aristocrats were altogether too exalted for me) but also that there was no chance of getting myself out of debt.
>
> In the Mess, officers would play picquet with one another, gaining or losing five hundred pounds an evening, nearly three times my gross annual pay. They kept cars, owned racehorses, went to their country homes at the week-ends, helped themselves to women (I guessed) and were familiar with all the luxuries of life.

Bulteel concluded:

> This was a world in which I had no place. I had joined up, I thought, to fight in a war. But there was no war for soldiers, as yet, and there never would be for these high-living drones.[21]

Michael Howard recalled being introduced to the many taboos of the tribe as a young ensign in the Coldstream Guards. There was a minefield of social etiquette and conventions that governed every aspect of an officer's life in the 'Brigade' (never to be mistakenly referred to as the 'Guards'). Howard explained that anyone who broke these taboos did not belong to the tribe and believed the British Army consisted of umpteen such tribes. However, Howard questioned the value of such tribalism in bonding fighting men together when weighed against its divisiveness.[22]

Eventually, as the war took its toll on the army's available manpower, the Guards had to seek recruits from a wider social pool than the British upper classes. However, it seems that a more egalitarian and socially diverse Brigade of Guards was not to last long after the end of hostilities. A 2014 research study into the relevance of social differences at the Royal Military Academy Sandhurst found that around 42 per cent of officer cadets had attended private schools. Although many cadets stated that they did not believe social class influenced the training given at Sandhurst, it did have an impact on regimental allocation. One cadet commented that getting into the Guards was like getting into Oxford or Cambridge. Another cadet suggested candidates often excluded themselves from applying to certain regiments such as the Guards because of the associated expenses, and through a fear of class or group prejudice, either real or imagined. The research also found that the persona of certain regiments often encouraged or discouraged certain types of officer candidates from applying. One cadet observed that the Guards were seen as quite strict and particular in everything they did, and very keen on drill, while the Parachute Regiment, for example, was viewed as a more action-oriented than cerebral organisation. The research also found that some of the most senior regiments in the British Army including the Household Division (formerly the Brigade of Guards, which was renamed the Guards Division during the army reforms of 1968) tended to select officer cadets based on whether they were a good fit with the organisational culture, and so maintain the status quo, rather than other factors such as academic achievement.[23]

In 1941, the newly formed Guards Armoured Division quickly realised that those battalions converted to tanks would require men of intelligence, initiative, mechanical aptitude, and reliability. The 1st (Armoured) Battalion, Coldstream Guards, were instructed to reassign or otherwise remove NCOs and men who had performed poorly in intelligence tests no matter how long they had served in the peacetime army:

> For tank commanders and crews, the first essential is that they must be capable of handling their tank in battle.
> Any N.C.O. or man who is mentally not up to the job, no matter how good a soldier he is in barracks, will be a danger to his comrades in action.[24]

The War Office's new intelligence and aptitude tests helped the armoured battalions identify those men best suited to the various technical and mechanical roles that had to be filled such as fitters, electricians, mechanics, and wireless operators. Besides the numerous technical and mechanical trades required to maintain a squadron of tanks, the Guardsmen would have to learn many operational and tactical lessons to successfully fight their tanks in battle. A tank commander, for example, required a multitude of skills. They had to be mentally agile, decisive, capable of reading the terrain in front of them, and able to assimilate lots of information quickly.

In June 1942, all squadrons including officers of 2nd (Armoured) Battalion, Irish Guards, underwent Raven's Progressive Matrices (RPM) tests. The RPM was a tool to measure general human intelligence and abstract reasoning ability, developed by John C. Raven in 1936.[25]

According to the Irish Guards, war diary' the tests could predict with 95 per cent accuracy the suitability of a candidate for certain types of job. The diarist explained that the test consisted of around sixty sets of drawings from which one was missing. At the foot of the page there were six to eight possible choices for the missing figure in the set. The test subject was asked to select the most appropriate and logical to fill the space. A score of fifty-four or above was Class I (capable of raising to any heights), with classes two, three plus, three minus, four, and so on. The diarist recounts that there was a certain amount of friendly rivalry among the officers tested:

> Of the officers tested, Jack Reynolds came out top with 58, Desmond Fitzgerald and Paul Stobart tying for second place with 57. There were no appalling disasters.[26]

Between 1941 and the summer of 1944, the Guards Armoured Division 'combed out' officers, NCOs and men who had been identified as unsuitable for service with an armoured battalion.

On Sunday, 13 December 1941, Sergeant Murrell confided to his diary that the Prince of Wales (PoW) Company's Captain of the Week was the worst type of Guards officer, a man devoid of all character who believed in his own divine right to command. However, Murrell went on to say that thankfully this officer was one of the few 'Blimps' left in the battalion.[27] The term 'Blimp' was a reference to a First World War character created by cartoonist David Low, Colonel Blimp, who by the 1930s had come to epitomise a public perception of British Army officers as being upper class, blustering, officious halfwits.[28]

As the war progressed, so the Guards gradually accepted 'Citizen Officers' into its ranks. These were men who joined the army and were awarded a commission for the duration of hostilities. In an assessment of the training of 2nd Battalion, Welsh Guards, it noted that this intake of new citizen officers thought the Guards' obsession with drill was a waste of time, and they were not averse to expressing their opinions.[29] Nevertheless, the Brigade of Guards did its best to instil its ethos into new subalterns. In August 1944, during Operation BLUECOAT, Sergeant Murrell, attached to 2nd Battalion HQ, recalled the arrival of two replacement officers while he was busy making wooden crosses for the graves of recently killed Guardsmen. He observed how the young officers, little more than schoolboys, maintained the usual flow of flippant conversation that all Guards' officers adopted.

> But war inevitably imposes some familiarity between officers and men – even in the Guards – and these subalterns who join us now are war intakes – all have been through the Guards Depot, and served as rankers. They know our patter and our way of life. Some come from less grand public schools than did our peacetime officers, and sometimes stoicism and reserve give way almost to confidences.[30]

From the start of the conflict, the war created certain recruitment challenges for the Brigade of Guards. The British Army, by and large, held little attraction for many people compared with the Royal Navy and Royal Air Force, who took the pick of available recruits.[31] Once in the army, a significant number of the brightest and the best officers and rankers were siphoned off to special forces such as the Commandos and Airborne. Just over 28,000 men served in Britain's two parachute divisions and an independent parachute brigade.[32] As we have seen, the Guards had something of a public image problem. As an institution, the Brigade of Guards was often seen as being a unit that was obsessed with parade ground drill; rigid disciplinarians and social elitists, where money and status mattered more than military skill and ability. Although the formation of the Guards Armoured Division was, to some extent, meant to demonstrate the Brigade of Guards' ability to change, embrace modernity, and preserve its elite status within the army, it was not wholly successful.

In early 1942, it was hoped the public announcement and subsequent newspaper coverage of the formation of the Guards Armoured Division would dispel the old 'spit-and-polish' perception of the Foot Guards and replace it with a new, technically advanced, more egalitarian one.[33] However, in October 1944, Sergeant Murrell was smarting with annoyance having read a newspaper column that joked that the Guards Armoured Division had performed well in battle but suffered heavy casualties because tank crews regularly hit their heads on the inside of their vehicles because they instinctively jumped to attention at the sound of an officer's voice on the radio network.[34] Joking aside, the Guards ethos, which gave the Guards armoured formations much of their internal strength, unity of purpose and organisational identity, was all too easily misunderstood and misinterpreted by outsiders. What Lieutenant General Sir Brian Horrocks, 30 Corps, observed as the Guards' fetish for understatement and practice of never showing any emotion under any circumstances was just as easily misread by outsiders as arrogance, snobbery and even incompetence.[35] Perhaps putting Guardsmen into tanks and hoping to recast them in a similar image of heroic modernity as the dashing fighter pilots and oily mechanics of the RAF was an impossible task. The Brigade of Guards certainly appeared to have suffered from organisational dissonance, a bastion of the British establishment on the one hand while trying to cast themselves in a range of new and experimental roles on the other. Besides armour, the Guards played a prominent role in the formation and evolution of various special forces during the war including the Parachute Regiment, the Long Range Desert Group (LRDG) and Special Air Service (SAS). Perhaps because of their elitist nature and sense of entitlement, the Guards possessed a unique belief that there was no challenge they could not overcome and no aspect of modern warfare they could not eventually master.

The Guards Manpower Crisis

During 1943, the heavy fighting in Italy and the subsequent toll of casualties created a replacement crisis for front-line Guards battalions in the Mediterranean. Due to the shortage of trained Guardsmen available to fill the depleted ranks in Italy, it was suggested that either the Guards Armoured Division or the 6th Guards (Tank) Brigade be broken up to provide the necessary replacements.[36]

A letter from the Secretary of State for War pointed out that because Guardsmen were not regarded as regular infantry, it was not possible to transfer men from other line regiments to make up for the shortfall in Guards replacements. However, the prime minister resisted the notion of breaking up either of the Guards armoured formations, and an increase in the draft of recruits into the Guards provided a temporary solution.[37]

During the build-up to D-Day, the 6th Guards (Tank) Brigade was once again threatened with disbandment as a possible source of replacements for men lost in Italy and anticipated casualties for the Normandy campaign. In March 1944, the secretary of state for war wrote to the prime minister recommending the running down of six divisions, reducing anti-aircraft defences, abolishing the Guards (Tank) Brigade, and disbanding the 10th Armoured Division. In response, the prime minister suggested that the Guards Armoured Division and 6th Guards (Tank) Brigade be amalgamated. The prime minister's idea was that the new enlarged Guards formation would provide its own casualty replacements until this became unsustainable.[38]

On 5 April, General Montgomery rejected the idea of an enlarged Guards formation. Next, Jock Colville, the prime minister's assistant private secretary, became involved in the debate. Colville consulted the Brigade of Guards and stated that disbanding the 6th Guards (Tank) Brigade would have a 'catastrophic effect on morale' and waste years of specialist training on Churchill tanks.[39]

The prime minister remained obdurate. He insisted there was no question of the 6th Guards (Tank) Brigade being abolished. Instead, he wanted men transferred from line regiments and the RAF Regiment to ensure Guards battalions were maintained. Initially, there was some resistance from the Air Ministry to the prime minister's demands. Nevertheless, by the end of June 1944, 2,000 RAF Regiment personnel had been transferred to the army. Eight hundred men were described as of full Guards standard and the remainder as just infantry standard.[40] The majority of RAF personnel who arrived at the Guards Depot in June for basic training had been assimilated successfully by September 1944.[41]

Precisely what motivated the prime minister's determination to maintain the integrity of Guards armoured formations, even at the expense of line regiments and the RAF, remains unclear. The Guards sat at the top of the army's social hierarchy due to their long lineage and close association with the monarchy. Indeed, the Brigade of Guards could exert political influence. Of course, the prime minister's bias in favour of the 6th Guards (Tank) Brigade might simply have been an expression of his vanity. After all, they were equipped with Churchill tanks. However, Montgomery was irritated by Churchill's interference and subsequently removed the 6th Guards (Tank) Brigade from his order of battle for Operation OVERLORD. Charles Farrell argues that Montgomery's desire to 'melt down' the 6th Guards (Tank) Brigade was motivated by the projected casualty figures for tank crews during the Normandy campaign, which proved incorrect. Finding replacement tank crews never proved a serious issue during the campaign for north-west Europe, while infantry casualties were alarmingly high and remained a cause of concern until the end of the war. Of course, one can only speculate about what might have happened if the two Guards armoured brigades had been broken up as Montgomery wanted.[42]

Chapter Eight

Tanks: Covenanter to the Sherman

Those Guards battalions earmarked for conversion to armour started their training on the much-maligned Covenanter Cruiser tank. Major General Adair described the Covenanter as fast but unreliable, although only ever intended for training purposes.[1] A member of the 2nd Battalion, Welsh Guards, simply described the Covenanter as the worst Cruiser tank ever made.[2] Perhaps its only saving grace, the Covenanter provided its tank crews with ample opportunities to test their newly acquired skills in diagnosing and fixing mechanical faults. Before the end of 1942, the Division's armoured battalions received Crusader tanks, armed with an effective 6-pounder gun, but the Crusader were generally considered underpowered and outdated by 1st (Armoured) Battalion, Coldstream Guards. In 1943, the Guards Armoured was equipped with the American M4 Sherman, classified by the British as a Cruiser tank. The Sherman was mechanically much more reliable than anything British tank manufacturers had produced up to that point. The Sherman was armed with a dual-purpose 75mm main gun capable of firing both AP and HE shells. However, the Sherman was not universally accepted by members of the Division as a panacea to German armour and anti-tank guns, which were regarded as superior.[3]

William (Bill) Anstruther-Gray was the member of parliament (MP) for North Lanark. He had commanded a squadron of Sherman tanks in Tunisia, where he had won the Military Cross (MC). According to Robert Boscawen, 1st (Armoured) Battalion, Coldstream Guards, Anstruther-Gray attended two 'Secret Sessions' held in the House of Commons, where he told the minister of war, P.J. Grigg, and Prime Minister Winston Churchill about what he believed to be the Sherman's inadequacies when confronted by German 88mm anti-tank guns and the new German Tiger tank. It seems that neither minister liked what Anstruther-Gray had to say.[4]

The M4 Sherman

American armoured doctrine of the inter-war years viewed the tank as an infantry support weapon. Armour was a subordinate branch of the infantry due to a congressional amendment to the National Defence Act of 4 June 1920. It was not until July 1940 that Army Chief of Staff George C. Marshall ordered the creation of an Armoured Force independent of infantry or cavalry control. However, American doctrine was influenced by the early successes of the German Panzer Divisions in 1939 and 1940.[5] The development of American medium tanks focused on the needs of armoured divisions, which would play a similar tactical role to horsed cavalry. The infantry would accomplish the breakthrough, and the armoured divisions would exploit the penetration in the enemy's line.

Because of its need for mobility, the new medium tank's design somewhat sacrificed armoured protection. In terms of firepower, the U.S. Army wanted a good dual-purpose gun that could engage a variety of soft targets and fire an armour-piercing shell. However, there was a view that tank-on-tank engagements would seldom occur, and so the armour-piercing capabilities of the tank's gun were given secondary consideration. The first significant medium tank to be produced was the M3 (Lee) in its basic American version and M3 (Grant) with a British-designed turret. Following the shock defeat of France in 1940, the design of the M3 was rushed into production. U.S. Army Ordnance had no experience of building a tank turret capable of housing a 75mm main gun, so the expedient solution was to house the gun in a sponson (a gun platform standing out from the tank's side). The new tank was in production by June 1941, less than nine months after the initial design. In August 1941, Major General Jacob Devers was appointed head of the U.S. Army's Armored Force (sic). Devers was a proponent of replacing light and medium tanks with a single universal or multi-role tank design. However, the U.S. Army and Britain wanted an adequate tank now rather than something near-perfect later. Although the M3's sponson-mounted 75mm gun had helped the British in North Africa answer the threat posed by German anti-tank guns, it was not an ideal configuration.[6] U.S. Ordnance quickly started working on a new medium tank design with a turret-mounted main gun. The new medium tank, which was accepted into U.S. military service in December 1941, was designated the M4. The British named it the Sherman. The design, approval, and production of the M4 was not straightforward. U.S. Ordnance had very little experience of building tanks. They persistently failed to design tanks capable of meeting tomorrow's military threats rather than yesterday's.[7] The development of the M4 was further hindered by inter-service bickering, rivalries, and bureaucracy, which negatively affected design and production decisions. In many ways, the Sherman was designed by committee.[8]

Major General Devers saw the M4 Sherman as a replacement for the M3 Grant. He also significantly changed the structure of the armoured division, making it a more balanced formation with more medium and fewer light tanks, increasing the armoured infantry component, and replacing artillery with self-propelled guns.[9] The armoured force employed armoured divisions to exploit breaches in the enemy's lines and disrupt command and control. The main striking force of the armoured division was the medium tank. Those units detailed with making the initial breach in the enemy line were assigned tanks from the GHQ reserve, a similar idea to the British Infantry tank concept but without a heavily armoured vehicle for the purpose. Armoured Divisions and Corps were assigned to Infantry Corps or Armies predominantly.[10] The medium tank had two principal roles to perform: infantry support and exploitation. Consequently, the medium tank was designed for speed and mobility. Curiously, tank-on-tank engagements were considered unlikely, and so anti-tank defence was assigned to tank destroyer units equipped with specialised vehicles.[11]

New Equipment, Same Tactics

The M4 Sherman was equipped with a reliable, dual-purpose 75mm gun capable of firing AP and HE shells. However, the short barrel and low muzzle velocity of the Sherman's main gun meant that it was at a distinct disadvantage when engaging German Panther and Tiger tanks.[12] Regrettably, there was no corresponding change in tactics or training methods to accompany the upgrade in equipment. The Guards Armoured Division continued to practice either hull-down (where the tank's hull is concealed by the terrain and only the turret is visible) static fire support or charging the enemy line in a massed assault.[13]

As well as the standard M4 Sherman, a late addition to the Guards' arsenal was the Sherman Firefly. These Sherman tanks were modified to house the British 17-pounder anti-tank gun. One Firefly was allotted to each troop to perform an overwatch function. When possible, the Firefly remained at the rear of the troop and then came forward to engage any German armour that posed a threat.[14]

The Guards Armoured received no training to prepare itself for the closed Norman countryside known as the bocage. The Normandy bocage was a patchwork of small fields bordered by steep earth banks and impenetrable hedgerows, criss-crossed by sunken lanes. The terrain gave every advantage to the defender and severely limited the deployment of tanks.[15]

The Guards Armoured Division seemed to follow War Office directives on organising and operating an armoured division. However, they were hobbled, first by their own inexperience and a lack of tanks, equipment, and suitable training areas. Later, there seems to have been a collective failure to appreciate many of the lessons learned in North Africa and Italy. In addition, the tendency to devolve training responsibilities to battalion commanders created an imbalance, where some units were better trained than others. The most serious deficiency in training was the lack of infantry and armoured co-operation. However, inconsistent training was not confined to the Guards; it was more widespread across the British Army. In *Clash of Arms*, Russell Hart argues that the British Army's inability to master close all-arms co-operation remained a problem throughout the Normandy campaign:

> British forces rarely displayed combined-arms proficiency because regimental parochialism and the absence of holistic doctrine led armor [sic] and infantry to fight their own separate wars. Lack of an interarms tradition meant it took long association – years in fact – for Commonwealth forces to developed combined arms proficiency.[16]

In contrast to the Guards Armoured, the 11th Armoured Division spent nearly four years under intensive training, including exercises to ensure close infantry and tank co-operation.[17] In June 1944, on the eve of Operation OVERLORD, British armoured divisions still maintained a separation between infantry and armoured brigades. Commander of the 4th Armoured Brigade, Brigadier Michael Carver (later Field Marshal Lord Carver), explained that Montgomery's strategic plan for the Normandy campaign stuck rigidly to what many veterans by then considered an outdated orthodoxy:

> Much discussion as to whether, as a result of the lessons we had learned in Italy, the organization of the division should be changed to one which gave a more even balance of infantry and tanks than the official one of an armoured brigade of three tank regiments and one motor infantry battalion, and an infantry brigade of three infantry battalions, carried in three-ton lorries, and no tanks. Under terms of great secrecy, within the confines of Cambridge college, we were initiated into Montgomery's plan, which forecast that, after a short period of battle in the close 'bocage' country of Normandy, we should break out into the open country of Northern France, ideal for tank action. It was therefore generally accepted that we should stick to the official organization of the division, although it was clear that one of the tank regiments, initially at least, would have to be attached to the lorried infantry brigade.[18]

Although British commanders had learned many lessons from earlier campaigns, they had failed to appreciate that an armoured division is an integrated and flexible all-arms formation.[19] The Guards Armoured Division would not adopt an all-arms co-operative system until after its baptism of fire during Operation GOODWOOD.

The Churchill Infantry Tank

As we have already seen, British military thinking about the development and deployment of tanks had settled upon the idea of three role-based vehicle designs. First, the army would need a small, light-weight tank for reconnaissance purposes. Next, a heavily armoured infantry support tank was required to achieve break-in attacks on the enemy line. Finally, the army wanted a fast, agile but lightly armoured Cruiser tank that could exploit any breach in the enemy lines and perform a similar role to that of traditional horsed cavalry.

At the start of the war, the Matilda and then Vickers Valentine took up the mantle of infantry support tanks, although the Valentine would eventually be redesignated as a Cruiser. Next, the Special Vehicle Development Committee (SVDC) sanctioned the development of an experimental tank design that harked back to the First World War rather than looking forward to the needs of the current conflict. The experimental super-heavy infantry tank became known as TOG (The Old Gang), because the development group was made up of people who had worked on the earliest British tanks. Shipbuilders Harland and Wolff also put forward a design for an infantry tank designated the A20. However, while the development of the TOG was soon abandoned, the A20 was considered to have some latent promise, and its development was taken over by Luton-based car manufacturer Vauxhall Motors. Under immense pressure from the prime minister and the Tank Board, Vauxhall hurried into production the newly designated A22 or Churchill Mark I Infantry tank. In appearance, the Churchill resembled its First World War predecessors. The Mark I was armed with a 3-inch howitzer, 2-pounder gun and Besa machine gun. The Churchill had a crew of five and weighed 38.5 tons. The 3-inch howitzer was removed from the Churchill Mark II, replaced by a second hull-mounted machine gun. Next, the Churchill Mark III got a new turret designed to accommodate a 6-pounder gun. In the Mark IV, the plate-welded turret was replaced with a cast one. However, the new tank was plagued by many mechanical faults.

Having been rushed into production during the early days of the war, when Britain faced the imminent threat of invasion, the early versions of the Churchill tank were mechanically unreliable. In January 1942, a report stated that 42 per cent of Churchills were unavailable for service due to technical problems. Because of its pitiful record of mechanical unreliability, Churchill production was expected to be cancelled. Nevertheless, while the War Cabinet pondered the tank's fate, 300 Churchills were adapted to take a 95mm close-support howitzer, replacing the 6-pounder gun. The Churchill Mark VI was equipped with a 75mm gun. In 1943, a new 'heavy' Churchill (A22F) was built, which carried 6-inch frontal armour and a range of other modifications and improvements.

Finally, the Churchill Mark VII and Mark VIII, the former mounting a 75mm gun and the latter armed with a 95mm howitzer, would be the Infantry tanks used throughout the campaign for north-west Europe. Many of the earlier-production models of the Churchill were adapted for specialist tasks such as bridge layers with the 79th Armoured Division. Perhaps the most famous and feared specialist adaptation was the flamethrowing Churchill Crocodile. The Churchills that saw service in north-west Europe from D-Day onwards were much more reliable than their predecessors. Additionally, the Churchill possessed good off-road performance and an ability to climb steep gradients and cross ditches that confounded other tanks.

In December 1944, the anecdotal evidence of the Churchill's remarkable cross-country performance was substantiated during a series of qualitative performance trials of various Allied and Axis tanks. During the trials held on Chobham Common, tanks including the Panther, Tiger, Churchill, Cromwell, Sherman, and T-34 had to navigate a muddy, waterlogged defile, transverse a small valley, and finally climb straight up a hillside.

Across the three tests, the German Tiger tank was reported as easily being the worst performer. The Churchill and Panther proved the only two vehicles capable of successfully negotiating the rough, undulating ground of the second test site, which quickly deteriorated into a morass after heavy rain. Overall, the Churchill tank completely outperformed all other vehicles when required to negotiate wet, slippery ground and various gradients. The report also found the American Sherman demonstrated poor track adhesion regardless of the track configuration used on the vehicle.[20]

Generally, the Churchill proved a popular vehicle with the 6th Guards (Tank) Brigade, unlike the Sherman with the 5th Guards (Armoured) Brigade. Perhaps the Churchill's principal defect was it remained under-gunned throughout its service life. The size of the tank's turret ring meant that it could not accommodate the more powerful 17-pounder gun that was fitted into the Sherman Firefly.[21]

The Churchill tank had a crew of five. The commander, wireless operator/loader and gunner were situated in the turret. The driver and co-driver, who also operated a Besa machine gun, occupied the tank's hull. Typically, a tank battalion was organised into a Headquarters Squadron and three subordinate Squadrons, numbered one to three. In the case of the 3rd (Tank) Battalion, Scots Guards, the Squadrons were designated Right Flank, Left Flank, and 'S' Squadron. The Battalion Headquarters had four Churchill tanks; each of the three Squadrons had three tanks at Headquarters and five Troops of three tanks each. In total, a battalion would have a fulfilment of around fifty-eight Churchill tanks plus an assortment of reconnaissance vehicles including scout cars and M3 Stuart light tanks, known as Honeys to British formations. However, casualties often reduced Troop numbers during operations.[22]

The Churchill tank was not produced in sufficient numbers to equip the eight independent tank/armoured brigades that were deployed to Normandy, so only three tank brigades fought in the campaign equipped with the type. In fact, only 350 Churchill gun tanks saw front-line service at one time, while the rest were employed in various specialised roles.[23]

Section Two

Into Battle and Lessons Learned

Chapter Nine

Operation GOODWOOD

Normandy

The D-Day landings, the battle for Normandy and the campaign for north-west Europe have all been written about extensively by others. In this book, I have restricted myself to writing brief descriptions of various military operations undertaken by the Guards Armoured Division and the 6th Guards (Tank) Brigade to provide the necessary context for my examination of their combat performance, and ability to adapt to changing circumstances on the battlefield based on lessons learned.

OVERLORD

The campaign for the liberation of north-west Europe started on Tuesday, 6 June 1944 with a massive air and amphibious assault on a 50-mile stretch of the Normandy coastline divided into five designated beaches code-named Utah, Omaha, Gold, Juno, and Sword. The D-Day landings of Operation OVERLORD and subsequent fighting secured a bridgehead for the western Allies, although not all D-Day objectives, such as the capture of the port city of Caen, were achieved. The Allied ground forces enjoyed several advantages over the German defenders, including a protective umbrella of naval gunfire and almost complete air superiority. Having got ashore successfully, the Allies had to win the battle of the build-up. Basically, the Allies had to pour more men, vehicles, ammunition, food, and fuel into the battlespace faster than the Germans could respond. To help win the logistics battle of the build-up the Allies constructed two prefabricated Mulberry harbours. By 18 June, the Allies had landed 218,000 tons of supplies, 95,000 vehicles and 628,861 troops across the beaches.[1]

By the time the Guards Armoured Division joined General Montgomery's 21st Army Group in Normandy, Operations PERCH and EPSOM had achieved enough to consider a breakout from the bridgehead. However, the early Anglo-Canadian operations fought during the Normandy campaign revealed several tactical and operational shortcomings such as poor co-ordination of infantry and armour. Having failed to outmanoeuvre his opponents, Montgomery revised his plans and adopted new tactics that utilised the Allies' strengths in artillery firepower and aircraft. The 21st Army Group would fight a series of pitched battles with limited objectives where the enemy would first be 'softened up' by stupefying air bombardments and artillery barrages before being battered by the infantry and armour. Montgomery's brutally simple plan was to win through attrition, gradually denuding the enemy of troops, materiel, and, ultimately, its ability to resist.[2]

Prelude to GOODWOOD

In the month since D-Day, the Allies had built up enormous material resources of men and equipment, lodged into a small and increasingly crowded bridgehead.[3] In the west, American forces under General Bradley had been making limited progress through the dense terrain of the Normandy bocage. In the east, the British and Canadians faced the bulk of the Germans' armoured formations, fighting to maintain their hold on Caen. In early July, General Bradley proposed a plan enabling the Americans to break out of the Cherbourg peninsula. Code-named Operation COBRA, the American offensive was due to start on 18 July 1944. To give the operation its best chance of success, it was important that German armoured formations remain engaged in the east, around Caen, rather than redeploy to meet the American threat.[4]

In response to General Bradley's proposed plan, General Dempsey, commander of the British 2nd Army, suggested a new breakout offensive east of the River Orne. Initially, General Montgomery, Commander-in-Chief of Allied land forces, was unenthusiastic about Dempsey's idea. However, later, Montgomery reconsidered Dempsey's plan as a subordinate operation to support the main American effort.[5]

The Operational Challenges of GOODWOOD

The basic plan for GOODWOOD required three British armoured divisions to cross two water obstacles the Orne River and Caen Canal. Next, each Division would have to navigate narrow lanes through British minefields laid earlier in the campaign. Once through the minefields, the battlespace itself was extremely limited, barely wide enough for two tank squadrons (about forty tanks) to advance line abreast.[6] The ground sloped gently upward from around Cuverville south-west towards Cagny and Bourguébus. The battlefield was bisected, east to west, by two railway lines on embankments. The axis of advance was also flanked by several Norman villages, woods, and orchards. Overall, the ground gave every advantage to the defender. The staging area for GOODWOOD, the Orne bridgehead, was under observation by the Germans who held the Colombelles industrial area of Caen's north-eastern suburbs.[7] The Canadian 2nd Corps launched Operation ATLANTIC, synchronised with GOODWOOD, to capture the Caen suburbs south of the Orne. Intelligence assessments and aerial reconnaissance revealed 'that the 8 Corps attack would have to reckon with a very strong enemy defensive position sited in considerable depth'.[8]

The ground assault for GOODWOOD was preceded by a massive air bombardment, numbering over 2,000 heavy and medium bombers. An intricate artillery fire support plan followed the air bombardment. However, the narrowness of the Orne bridgehead meant that most of the heavy and medium artillery (760 guns) had to be sited on the west bank of the river, which limited their effective range to a line just short of the Bourguébus Ridge. The physical limits imposed by the terrain and difficulties of approach to the start line meant that 8 Corps would have to advance 'one division up' in echelon: 11th Armoured Division, Guards Armoured Division and 7th Armoured Division.[9]

The Guards at GOODWOOD

Operation GOODWOOD was the Guards Armoured Division's first battle. The following is a summary of the Guards' first action during GOODWOOD, not a retelling of the entire operation.

On 18 July 1944, the Grenadiers Guards moved south-east toward the village of Cagny on the left flank of the advance. The Grenadiers were about 2,000 yards short of the village when they met anti-tank gunfire, which knocked out two tanks. Attempts to outflank the village were unsuccessful and the advance stalled. Next, tanks of No. 1 Squadron, Grenadier Guards, moved to the left of the village and eventually worked their way to the edge of Cagny by 1600hrs. The operation to invest the village then began. The attack on Cagny was completed quickly as the German defenders had already withdrawn, leaving behind three dual-purpose 88mm anti-aircraft/anti-tank guns and other equipment. Later, the Coldstream Guards moved south around Cagny and engaged German tanks concealed in an orchard south of a railway embankment. The result of this action was a stalemate.

Throughout the day 32nd Guards Infantry Brigade made slow, fitful advances due to limited space and traffic congestion within the Orne bridgehead. The Guardsmen mounted in lorries were shelled and mortared. It was nearly evening before the infantry finally reached the armour.

By evening, 1st Battalion, Welsh Guards, relieved the Grenadiers in Cagny. The Coldstream Guards dug in east of the village. The 3rd Battalion, Irish Guards, moved to invest Frénouville, screened by the 2nd Battalion's tanks on

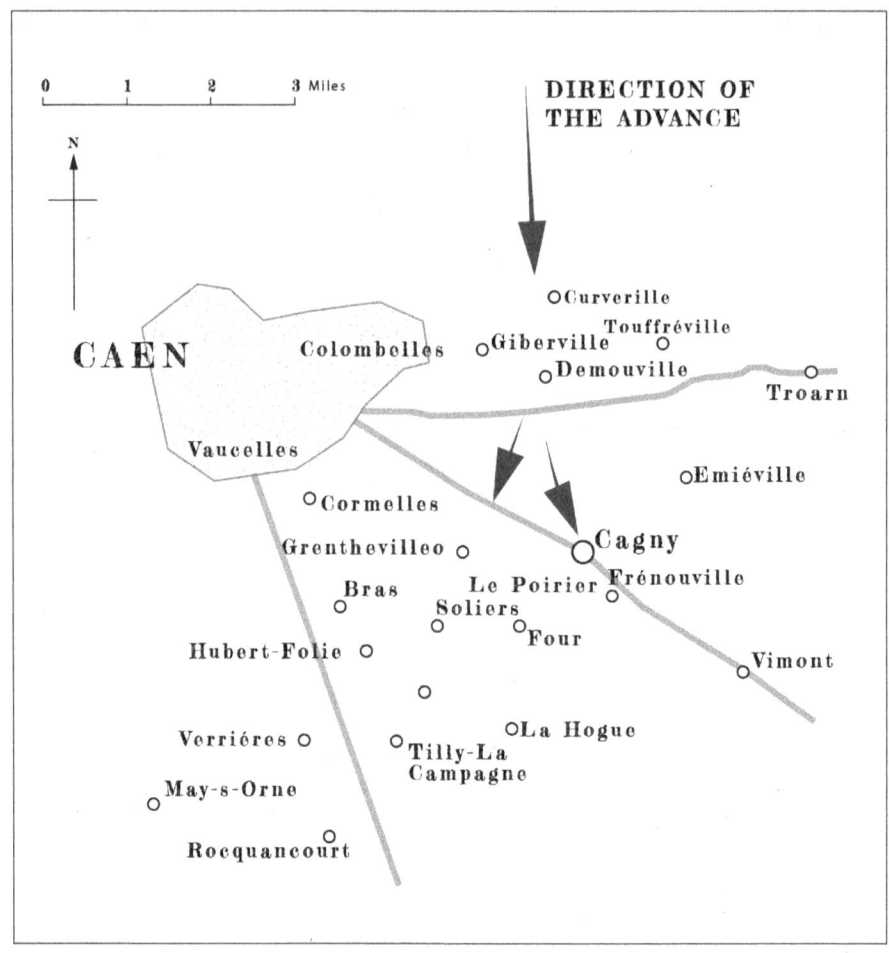

Map 1. Operation GOODWOOD, 18 – 20 July 1944, Guards Armoured Division.

the Vimont Road. Having met resistance from Frénouville, the Irish Guards dug in for the night.

On 19 July, the 1st Battalion, Welsh Guards, successfully attacked the village of Le Poirier. Next morning, 5th Battalion, Coldstream Guards, occupied Frénouville. Both battalions dug in and held their positions for three days until relieved.[10]

Operation GOODWOOD advanced the Orne bridgehead about 7 miles deep across a 6-mile front with 2,500 prisoners taken and approximately 100 enemy tanks destroyed.[11] The operation cost the Guards Armoured Division 330 casualties: 79 killed, 226 wounded, and 25 missing.[12]

Assessment and Legacy of GOODWOOD

Today, Operation GOODWOOD generates much historical debate and controversy regarding its planned objectives and results. Subsequently, it has become a popular subject for writers, journalists, historians, and military theorists. For example, in 1980, General Sir William Scotter proposed that German defensive tactics used at GOODWOOD might provide a template for NATO forces to repel a Soviet armoured offensive in north-west Europe.[13] In 1982, Charles Dick sought to refute the 'GOODWOOD concept'.[14] Nevertheless, a generation of British Army officers visited the GOODWOOD battlefield, escorted by key protagonists such as Major General Roberts, commander of 11th Armoured Division, and Colonel Han Von Luck, 21st Panzer Division.[15]

British military historian Ian Daglish suggested that Operation GOODWOOD was unusual because it did not conform to Montgomery's 'set-piece' battles and presented major logistical difficulties. However, GOODWOOD was General Miles Dempsey's plan, not Montgomery's. Nevertheless, Charles Forrester and John Buckley broadly concur with Daglish's assessment, but for different reasons.

Daglish says the operation yielded impressive casualties and heavy tank losses but failed to deliver the dramatic breakthrough that many had expected. Matters were made worse by early reports of a breach in the German defences, which proved unfounded. Montgomery's over-optimistic predictions for the operation also caused a rift between the British and American military leadership.

Daglish describes GOODWOOD as an experiment in armoured warfare. Dempsey believed he could substitute machine power for dwindling British manpower to achieve GOODWOOD's aims. He also assessed the open rolling countryside of the GOODWOOD battlefield as 'good tank country'. However, with limited space for the armoured divisions to deploy and uninterrupted fields of fire for the German anti-tank guns, the terrain proved a killing ground for British tanks.[16]

Forrester broadly agrees with Daglish's assessment that GOODWOOD was a test and incubator of British armoured doctrine. The idea that tanks could operate divorced of supporting infantry and save on casualties proved unfounded. However, Forrester saw GOODWOOD as a seminal operation that allowed middle-ranked officers (division and brigade commanders) to quickly apply lessons learned to subsequent actions in Normandy, such as BLUECOAT. The British Army's decentralised command structure possibly helped facilitate what Forrester describes as the 'bubbling up' process of battlefield adaptation while still adhering to Montgomery's functional doctrine of combined arms operations.[17]

John Buckley argues that GOODWOOD was a flawed operation that fell between two stools, neither conforming to the prescribed method of operations nor working through the tactical implications necessary to break the mould. Nevertheless, Buckley concedes that the operation contributed to the overall success of the Anglo-Canadian strategic effort around Caen.[18] Similarly, Daglish believed GOODWOOD did succeed in its strategic aim of fixing the bulk of German armour on the eastern flank, enabling the Americans to break out in the west. However, he denigrated the GOODWOOD concept of the 1980s.[19]

Buckley points to the changes in Dempsey's original plan for GOODWOOD and Montgomery's later downgrading of the operation as a prime source of later controversy. He explains that Montgomery's changes to the plan were not communicated to the Corps commanders or outside the 2nd Army. This communications failure led General Eisenhower and SHAEF (Supreme Headquarters Allied Expeditionary Force) to believe GOODWOOD was intended to break the German line and advance toward Falaise.[20] It is possible that Montgomery purposely kept SHAEF in the dark about his altered plans for GOODWOOD to ensure the operation still received the massive air support requested.

Dempsey argued that confusion at SHAEF and in the press about GOODWOOD's true intentions misled the enemy and was entirely beneficial to the Allies. He said the press coverage helped convince the Germans that the British were trying to break out in the Caen area.

Dempsey insisted that he confined himself strictly to Montgomery's instructions when preparing the GOODWOOD plan. Nevertheless, he confessed that the possibility of a German collapse and exploitation toward Falaise was in his mind, but he did not disclose it or discuss it with his subordinates.[21]

Dempsey believed that the attack he put in on 18 July 'was not a very good operation of war tactically, but strategically it was a great success, even though we did get a bloody nose'.[22]

Stephen Napier's study of tank loss estimates for GOODWOOD suggests that the commonly quoted figure of between 400 and 500 tanks knocked out during the operation was excessive. Napier proposes that an adjusted figure of 275 tank casualties is a more accurate figure.[23] However, he also argues that the British Army in Normandy was short of Sherman tanks by the end of July because of GOODWOOD.[24] In contrast to the lower number of tanks lost, GOODWOOD produced 5,537 man casualties, which the 2nd Army could ill afford.[25] If correct, Napier's figures make a nonsense of Dempsey's assertion that he could lose a couple of hundred tanks to preserve manpower during GOODWOOD.

GOODWOOD Lessons Learned

Major General Adair said that 8 Corps designed the GOODWOOD operation poorly but did not clarify this statement in his memoir. Without any sense of irony, he also condemned the Guards' advance as being like a cavalry charge. However, Adair had previously been the proponent of 'good tank gallops' during exercises on the Yorkshire Wolds. He was also critical of the Sherman tank, which he described as no match for the German tanks.[26]

The secondary literature to date overwhelmingly suggests that the main lesson learned by the Division was the need for greater integration of infantry and armoured battalions. As Rosse and Hill explained:

> The armoured brigade had outstripped the infantry brigade, which had no chance to close up and influence the battle at the vital moment. Consequently, this was the last, as well as the first, occasion on which we fought on the lines according to which we had been trained.[27]

However, days before Operation GOODWOOD, training was already under way to improve infantry and tank co-operation in anticipation of the difficulties of fighting in the Normandy bocage. On 13 July, the war diary of 5th Battalion, Coldstream Guards, stated that all officers must attend a demonstration arranged by Brigade of 'Tank and Infantry co-operation in close country fighting, designed to meet our needs in the Bocage district which lies ahead'. The following day the war diary sets out the main items of the training programme, which include companies to practise bocage fighting in co-operation with 1st (Armoured) Coldstream Guards, and parties to visit local battlefields. It is also clear that training to improve infantry and tank co-operation was a division-wide initiative.[28]

On 10 July, the war diary of the 2nd (Armoured) Battalion, Irish Guards, states that all squadron leaders should conduct TEWTs on the co-operation of infantry and tanks in close country. The squadron leaders then performed a similar exercise with the tank commanders over the following two days.[29]

On 13 July, the war diary for Headquarters, 32nd Guards Brigade, refers to a demonstration of tank and infantry co-operation being conducted by the 1st (Armoured) Coldstream Guards and 1st Welsh Guards.[30] The war diary for the 1st (Motor) Battalion, Grenadier Guards, contains the same order that all officers were to attend the demonstration.[31]

The main result of the lessons learned from GOODWOOD was a reorganisation of the Division into three 'bocage battlegroups'.[32] The 5th Guards Brigade combined the 2nd (Armoured) Irish Guards with the 5th Battalion,

Coldstream Guards. In 32nd Guards Brigade, the 2nd (Armoured) and 1st (Motor) Battalion, Grenadier Guards, formed the second battlegroup and the 1st (Armoured) Coldstream and 3rd Battalion, Irish Guards, the third. The Welsh Guards remained ungrouped.[33] Nevertheless, before GOODWOOD, the Guards had already acknowledged the need for closer infantry and armoured co-operation in anticipation of fighting in the Normandy bocage.

There is a discrepancy in the literature about who was the true architect of the bocage battlegroup. Both Major General Roberts[34] and Adair[35] claimed the battlegroup was their invention. However, Stephen Napier says that the Guards Armoured Division was reorganised after GOODWOOD at the specific instruction of Lieutenant General O'Connor. The reorganisation was done in great haste, just ninety minutes.[36] John Buckley suggests that Adair and Roberts had reached the same conclusion about the need for greater infantry and armoured co-operation when fighting in Normandy before GOODWOOD.[37] According to Rosse and Hill, the Division's tanks and infantry had only trained together in the last weeks on the Yorkshire Wolds. Once deployed to Normandy, it quickly became apparent to the Guards that greater infantry and armoured co-operation would be required.[38]

The bocage battlegroup provided only a limited solution to the problem of better infantry and tank co-operation. Only the lead squadron of tanks moved with the infantry riding on the hulls while the rest travelled in troop-carrying lorries (TCL).[39] The lorries proved highly vulnerable to small arms, mortar, and artillery fire. They also possessed no off-road capability.

Lord Carrington pointed out that the reorganisation of the Division into battlegroups created its own set of problems. He says that the brigades' new arrangement into one armoured battalion and one infantry battalion was inflexible. Lord Carrington explained that operational necessity would sometimes require more men or more tanks or other support services. However, he did concede that the reorganisation created a better situation than had existed before.[40]

Sir David Fraser also thought the two-battalion battlegroup was not always the most efficient or economic use of resources but did ensure that tanks and infantry moved, lived, and fought together. However, he queried why the Division had not segregated into Regimental Battlegroups immediately instead of waiting until the end of August 1944.[41]

On balance, Carrington's and Fraser's criticisms appear valid. An armoured division was a flexible formation, not a unit. It was a collection of fighting arms and ancillary services, sometimes only temporarily brought together to tackle a specific objective. However, the Guards did seem slow in appreciating the inherent flexibility of their formation and how to apply the right balance of forces to meet particular challenges. For example, the 5th Guards Armoured

Brigade did not issue its directive on fighting in the Normandy bocage until 15 August 1944.[42]

Conversely, the Guards appeared to have had a natural advantage over other formations in that their infantry and armoured battalions came from the same regiments. Indeed, it would seem to make sense to group officers and men who knew each other well and shared much in common into the same battlegroups. Nevertheless, this was not done until the end of August, and the revised composition of brigades was not confirmed until 30 November 1944.[43] It seems unlikely that reorganising battalions along regimental lines would have been an arduous logistical undertaking, suggesting some other reason. Perhaps no one thought to raise the idea of Regimental Battlegroups until after the fighting in Normandy was over. Nevertheless, it does seem extraordinary that the lessons learned in training by the armoured and infantry battalions of the Irish Guards, who first conceived the idea of Regimental Battlegroups back in 1943, appeared to have been completely forgotten.[44]

Chapter Ten

Learning to Fight in the Bocage

On 15 August 1944, the 5th Guards Armoured Brigade distributed a directive entitled 'Fighting in Bocage Country'. It concisely outlined the challenges of operating in Normandy and what the brigade had learned. The document described an environment that overwhelmingly favoured the defender, where 3,000 men and 100 guns could be held up for half an hour by ten men and one gun. The document explained how to use demolition charges to blast holes in the large, impenetrable bocage hedgerows to bypass blocked roads and obstacles. The author also mentioned Rhino tanks, an American adaptation of the Sherman fitted with an improvised hedge-cutting device that resembled tusks.[1]

The Brigade had learned that it was better to advance on multiple centre lines or columns. In this way, at least one column would generally find a route around any German opposition, and flanking attacks could quickly eliminate pockets of resistance.[2]

In terms of the order of march, the directive explained that the leading column should consist of one infantry battalion and one armoured battalion, sub-divided into three groups. Each group should have a vanguard of one troop of tanks and one platoon of infantry. The main group consisted of Guardsmen, a squadron of tanks and support units of artillery and engineers. The author makes it clear that boldness, situational awareness, and flanking attacks generally won the day. They also emphasised the importance of the closest possible co-operation between the company and squadron commanders.[3]

Rather than pushing tanks forward in cavalry-style charges, the Brigade had learned that it was better to keep most tanks back from the leading edge of the advance. In this way, tanks could be fed into an engagement as the situation required. The document discusses the use of artillery, engineers, traffic discipline, bypassing enemy forces and the importance of reporting the position of forward elements accurately (presumably to avoid friendly-fire incidents). It pointed out that the Germans typically pre-registered approach roads and junctions for artillery and mortar bombardment, so it was safer to move off-road until an enemy position was overcome. The directive was circulated throughout the Division.[4]

A Summary of Lessons Learned

As we have seen, the War Office produced a series of military training pamphlets that were a distillation of lessons learned from various operational theatres. However, the army tended to devolve training responsibilities to individual divisions and unit commanders. The German army operated a similar decentralised approach to training, with one significant difference. The German army had a clearly defined doctrine to frame their training efforts, while the British did not.[5] The Headquarters of the Guards Armoured Division took a distinctly non-interventionist approach to how training was conducted.[6] Without the benefit of a guiding doctrine, this devolution of training responsibilities must inevitably have led to a great deal of inconsistency in units' preparedness for battle. As a result, Williamson Murray believed, 'Most British units had to learn many of their basic tactical skills on the battlefield – an expensive school.'[7] Williamson Murray's opinion of British units' combat readiness appears overly critical. The 11th Armoured Division, for example, had practised the type of close infantry and armoured co-operation they anticipated would be required of the fighting in Normandy.[8] They also benefited from having a cohort of battle-experienced officers to guide their training. Once committed to action, the 11th Armoured quickly realised that much closer infantry and armoured co-operation would be required for operations over the dense Norman terrain, down to the squadron/company and platoon/troop level with infantry often riding on the tanks.[9] Similarly, the 4th Armoured Brigade rightly identified the need for much closer infantry and armoured co-operation when operating in the Normandy bocage based on their experiences of fighting in Italy. However, when they suggested a reorganisation of the brigade to form a more balanced formation of infantry battalions and armoured regiments, the idea was dismissed by Montgomery as unnecessary. Prior to D-Day, he remained convinced of his own plan. He believed the Allies would quickly break out of the bocage and sweep all before them across the open country of northern France.[10] In 1943, during training exercises, the Irish Guards had quickly realised that much closer armour and infantry co-operation would be required to overcome an enemy in prepared positions concealed in woodlands, for example.[11] It seems clear that regardless of the British Army's preference for a decentralised approach to training, many armoured and infantry formations arrived at similar conclusions about the best ways to achieve operational objectives. However, the British Army's training system seems to have faltered or failed when it came to disseminating tactical and operational lessons.

Issued in 1943, Military Training Pamphlet No. 41 focused on the tactical handling of an armoured division and its components. The document covers a variety of subjects, including the development of battle drills to ensure uniformity of action in response to likely combat scenarios. The author repeatedly highlights the need for all-arms co-operation to achieve operational objectives.[12] However, the author was aware of a deficiency in the organisation, training, and culture of the British Army, whereby units tended to focus on performing their specific roles at the exclusion and quite possibly the detriment of everything else. In the section of the pamphlet entitled 'Co-operation with other arms', the author writes this stinging rebuke:

> The British character is naturally not inquisitive enough and individual officers and soldiers tend to shirk inquiry into matters which they consider the business of other people. It is the business of everybody to win the war, and in particular to win the actions in which they are engaged, and this can only be done by the closest co-operation of all concerned.[13]

In May 1944, the War Office published Military Training Pamphlet No. 63, which was probably too late to have any meaningful impact on the training of troops destined for Normandy. The subject of this pamphlet was the co-operation of tanks with infantry divisions. The pamphlet briefly explains the dual-tank approach to armoured doctrine and explains Infantry and Cruiser tanks' different roles. Once again, the pamphlet's authors emphasised the importance of close co-operation between infantry and tanks to achieve the best operational results. However, the pamphlet does endorse infantry and tanks echeloned separately for a staged attack rather than integrating them.

Nevertheless, the pamphlet contained many useful recommendations for operating in terrain like the bocage, such as pressing the infantry forward and holding tanks back for support. The pamphlet also recommends using flank attacks to overcome enemy strongpoints and has a section on infantry riding tanks into battle. However, it discourages the practice of tank riding and highlights the dangers involved, such as infantry exposure to small-arms fire and air-attack.[14]

The war diary of the 1st (Motor) Battalion, Grenadier Guards, contains an account of the action at Drouet Woods, which indicates that the adopted tactics set out in 'Fighting in Bocage Country' worked:

> Many times during the day the situation was saved by having the tanks well back, and moving them up on our flanks as required, rather than keeping them forward all the time.[15]

However, it is possible to interpret the 'Fighting in Bocage Country' directive in two ways. First, the document's authors might have incorporated the War Office's advice and recommendations into their lessons learned. Alternatively, the 5th Guards Armoured Brigade had overlooked or disregarded much of the contents of the various military training pamphlets published and instead learned the hard way, through experience, how to fight the Germans in the Normandy bocage.

A Failure of Application

One of the operational failures of Operation GOODWOOD was the separation of infantry and armour, partly due to the inadequacies of the motor transport available.[16] However, Military Training Pamphlet No. 63 contains a perfectly suitable alternative to moving troops forward using lorries. Instead, the infantry could have ridden into battle on the back of the tanks and been immediately available when needed most. For example, an article in *The Scotsman* newspaper from December 1943 described how the 'Eighth Army infantry, riding into battle on tanks, smashed a determined last-minute attempt by the Germans to prevent a breakthrough' at Fossacesia, Italy.[17]

During Operation GOODWOOD, the armoured divisions had no control over separating infantry and armour onto different objectives. Nonetheless, Major General Roberts, 11th Armoured, protested to the Corps commander about being tasked with taking the village of Cagny without his infantry.[18] However, Major General Adair made no such protests about his division's assignments even though the Guards had practised a similar scenario during Exercise SPARTAN in 1943 with disastrous results.[19]

In the days before GOODWOOD, it is clear the division was training to improve infantry and armoured co-operation in anticipation of fighting in the dense bocage countryside. Nevertheless, they seem to have taken a retrograde step at GOODWOOD and acquiesced to fighting as they had trained with infantry and armour separated. Following GOODWOOD, the division reorganised itself into bocage battlegroups to improve its balance of forces and ensure closer infantry and armoured co-operation. It also appears to have quickly improved its ability to collect, disseminate and adapt lessons learned to enhance its tactical and operational efficiency. However, there does seem to have been a collective failure by the Guards to retain and assimilate lessons learned during training, from War Office pamphlets, the experiences of other formations, and even the newspapers. Instead, it seems the battlefield would assume the role of schoolmaster, a harsh teacher, quick to punish any mistake.

Chapter Eleven

Operation BLUECOAT

On 25 July 1944, albeit belatedly, the U.S. Army's Operation COBRA finally got under way. The American ground assault was preceded by waves of Allied bombers. The Americans were able to create a breach in the German defences and break out across the Cotentin Peninsula of Normandy. To tie down German armoured forces and give the American operation time to develop, General Dempsey instituted Operation BLUECOAT. On 28 July, Dempsey set out his intentions for BLUECOAT at a conference of all corps commanders.

The tasks:

To draw onto itself the maximum German strength – particularly armour – and weaken it.
To hold the pivot secure, for on this the whole operation depends.
To help the US First Army in every way to get Brittany.
To pivot, first north of Caen, then on Caen, and then south of Caen.[1]

On 30 July, Operation BLUECOAT began with another massed air bombardment by more than 1,000 Allied bombers. British 30 Corps led the attack with 8 Corps on its right flank with the Guards Armoured Division in corps reserve. However, the nature of the terrain as much as the German defences meant that BLUECOAT got off to a less than auspicious start. The Normandy bocage with its narrow sunken lanes and thick hedges made the deployment of armoured forces extremely difficult. On 2 August, Sergeant Charles Murrell, Welsh Guards, wrote in his diary about some of the difficulties of fighting in the bocage for his battalion:

> In this *Bocage* it's a bit like being in a jungle – everything is close and confined – it's not like a battlefield – we here see nothing of the enemy – or even our own rifle companies – the orchards and woods and tiny fields bounded by trees growing out of 8 feet high banks – just seem to have swallowed up, not just our own battalion, our brigade and division, but the whole German and British armies on this front.

Murrell went on to explain why the closed terrain was ideally suited for defensive operations:

> One is right on top of the enemy before one realizes it, and tanks in attack are pretty useless, though in defence they can be deadly. It is infantry country that demands good reconnaissance for success. It is 'cat and mouse' terrain, and all the advantage lies with the mice.[2]

On 31 July 1944, the 11th Armoured Division, on the left of the 15th (Scottish) Division supported by the Churchill tanks of the 6th Guards (Tank) Brigade, overcame minefields and dug-in tanks. The 11th Armoured was able to exploit a gap in the German inter-army boundary, finding an undefended bridge that enabled them to cross the River Souleuvre. The 30 Corps, in the centre, made limited progress. The villages of Le Beny Bocage and Jurques fell to 8 Corps and 30 Corps respectively.

On 3 August, the 11th Armoured Division crossed the Vire-Condé-sur-Noireau road. The Guards Armoured Division moved up on its left. Three days later the 11th Armoured Division held a German counter-attack east of Vire. The 43rd (Wessex) Division took and held Mont Pinçon, the highest point in Normandy.

The German left flank was now in the air and could not hold around the city of Caen. At this juncture, the strategically prudent option would have been for the Germans to pull their forces back to a more defensible line on the River Seine. Instead, Hitler ordered a counter-attack by the remnants of six panzer divisions through Mortain towards Avranches with the intention of splitting the American forces.

On 7 August, the German panzer attack succeeded in taking Mortain. However, Allied airpower proved decisive in repelling the German attack, and it was quickly recaptured. Next, the 1st Canadian Army launched a successful attack south of Caen. The German 5th and 7th Armies began to disintegrate as they found themselves squeezed into a pocket between Falaise and Argentan. By the end of August, the battle for Normandy was over.[3]

Operation BLUECOAT succeeded in fixing the German armoured formations on the British eastern front, where they were remorselessly ground down. In turn, this helped enable the American breakout at Avranches. However, Operation BLUECOAT was also extremely costly in terms of British casualties. The 30 Corps had made slow, faltering progress that eventually led to the sacking of Lieutenant General Gerard Bucknall, who was replaced by Brian Horrocks. Similarly, the 7th Armoured Division, the famous Desert Rats of North

Africa, saw their commander Major General George 'Bobby' Erskine replaced by Brigadier Gerald Lloyd-Verney, formerly of the 6th Guards (Tank) Brigade.[4]

Battle of Caumont

During Operation BLUECOAT, 30 Corps' objective was to punch a hole through the German front lines towards Cahagnes and then on to map reference Point 361, which was a feature to the east of the Bois du Homme ridge. The 8 Corps was to protect 30 Corps' right flank while exploiting any opportunities that might allow for an armoured breakout.

The 15th (Scottish) Division had seen action during Operation EPSOM at the end of June. The Division had also been involved in fighting around the Odon River valley. Now, during Operation BLUECOAT, the 15th (Scottish) and the recently arrived 6th Guards (Tank) Brigade would be reunited after General Montgomery had replaced the Guards in his original order of battle for the Normandy invasion. As we have already seen, the 15th (Scottish) and 6th Guards had previously trained extensively together. The Guards were placed under the command of the 15th (Scottish) for the forthcoming operation. At the time, British forces occupied positions along the Caumont ridge, a feature about 8 miles south-west of Caen.

After the Americans had taken the town of Saint-Lô, they started their breakout operation on 25 July 1944. However, by 28 July, the American offensive was threatened by German forces who occupied the high ground on their left. To alleviate the threat to the Americans, General Montgomery ordered General Dempsey, 2nd Army, to launch an operation that would advance around 6 miles south of the Caumont ridge toward the town of Vire.

Today, according to the tourist literature, the area known as Suisse Normande (Norman Switzerland) is described as wild and hilly, ideal for outdoor pursuits such as canoeing, kayaking, hiking, and rock-climbing. This wild and hilly terrain did not lend itself to the accomplishment of swift military operations. Unfortunately, the urgent need to relieve the threat to the American offensive meant that there was little time for reconnaissance and planning.

Major General MacMillan, 15th (Scottish) Division, devised a multi-phased attack on a narrow front with two infantry battalions leading the assault. The 4th (Tank) Battalion, Grenadier Guards, with support from mine-clearing flail tanks and flamethrowing Churchill Crocodiles, were to capture Lutain Wood and the village of Sept-Vents with the 227th Highland Brigade including the Cameronians under command. Having achieved these initial objectives, the operation would then start in earnest. Two battalions of the 227th Highland Brigade supported by the 4th (Tank) Battalion, Coldstream Guards, and the 3rd

(Tank) Battalion, Scots Guards, would cross the operation's start line at 0955hrs. The infantry and tanks would then advance together around 2½ miles to the village of Les Loges and a hill marked on the maps of the day as Point 226. Once these objectives were reached, the infantry of 46th Brigade would pass through in their turn and advance to secure a Point 309 known as Quarry Hill.[5]

By this stage of the Normandy campaign, it was standard British practice to launch massive air and artillery bombardments to 'soften up' the enemy prior to launching a large-scale attack. On the morning of 30 July, smoke from the artillery barrage filled the valley and reduced visibility to nil. Nevertheless, at around 0800hrs the Guards' Churchill tanks lumbered forward over the ridge and into the valley. The 1st and 2nd Squadrons of the Grenadier Guards and the 9th Cameronians headed for Sept-Vents. The 3rd Squadron of the Grenadiers and the 2nd Gordon Highlanders attacked Lutain Wood.[6]

During the attack on Sept-Vents, five Grenadiers tanks were disabled by mines in quick succession. The flail tanks of the Lothian and Border Yeomanry were called forward to deal with the mines. By 0830hrs, when B Company of the Cameronians reached Sept-Vents, only one Churchill tank remained in support. After the Churchills of No. 2 Squadron were called forward, it took until around 1500hrs for the infantry to clear the village of enemy troops.

Two troops of tanks from No. 3 Squadron, Grenadier Guards, supported A and B Companies of the Gordon Highlanders with their attack on Lutain Wood. The infantry encountered minefields and enemy machine-gun nests, which slowed their progress. Next, C and D Companies of the Gordons passed through their sister companies, and advanced into the wood supported by a squadron of Crocodile flamethrower tanks. A troop of three Grenadier Guards tanks then managed to advance into the wood and manoeuvre into a position behind the German defenders. One of the Churchill tanks was knocked out by enemy fire, and soon afterwards the Troop Leader was killed. Nevertheless, Lance Sergeant Kingston kept his lone tank in position, pouring high-explosive shells and Besa machine-gun fire into the enemy rear until their opposition waned. The first objectives of the plan had been reached, but the operation was already behind schedule.[7]

Following the aerial bombardment, the second phase of the operation would be supported by a creeping artillery barrage. As soon as the bomber aircraft had dropped their payloads, the Highland Light Infantry (HLI) and the Argyll and Sutherland Highlanders moved off. However, the infantry almost immediately ran into trouble. The Germans had prepared stout defensive positions, and the terrain proved a natural barrier to both infantry and the Scottish Division's motor transport. The Guards supporting this phase of the operation had crossed the start line roughly on time. The 4th (Tank) Battalion, Coldstream Guards, and the 3rd (Tank) Battalion, Scots Guards, accompanying the HLI and Argylls respectively. However, because the infantry was having trouble maintaining contact with the tanks, it placed this phase of the operation in jeopardy. Brigadier Verney now had to decide whether to halt his tanks and wait for the infantry or press on without them under the cover of the scheduled artillery support. Although his decision ran contrary to doctrine, Brigadier Verney decided the tanks should continue alone.

By around 1130hrs, the tanks of the Coldstream Guards had reached an important cross-roads at Hervieux. Soon afterwards the HLI caught up with the tanks and together they reached their final objective, which was some high ground about eight hundred yards further south. The Argylls did not reach the start line until around 1300hrs. They then halted while artillery support was organised for them. However, the Scots Guards continued to advance without infantry support. At around 1430hrs, the Scots Guards were on their objective of Hill 226. An hour later, the Argylls came forward, cleared the village of Les Loges and joined the Guards on Hill 226. As the Argylls had not been able to bring their anti-tank guns forward to help secure their positions, the Scots Guards remained on station rather than retire.[8]

The Coldstream Guards secured Hill 309 (Quarry Hill), which was a dominant peak midway between the German strong points of Saint-Martin-des-Besaces and the Bois du Homme massif. The Coldstream Guards were able to reach their objective mainly due to the skill of the tank crews and the excellent cross-country ability of the Churchill tank.

At around 1830hrs, the British positions on Hill 226 came under enemy artillery and mortar fire, catching some of the Guardsmen out of their tanks. Next, two German Jagdpanther self-propelled anti-tank guns advanced while a third vehicle provided covering fire. The Jagdpanther was equipped with the infamous long-barrelled 88mm PaK43/3 gun, which was more than capable of destroying the heavily armoured Churchill tank. In just a few minutes, twelve tanks of 'S' Squadron, Scots Guards were knocked out as well as the tank of Major Sydney Cuthbert, the battalion's second-in-command. William Whitelaw, a junior Scots Guards officer, later to become a Conservative MP, cabinet minister, and viscount, described seeing Major Cuthbert's tank hit:

> All at once on my right I saw something so horrifying that my senses were completely dulled. The turret of Sydney Cuthbert's tank was lifted clean off as the vehicle burst into flames. At that moment it never occurred to me that for an armoured turret to be lifted off and deposited on the ground the tank must have suffered a direct hit from a heavy shell, nor did I realise then that a great friend and his crew must have been instantly killed.[9]

Any illusions about the Churchill tank's ability to resist the kinetic energy of either a 75mm or 88mm anti-tank gun were immediately dispelled on this first day of fighting for the 6th Guards (Tank) Brigade. Confidence in the tank's armoured protection was replaced by the stark realisation that 'every member of the Brigade knew that his passport to heaven was engraved with a large 88 and that round every corner and over every hill it might be handed to him by a gunner of the German army'.[10] Perhaps some cold comfort to the young William Whitelaw, but two of the Jagdpanthers were later found destroyed and abandoned by their crews.

During a later phase of BLUECOAT, the 6th Guards (Tank) Brigade and Guards Armoured Division operated together for the first and only time. The objectives of the operation were Le Haut Perrier, Chênedollé and Le Boulay aux Chats. The village of Chênedollé overlooked the strategically important Vire to Falaise road, which was just to the south. The Le Boulay aux Chats was high ground to the south of the highway. The tanks of the 3rd Battalion, Scots Guards, married up with the 1st Battalion, Welsh Guards, infantry. However, even though the Welsh Guards were part of the Guards Armoured Division, they had no experience of close co-operation with tanks.

At around 0300hrs on 11 August 1944, the Scots Guards moved to their forming-up positions. By 0630hrs, 'S' Squadron was divided into two halves, each supporting a company of the Welsh Guards. On the left, the attack went well, but on the right the Guards found themselves opposed by several Panther tanks. Next, 'S' Squadron and Right Flank, Scots Guards, moved around the flanks of Chênedollé before the infantry of the 5th Battalion, Coldstream Guards, took the village itself. Right Flank met stiff opposition, which was overcome by positioning the tanks in front of the infantry and close behind an artillery barrage. Overall, the attack on Chênedollé proved successful. Hundreds of German troops were killed, wounded, or captured and several Panther tanks were either knocked out or destroyed and abandoned by their crews.[11]

After the battle of Caumont, Brigadier Verney replaced Bobby Erskine as GOC of the 7th Armoured Division. Unfortunately for Erskine, the famous Desert Rats of North Africa had become the ineffectual Normandy mice of Villers Bocage. Lieutenant Colonel Sir Walter Barttelot, Coldstream Guards, assumed command of the 6th Guard (Tank) Brigade. However, on 18 August, the brigadier was killed when his scout car drove over two Teller mines. Two days later, Colonel Greenacre, Welsh Guards, arrived from the Guards Armoured Division to take command of the Brigade. After the first day's fighting south of Caumont, the 6th Brigade remained in continuous action for around three weeks. As always, the Germans fought stubbornly but were gradually pushed back and worn down until they were nearly encircled in the Falaise pocket. At around the same time, 19–25 August 1944, Paris was liberated. The German tenure of France was by and large over.[12]

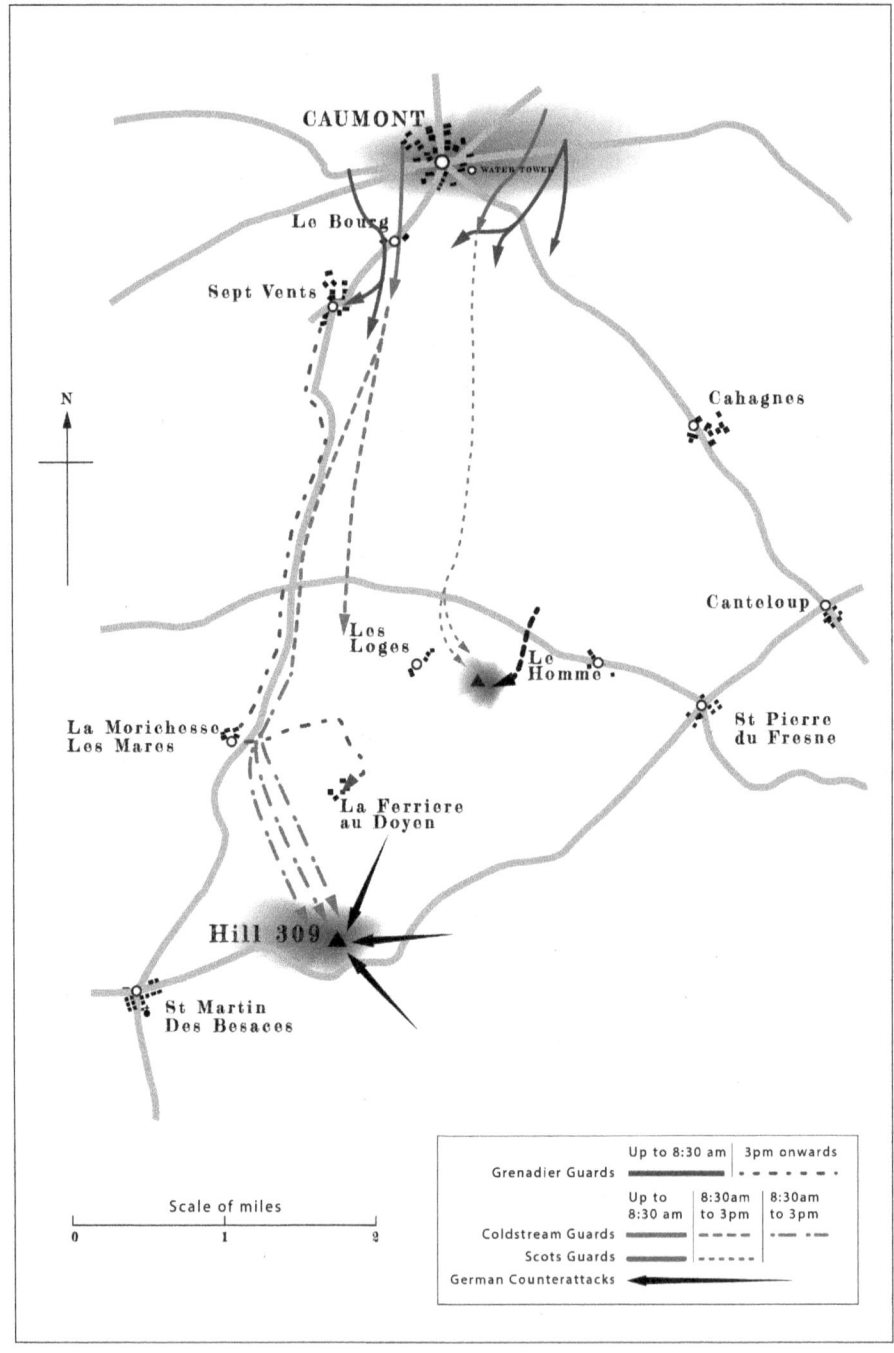

Map 2. Operation BLUECOAT, Caumont, 30 July – 7 August 1944, 6th Guards (Tank) Brigade.

Lessons Learned by the 6th Guards

Among the lessons learned during Operation BLUECOAT was the importance of the closest possible co-operation between tanks and the infantry they were supporting. Ronald Buckland, an intelligence officer with the 4th (Tank) Battalion, Coldstream Guards, believed that the Brigade's success at Caumont was a direct result of the joint training conducted with the 15th (Scottish) Division. Interviewed decades later by the Imperial War Museum, Buckland said that operations never seemed to run smoothly whenever the Brigade worked with an infantry formation they did not know or had no previous experience of operating with tanks.[13]

According to their war diary, the 3rd (Tank) Battalion, Scots Guards, had learned three valuable lessons from the Caumont operation. First, that the cross-country performance of the Churchill tank completely surprised the Germans, who considered the ground crossed by the Guards as tank proof and so concentrated their anti-tank guns on the roads and tracks. Next, the Guards had learned that when properly co-ordinated, the combined firepower of a squadron of Churchill tanks was enough to completely demoralise unsupported infantry. Third, it was necessary to have some form of reconnaissance vehicle capable of keeping up with Churchill tanks when operating in closed country like the Normandy bocage.[14]

Later, the fighting at Chênedollé taught the Scots Guards that if its tanks and the infantry could stay close enough to a creeping artillery barrage then even the best enemy troops, such as elements of the 9th SS Panzer Division, could be overrun. The Guards also learned that Panther tanks were vulnerable to flank attacks, and that spotting the enemy before they spotted you was often the decisive factor in an engagement. The Guards were also pleased to discover that Panther tanks were definitely not cross-country vehicles and appeared to struggle with the challenges of the Suisse Normande terrain.[15]

Although an obsolete design by 1944, under-gunned and slow, the Churchill tank proved itself quite capable of taking on the enemy in the worst of conditions, and prevailing. Perhaps most importantly of all, the Guardsmen of the 6th Guards (Tank) Brigade had faith in their tanks, the training they had undergone, and their leadership. When faced with challenges on the battlefield, the Brigade was willing to defy doctrine, take risks, adapt and innovate to gain its objectives.

Post-BLUECOAT Criticism

Regardless of the objectives achieved and valuable lessons learned from the hard fighting during Operation BLUECOAT, not everyone was impressed with the

British Army's performance. In a letter to Lieutenant General Martel, Liddell Hart was scathing in his criticism of Operation BLUECOAT. He remarked that even with every materiel advantage over the enemy in terms of air superiority, tanks and troops, the British found themselves repeatedly checked by relatively weak German forces. Liddell Hart assumed that a lack of drive among British troops was the only possible explanation for such poor battlefield performance throughout the Normandy campaign.[16] In fact, since the 1950s the British Army's whole approach to fighting the campaign for north-west Europe has been questioned and criticised as being slow, pedestrian and costly.[17] In Normandy, British armoured forces found that combat taught them new lessons from the ones they had learned in the classroom and on the training grounds. In response to lessons learned on the battlefield, the British armoured formations started to adapt and develop new tactical and operational methods.

In an account of the action fought by the 2nd (Armoured) Battalion, Grenadier Guards, during the clearing of Drouet Woods and Drouet Hill, between 2 and 4 August, Major J. Bowes-Lyon explained how his tanks were held back from the fighting until critical moments when they were thrust forward on the flanks to give vital support to the infantry. He went on to remark:

> The spontaneous co-operation between tanks, gunners and infantry left nothing to be desired, and I could never wish for more whole-hearted support than was given by my Motor Company.[18]

At first reading, Major Bowes-Lyon's statement might appear an endorsement of the Guards Armoured Division's ability to conduct all-arms operations. However, his use of the word 'spontaneous' to describe co-operation between tanks, gunners and infantry suggests this was something the various units involved in the action had not previously trained or planned for. Instead, they improvised a working solution to obtain their objectives.

Perhaps the pace of change could have been faster and more radical for the Guards Armoured Division and the British Army in Normandy. Nevertheless, Major J.J. How argues convincingly that of the final offensives during the Normandy campaign, Operation BLUECOAT did the most to ensure victory as it threw the German command into crisis and overshadowed all else in their reading of the battle.[19]

Staghound Armoured Car, Armoured Car Regiment, Guards Armoured Division. (*Photograph taken by the author*)

Sherman Tank, badged as 2nd (Armoured) Battalion, Grenadier Guards, Guards Armoured Division. (*Photograph taken by the author*)

Sherman Firefly, badged as 2nd (Armoured) Battalion, Grenadier Guards, Guards Armoured Division. Photograph taken by the author. (*Courtesy of The Tank Museum, Bovington*)

M4A4 Sherman Tank, 2nd (Armoured) Battalion, Irish Guards, Guards Armoured Division. Photograph taken by the author during Tankfest 2022. (*The Tank Museum, Bovington*)

Bedford QL Truck, Division Transport, Guards Armoured Division. (*Photograph taken by the author*)

The population of Aalst, south of Eindhoven, welcomes units of the Irish Guards, Guards Armoured Division, during Operation MARKET-GARDEN, 18 September 1944, photographed by Willem van de Poll. (*Courtesy of the National Archives of the Netherlands*)

Resident of Aalst hands out fruit to members of 2nd Household Cavalry Regiment, Guards Armoured Division, 18 September 1944, photographed by Willem van de Poll. (*Courtesy of the National Archives of the Netherlands*)

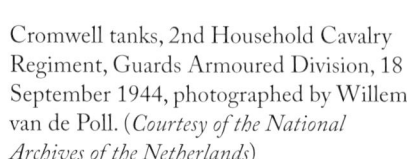

Cromwell tanks, 2nd Household Cavalry Regiment, Guards Armoured Division, 18 September 1944, photographed by Willem van de Poll. (*Courtesy of the National Archives of the Netherlands*)

A Sherman tank of the Irish Guards covering a road junction in Aalst, 18 September 1944, photographed by Willem van de Poll. (*Courtesy of the National Archives of the Netherlands*)

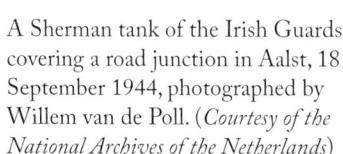

Irish Guards dug in at the edge of the Aalst Forest with residents nearby, 18 September 1944, photographed by Willem van de Poll. (*Courtesy of the National Archives of the Netherlands*)

An Irish Guardsman in conversation with a resident of Aalst, with Guardsmen washing in the background, 18 September 1944, photographed by Willem van de Poll. (*Courtesy of the National Archives of the Netherlands*)

Opening of the Liberation Museum in Nijmegen and commemoration of Operation MARKET-GARDEN: Sir Allan Adair (Guards Armoured Division) on the left and Lord Peter Carrington (Grenadier Guards) on the right, 17 September 1984. (*Photographed by Rob C. Croes, courtesy of the National Archives of the Netherlands*)

British Churchill tanks carrying infantry, Venlo, 24 November 1944, courtesy of the National Archives of the Netherlands.

Sergeant Bernard Hudson, 4th (Tank) Battalion, Grenadier Guards, 6th Guards (Tank) Brigade. (*Photograph courtesy of Bernie Hudson*)

Sergeant Hudson who commanded Churchill tank 'Guildford'. On 30 July 1944 during Operation BLUECOAT, Guildford, part of No. 8 Troop, No. 2 Squadron, 4th (Tank) Battalion, Grenadier Guards was knocked out by enemy gunfire. When Guildford was hit, L/Cpl. Francis Thorne, Gdsn. Maurice Bowler, and Gdsn. Albert Robertshaw were killed while Sergeant Hudson and Gdsn. Joseph Jacques managed to bail out. (*Photograph courtesy of Bernie Hudson*)

In response to the German Ardennes Offensive, also known as The Battle of the Bulge, on 22 December 1944, the Coldstream and Scots Guards moved to the suburbs of Maastricht. Photograph of Left-Flank, No. 11 Troop, Scots Guards at Valkenburg. Gdsn. Donald James Goodfellow, front row, right. (*Photograph courtesy of Philip Goodfellow*)

January 1945, Scots Guards tanks in the snow at Geilenkirchen, Germany, during Operation BLACKCOCK to clear enemy troops from an area bounded by the rivers Roer, Wurm and Maas. (*Photograph courtesy of Philip Goodfellow*)

The 6 Guards Tank Brigade captured Munster with infantry of the U.S. 17th Airborne Division.

Chapter Twelve

Tank Casualties and Loss of Confidence

Even before Operation GOODWOOD, the 5th Guards (Armoured) Brigade were sceptical about the M4 Sherman's ability to go toe-to-toe with the latest German tanks. Operation GOODWOOD simply reinforced what the Guards had previously suspected about the Sherman, that it lacked sufficient firepower and armoured protection for its crews. The Germans had nicknamed the Sherman 'Tommy Cooker', a macabre reference to the tank's unfortunate propensity to burst into flames when hit. According to Robert Boscawen, Coldstream Guards, the Guardsmen of the armoured battalions believed the Tommy Cooker epithet was a fitting description of the tank. To make matters worse and further undermine confidence in the Sherman, the British prime minister had made a statement in the House of Commons saying that British tanks were superior to German tanks. The Guardsmen in the armoured battalions knew this to be untrue.[1] During the bitter, often confused fighting south of Caumont during Operation BLUECOAT, members of the Irish Guards observed 'no matter what is said in Parliament, the German guns penetrate our armour, and our 75mms do not penetrate theirs'.[2]

The Guards' lack of confidence in the Sherman, dramatically reinforced by Operations GOODWOOD and BLUECOAT, must have had a negative effect on morale and the psychology of tank crews. Exactly how this loss of confidence in the Sherman affected the operational performance of the armoured battalions is not so easily discerned. It is likely that some crews adopted an overly cautious approach to operations while others turned to tactical and technical refinements to compensate for the Sherman's shortcomings. Whatever the Guards might have thought of the Sherman, perception is not reality. At the end of the war, Operational Research produced two reports on Sherman tank casualties. These help create a more balanced assessment of the Sherman's operational utility and survivability.

A report on Sherman tank casualties between 6 June and 10 July 1944 found that of the forty-five tanks examined, thirty-seven had 'brewed up', the colloquial term for a tank fire.[3] The report found that 82 per cent of the tanks penetrated were hit by a 75mm AP round, while 88mm shells accounted for 18 per cent of those knocked out. Only 5 per cent of hits failed to penetrate the Sherman's armour, and these were all 75mm rounds.[4] However, the most concerning statistic was that 82.2 per cent of the tanks hit had burned.

In the discussion section of the report, the authors ask whether more could have been done to mitigate the risk of tanks catching fire when hit. The report mentions that during Operation BLUECOAT the 1st (Armoured) Battalion, Coldstream Guards, experienced fewer brew-ups than other units. The Coldstream Guards attributed the low instance of tank fires to the fact that they carried no extra ammunition outside of the armoured bins. Although not recommended, it was a common practice for tank crews to keep several shells outside of the protective stowage bins so that they could reload the gun as quickly as possible during combat. Tank crews also had a habit of overloading on ammunition in case of resupply problems. The report points out that the applique armour fitted to the sides of Sherman tanks with the intention of providing extra protection for the ammunition appeared to have failed to prevent or reduce the instances of rounds penetrating. The report concludes that by keeping rounds stowed until needed they remained protected from any flying fragments once a shell had penetrated the tank's armour. The inference was that loose, unprotected shells on the floor of the turret or elsewhere were more likely to ignite immediately after a penetrating hit, which in turn caused the tank to brew up.[5] Some later models of the Sherman were fitted with 'wet' stowage. In 1945, research by the U.S. Army found that this reduced the likelihood of tank fires to around 15 per cent. In contrast, between 60 and 80 per cent of Shermans fitted with dry stowage caught fire once penetrated by an AP round or hollow charge (HC) projectile.[6]

Sherman Pros and Cons

Every tank design is something of a compromise based on the vehicle's combat role. A reconnaissance tank, for example, requires good speed, mobility and radio communications, which will mean compromising on armour and firepower to a certain extent. The British classified the Sherman as a Cruiser tank, which was issued to armoured divisions based on their primary purpose of exploitation and pursuit of the enemy after a decisive breakthrough had been achieved. The Sherman was never designed to challenge enemy tanks in single combat. As we have seen, American armoured doctrine, which dictated the design of the Sherman, believed tank-on-tank engagements unlikely and best left to purpose-built tank destroyers like the M10 (designated the Achilles by the British). Overall, the Sherman was a very good design for its intended purpose. The Sherman possessed good speed (between 25 and 30mph on a level road), range and reliability, but the tank was thinly armoured and tended to bog on wet, muddy ground due to the narrowness of its tracks. The Sherman was equipped with a quick-firing, dual-purpose M3 75mm main gun. In theory the Sherman could fire 20 AP or HE rounds per minute, although this rate of fire was seldom achieved, if ever. Additionally, the tank had a fast turret traverse, which meant the main gun could be brought on to targets quickly.[7] In many ways, tank warfare in the dense bocage countryside resembled a Hollywood western gunfight, where whoever fired first and kept firing tended to win the engagement. In his book *Brothers in Arms*, James Holland contests that, when used correctly, the Sherman was a match for any tank on the battlefield, even Tigers and Panthers.[8]

The report on Sherman tank casualties between June and July 1944 discusses the weaknesses of the vehicle's armour and makes several recommendations. The adding of more armour to the Sherman was likely to offer only marginal benefits in terms of crew protection. Instead, it was believed that adding a more powerful gun to the tank would be more advantageous. The authors believed it was better to try to make German tanks more vulnerable to the Sherman's firepower than attempt to increase its protective armour. The report also recommended more work be done to help British armoured units identify concealed enemy tanks and anti-tank guns in very close country like the Normandy bocage.[9]

Survivability

A survey conducted by No. 2 Operational Research Section of 21st Army Group looked at the human and vehicle casualties of twenty British armoured regiments between 24 March 1945 and the war's end. A total of 333 vehicles and 769 personnel casualties were examined. A total of 109, 32.73 per cent, of the vehicles examined belonged to the Guards Armoured Division. The total crew casualties numbered 371, of which 38 per cent were fatalities. Fifty per cent of the vehicles examined were Shermans, the remainder a combination of Cromwell, Comet, Challenger, and Stuart tanks.

The average range of an engagement was 600 yards (548.6m). The prevalent weapon used by the enemy was the German 75mm KwK 40, which was a vehicle-mounted gun. The KwK 40 was the primary armament of the Panzer IV medium tank, Sturmgeschütz III (StuG III) and Sturmgeschütz IV (StuG IV) tank destroyers/assault guns. Around 50 per cent of the tanks examined were only penetrated once by an AP round or HC projectile such as the warhead from a Panzerfaust or Panzerschreck handheld anti-tank weapon.[10]

Most of the tanks examined were hit in the front rather than sides or rear of the vehicle. Expressed as percentages, average crew casualties were 12 per cent killed, 14 per cent wounded, 6 per cent burnt and 68 per cent unhurt.

Overall, the survey found no difference among the incidence of casualties between the different vehicle types, except for the Sherman Firefly, which had a proportionally higher casualty rate. However, this anomaly is most likely due to the vehicle having a crew of four (no co-driver). A typical M4 Sherman had a crew of five; however, the Firefly was equipped with the British 17-pounder main gun, which fired a larger shell than the standard 75mm gun. To increase stowage for the larger shells, the co-driver position was removed.

The survey found, on average, that once a fire had started within a tank the crew had approximately two and a half seconds to escape without being burnt. The gunner was most likely to suffer burns due to their escape frequently taking five seconds as they had to wait for the tank commander to exit the turret before they could bail out.

Unsurprisingly, 84 per cent of casualties were caused when an AP round or HC projectile penetrated the crew compartment. In contrast, just 3 per cent of casualties were sustained in vehicles where the engine compartment was hit, for example.[11]

AP hits to the turret caused more fatalities than hits to a tank's hull. However, penetrating hits to a tank's hull tended to cause casualties among the entire crew, where hits to the turret generally only wounded or killed the commander, loader, and gunner, sparing the driver and co-driver.

The calibre of guns used against the tanks in the survey were 75mm and 88mm. However, in terms of lethality, the 88mm proved most effective. Of those tanks penetrated by an 88mm round, 41 per cent of the crew were killed. In comparison, around 26 per cent of the crew were killed when a tank was penetrated by a 75mm AP round.

An examination of vehicle hulks supported the widely held belief that Sherman tanks were more liable to catch fire when hit than other types of tanks employed. However, the survey also found that there was no greater occurrence of burns among Sherman crews than other types of vehicles sampled.[12] Having been penetrated by an AP round or HC projectile, the major cause of fire in the M4 Sherman was the ignition of ammunition. Anti-tank mines caused around 20 per cent of damaged vehicles examined in the survey but were only responsible for 8 per cent of casualties sustained.[13]

Although anecdotal, an explanation for the low casualty rate due to anti-tank mines might be a simple precaution taken by the tank crews themselves. In a letter written by Lieutenant N. Kearsley, 2nd (Armoured Recce) Battalion, Welsh Guards, he explained how tank crews placed four or five sandbags on the floor of the hull gunner and driver positions, which appeared to significantly reduce the likelihood of casualties when a tank hit a mine. However, the Welsh

Guards operated Cromwell not Sherman tanks, and it is unclear how common this practice was across the armoured battalions.[14]

Around 50 per cent of tank crews sustained their injuries inside the vehicle, 40 per cent outside of the vehicle and 10 per cent partially exposed, i.e. head out of the turret. A high proportion of officers/tank commanders were wounded or killed because of partial exposure during combat. However, it was often necessary for tank commanders to keep their heads exposed during battle to maintain situational awareness, identify and call out targets to the gunner. When the tank commander's hatch was closed, the Sherman was equipped with a periscope, but this provided a very restricted view of the battlefield. Of the 472 wounded crew members surveyed, 74 per cent returned to military duty.[15]

The Perception and Reality Gap

A general lack of confidence in Allied tanks often resulted in crews bailing out of vehicles without just cause. Research found that crews frequently abandoned their tanks immediately after being hit by a shell for two reasons. First, a fear of being burnt should the tank catch fire after being hit. Second, an expectation that the enemy gunner would quickly fire another shell to ensure the target was destroyed.[16]

Taken together, the two studies on tank casualties substantiate the belief that the Sherman was likely to catch fire after a shell penetrated the armour and ignited the ammunition. However, the Guards had found a simple and effective remedy to mitigate the chances of a tank fire by keeping ammunition stored in the protective bins until required. Similarly, they appear to have reduced crew casualties due to anti-tank mines by placing sandbags at the feet of the driver and co-driver. Whatever fears tank crews harboured about the inadequacies of the Sherman, and its ability to protect them, the statistics tell a different story. Most crew members (68 per cent) escaped from a tank unhurt after it had been hit. Nearly half of all crew casualties studied were wounded or killed when outside of the protective armour of their tanks. Certainly, being the point tank leading the advance in the dense Norman countryside must have been a nerve-racking experience for the crew. Nevertheless, statistically, a Guardsman was much safer in a tank than out of one. In Normandy, the infantry, who represented just a third of the British Army's strength, suffered 71 per cent of the total casualties. The same casualty rate was roughly true for the U.S. Army, although infantry divisions made up only 10 per cent of its total strength.[17]

Whatever the Guardsmen believed, there was not a German 88mm anti-tank gun or Tiger tank lurking around every corner and over every hill in Normandy, waiting to hand them their passports to heaven.[18] According to John Buckley, of the 2,500 German tanks available for action in Normandy between June and August, only 30 per cent could be classed as superior to Allied tanks. The German Panther and Tiger tanks were considered superior in terms of armament and armoured protection. However, both tanks left much to be desired in terms of speed, mobility, fuel consumption and mechanical reliability. Most German tanks encountered in Normandy, like the Panzer IV, were either inferior or equal to the Sherman, Cromwell, and Churchill. The Allies also possessed a significant three-to-one numerical advantage in tanks over the Germans.[19]

Although perceived as ideal defensive country, the Normandy bocage presented its own set of challenges for the Germans and their armoured forces. After the war, General Fritz Bayerlein, commander of the Panzer Lehr Division, wrote:

> Normandy was not tank country and it was very difficult to use even assault guns with their low silhouette, because turretless guns could not fire over the high hedge banks. The Panther was very difficult to handle because its long gun became tangled in the hedges, and the roads were too narrow to allow it to turn, and the hedge banks were too high for it to cross. The high silhouette of the Sherman was not a disadvantage in Normandy because of the thick cover and it often gave the tank commander better observation than was had from the Panther or MKIV.[20]

It was unfortunate that the armoured battalions of the Guards Armoured Division found themselves fighting a different type of war from the one they had expected or trained for. As the 1st (Motor) Battalion, Grenadier Guards explained, the lessons learned by the armoured formations on Salisbury Plain and the Yorkshire Wolds would have to be revised. Instead of sweeping across open terrain, the Division found progress was much slower and more methodical than had been expected, and its tanks were very suspectable to easily concealed anti-tank guns and bazooka men. Between 7 and 12 July, Divisional Headquarters held several conferences and then started to demonstrate new methods for better tank and infantry co-operation in close country. However, the new training never got under way before the Division received orders for Operation GOODWOOD.[21] As a result of its changed role and circumstances, the Division would have to reorganise its two brigades to create more balanced infantry and armoured battlegroups. The fast, reliable but thinly armoured Sherman tank was never designed for the jungle-like warfare of the bocage. Nevertheless, the Sherman too proved remarkably adaptable to the changing demands made upon it. Perhaps, changing the Guardsmen's negative perceptions of the Sherman proved the biggest challenge of all.

The Churchill Tank: Overcoming Obstacles

Hurried into production as the threat of invasion loomed, the cumbersome Churchill Infantry tank got off to an inauspicious start with its crews. As we have seen, the early Churchill variants were mechanically unreliable. However, Christopher Schofield, an officer with 4th (Tank) Battalion, Coldstream Guards, recalled how staff from Vauxhall Motors co-operated with his unit's fitters to identify and rectify the tank's numerous teething problems.[22] Similarly, Reg Sollitt, an NCO with the 4th (Tank) Battalion, Grenadier Guards, spent two months attached to Vauxhall Motors, where he learned all about the Churchill's inner workings, especially its engine.[23] Through a process of trial and error, Vauxhall Motors and those units equipped with Churchill tanks gradually modified and improved the vehicle. The staff at Vauxhall were also able to help the tank crews to get the most out of their vehicles in terms of performance. In April 1943, the war diary of the 4th (Tank) Battalion, Grenadier Guards, records that a Mr Hoy of Vauxhall Motors spent some days with the Battalion giving demonstrations and holding discussions on the Churchill tank.[24]

In his official history of the 6th Guards (Tank) Brigade, Patrick Forbes writes about the Churchill tank in the most approving terms. He clearly felt obliged to downplay the tank's many design, production, and operational shortcomings. Nevertheless, he does confess that the Brigade's tank crews did feel like guinea pigs as Vauxhall Motors sought to identify and eradicate various technical issues of the early production Churchills. Yet, with time, the tank crews developed an affection for the Churchill tank that Forbes likened to the relationship between a cavalryman and his horse. Each tank crew acquired an intimate knowledge of their own tank's idiosyncrasies, its maintenance needs, and how far they could push their vehicle in any given circumstance. Forbes also suggests that perhaps the greatest of all the Churchill's virtues was that the tank engendered confidence in its crews. He rightly points out that without confidence in a vehicle's ability to withstand the stresses of battle little was likely to be achieved. As we have already seen, those Guards battalions equipped with Sherman tanks had little confidence in them, which might well have resulted in an excess of caution on the battlefield.[25]

The study of casualties among armoured units who fought in north-west Europe by Wright and Harkness mainly examined Cruiser tanks damaged or destroyed during the conflict. However, a small amount of data was also obtained from British tank regiments equipped with Churchill Infantry tanks. The study found that 41 per cent of Churchill tank casualties were caused by AP shot, and 38 per cent of tank crew casualties were fatal. But the data also showed that overall, only half of all tank crew casualties were sustained while they were inside a vehicle. A total of 40 per cent of tank crews were either killed or wounded while they were outside of their vehicles performing other tasks or at leisure. The remaining 10 per cent of tank crews became casualties while they were partially exposed to enemy fire such as having heads and shoulders outside of the turret, for example. Overall, the ratio of killed to wounded among tank crews from all causes, from gunfire to handheld anti-tank weapons and mines, was 37 per cent killed to 63 per cent either wounded or unharmed. Although the sample size of Churchill tanks was smaller, the study found no difference in the ratio of killed to wounded to other types of Allied tank such as the Sherman and Cromwell when the armour was penetrated.[26] The study did note that the 4th (Tank) Battalion, Grenadier Guards, had about fifty tanks knocked out due to enemy action during the campaign for north-west Europe, but only six, or 12 per cent, of Churchill tanks caught fire after being hit. This suggests that the risk of fire was less in the Churchill than other types of Allied tank.

The study found that when a Churchill was penetrated by enemy fire into the crew compartment, on average half the crew members were wounded while the other half were unhurt. This statistic is roughly the same for other British and Canadian tank crews surveyed. Of the crew casualties, roughly half were killed, and about one third of non-fatal wounds were burns. Overall, the casualty picture of Churchill tank crews was consistent with the other types of tanks sampled in the study. However, the study was unable to assess the value, if any, of the Churchill's extra armour compared with Sherman and Cromwell tanks due to the limited sample size and type of data collected.[27] It seems unlikely that the Churchill's additional armoured protection provided any significant benefit to its tank crews, especially when operating in the closed country of the Normandy bocage, where engagements were often fought at close quarters. The extra weight of the armoured protection carried by the Churchill certainly limited its speed and manoeuvrability but then doctrine only required the tank to move at the walking pace of the infantry. The Churchill tank's extra thick frontal armour might have proved of some benefit when engaged by enemy tanks and anti-tank guns firing towards the limits of their effective ranges. An examination of 1,600 wrecked Allied tanks found that around 70 per cent of hits penetrated the armour of Sherman tanks, but only 50 per cent in the case of the Churchill.[28]

According to David Fletcher, author and military historian specialising in armoured warfare, the Churchill tank was by and large an obsolete vehicle by the time it reached Normandy in the summer of 1944. Nevertheless, the Churchill inspired a confidence in its crews and supporting infantry that the Sherman did not. The Churchill's ability to navigate rough terrain and climb the steepest gradients occasionally gave it a tactical advantage that surprised the enemy. However, perhaps the tank's biggest disadvantage throughout its service life was its lack of firepower. The Churchill gun tanks that went to war in north-west Europe were equipped with either the quick-firing 75mm gun or 95mm howitzer. Unfortunately, the 75mm gun proved largely ineffective when taking on German Panther and Tiger tanks. As the Churchill turret was unsuitable for conversion to the more potent British 17-pounder anti-tank gun, some units retained the 6-pounder, which they believed to be more effective against enemy tanks. Apparently, just after D-Day, the Tank Board discussed retrofitting 6-pounders to the Churchill fleet, but this idea never became policy.[29] According to David Erskine's history of the Scots Guards, the Churchill went through an amazing transformation from a dismally unreliable 40-ton waddling monster, equipped with a 2-pounder pop-gun, to an excellent tank and magnificent support to the infantry.[30]

Chapter Thirteen

The Liberation of Brussels

By the end of August 1944, the Guards Armoured had crossed the Seine.[1] The Division then advanced approximately 65 miles to the northern outskirts of Arras.[2] On 2 September, the Division prepared to move on Brussels in Operation SABOT. If the weather had remained fine, the Division's advance would have been preceded by a large airborne landing in the Tournai area supported by a heavy bombing programme. However, the airborne landings were cancelled at 0200hrs the following day.[3] The Division left Douai for Brussels on 3 September with the 32nd Guards Brigade on the right centre line and the 5th Guards Brigade on the left.[4] The Division drove, almost without stop, approximately 82 miles in thirteen hours.[5] After fighting three small actions, the Welsh Guards Group, 5th Guards Brigade, entered Brussels, winning the race with 32nd Guards Brigade by forty minutes.[6] The Division quickly secured all major administrative buildings and road junctions across the city and captured around 1,000 prisoners.[7] One can only speculate about what might have happened had the airborne landings taken place on 3 September. However, the fact that they did not take place probably contributed to the impetus for the ill-fated Operation MARKET GARDEN to proceed regardless of the risks involved.

Operation MARKET GARDEN

Operation MARKET GARDEN was one of the largest Allied operations of the Second World War. The operation intended to secure the key bridges over three major waterways in Holland, outflank the German defences of the Siegfried Line, cut off 250,000 German troops in the Netherlands, and accelerate the opening of ports such as Antwerp. The advance would follow the line Grave–Nijmegen–Arnhem.[8] The operation consisted of two parts. First, Operation MARKET would see 1st Airborne Corps commanded by Lieutenant General Frederick 'Boy' Browning, former Grenadier Guards, assault the key bridges by glider and parachute. The British 1st Airborne Division was to seize the bridge over the Neder Rijn at Arnhem; the U.S. 82nd Airborne Division would take the bridges at Nijmegen and Grave, and the U.S. 101st Airborne Division would secure Eindhoven and various canal crossings between there and Grave.[9] Next,

Operation GARDEN required the Guards Armoured Division, followed by the 43rd Infantry Division, to advance over the captured bridges to Apeldoorn, 35 miles north of Arnhem, and then turn east into Germany.

The operation faced three significant challenges. First, as the Allied advance slowed, it gave the retreating German forces time to recover, regroup and prepare a defensive front. Second, as Allied supply lines lengthened, it made the support of offensive operations more difficult. Third, the Guards Armoured Division's central axis of advance was along a single carriageway that prevented vehicle deployment off-road due to the marshy nature of the ground (Dutch polder).[10]

A cursory Internet search for 'Operation MARKET GARDEN' returns over forty history books. The debates over the causes of the failure of the operation continue to excite academics, popular historians, and readers alike. However, we will focus mainly on the Guards Armoured Division's operational role, performance, and lessons learned during MARKET GARDEN.

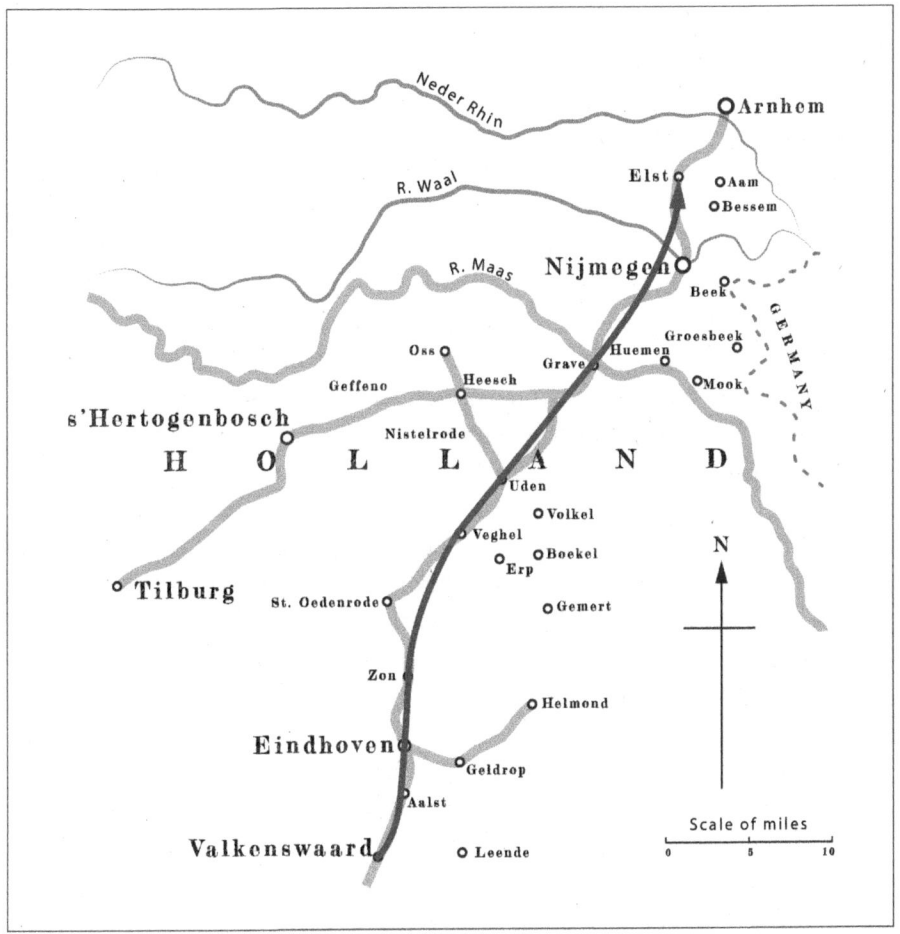

Map 3. Operation MARKET-GARDEN, 17 – 25 September 1944, Guards Armoured Division.

A Brief Historiography

Several common themes emerge from the various books on MARKET GARDEN and the role of the Guards Armoured Division. First, some historians question the sense of converting elements of the Guards into an armoured division. In *Operation MARKET GARDEN*, edited by John Buckley and Peter Preston-Hough, John Peaty questions whether elite forces such as the Guards Armoured Division and 1st Airborne Division would not have contributed more to the war effort as line infantry.[11] Peaty concludes that on balance neither the Guards nor Airborne made a sufficient contribution to the war effort to justify their elite status. On the contrary, he argues that diverting the best men into special forces harmed the army when its reservoir of trained infantrymen was dwindling. The elite status of airborne forces is not within the scope of this book. However, we will attempt to assess the overall contribution of the Guards Armoured Division during 1944 and 1945. One thing is certain: the Guards Armoured Division and 6th Guards (Tank) Brigade fought throughout the campaign for north-west Europe, once committed to battle. By comparison, the 1st and 6th Airborne Divisions were used sparingly.

In William F. Buckingham's book *Arnhem 1944*, the author describes the Guards Armoured Division's performance as tardy. The watchword for MARKET GARDEN was urgency, but the Guards chose to halt their tanks for maintenance once it got dark rather than continue the advance.[12] Given the urgency of the situation, the Irish Guards might have pressed on through the night. However, they were already battle fatigued and understrength. Tanks require continual preventive maintenance to keep them running, and the Guards were not used to operating their tanks at night at this stage of the campaign. In his book *Arnhem*, popular British military historian Antony Beevor questions the value of converting elements of the Guards into an armoured division. Beevor states that General Horrocks was criticised for selecting the Division to lead the advance rather than the 11th Armoured. Horrocks claimed he chose the Guards because he knew they could achieve the objectives regardless of cost.[13]

The most contentious and often repeated criticism of the Guards during MARKET GARDEN was their failure to continue to drive north towards Arnhem after the capture of the Nijmegen road bridge. William F. Buckingham and Antony Beevor claim the Guards tended to fight by the book and saw no urgency in reaching Arnhem.[14] They also assert that General Horrocks and Major General Adair failed to prepare a contingent force ready to advance once the Nijmegen road bridge was captured.[15] However, this assessment seems unfair considering the Grenadier Guards were still fighting to secure the town of Nijmegen. Moreover, the Irish Guards were very understrength, and most of the available forces were struggling west of Nijmegen.

In Robert Kershaw's study of the German response to MARKET GARDEN, *It Never Snows in September*, he briefly mentions the Guards Armoured Division. As part of his research, Kershaw, a military author and battlefield guide, found that the Guards did miss an opportunity to push a force into Arnhem. In Kershaw's assessment, between 1900hrs on 20 September and the following day, a determined force of tanks and infantry could have got through to Arnhem.[16] According to Max Hastings in *All Hell Let Loose*, debating whether the Guards could have advanced after taking the Nijmegen road bridge was irrelevant. The Germans had already overrun John Frost's men at Arnhem.[17] As tempting as it is to speculate about the Guards reaching Arnhem, Hastings's assessment that any scratch formation would have arrived too late to make any difference to the outcome seems accurate.

In Richard Mead's biography of Lieutenant General Sir Frederick Browning, he points out that Browning was a former Grenadier Guardsman and close personal friend of Major General Allan Adair.[18] Unsurprisingly, General Browning had every confidence in the Guards' ability to achieve their objectives during MARKET GARDEN. Mead suggests that General Horrocks should have pressed Major General Adair harder on the first day of the operation and got the Guards moving. He also thought General Horrocks should have made more effort to push available units straight up the road from Nijmegen to Arnhem but attaches no blame to the Guards for this decision.[19]

MARKET GARDEN Lessons Learned

In his book *The Last German Victory*, Aaron Bates argues convincingly that British Army training and doctrine focused too heavily on peacetime obsessions such as parade ground drill and the development of a 'proper soldierly bearing' rather than concentrating time and energy on realistic tactical training. Officers, NCOs, and other ranks were seldom encouraged to use their initiative or imagination to achieve objectives. Bates also argues there was still a reliance on the 'natural' leadership skills and decision-making abilities of men from the British upper classes who would always be able to find a solution and muddle through. Certainly, the British Army was dogged by antiquated training methods and social class bias in the selection of officers.[20] However, as we have seen, as the war progressed, and the casualties mounted, the army was forced to adopt new training methods and become a more egalitarian organisation. Nevertheless, the British Army never achieved parity with its German opponents in the training of junior officers and soldiers. The German Army rejected the idea that strict, centralised control at the tactical level was sensible or even possible for modern warfare. Instead of automatons, the German Army wanted soldiers, regardless of rank, who could think and act independently when the situation required them to do so. Unfortunately, the Guards were the epitome of the British Army's often backward approach to training and outdated belief in the inherent superiority of the aristocracy to command.[21]

In Normandy, the Guards developed an operational method that relied on set-piece attacks and the use of overwhelming artillery firepower to bludgeon the enemy. In consequence, the Division gained something of a reputation for slow, deliberate, perhaps overly cautious advances. Of course, the use of set-piece attacks with limited objectives, supported frequently by massed artillery and air support, was in accordance with Montgomery's own doctrine for the campaign in north-west Europe.[22] A summary of actions and lessons learned by the 2nd Household Cavalry Regiment (2HCR), the divisional armoured car regiment, which performed reconnaissance during MARKET GARDEN, mentions an incident when the leading armoured regiment was held up by German self-propelled guns at a bridge just south of Eindhoven. Although time was of the essence, the armoured regiment decided to stop and organise a set-piece attack supported by artillery to deal with the German guns. The report's author suggests that the set-piece attack would have taken at least an hour and a half to organise, perhaps longer. Instead, the armoured car troop leader was able get behind the enemy position and observe their exact strength and dispositions. However, he also discovered the enemy was in the process of withdrawing, although this movement could not be observed from the front. The troop leader's actions saved many hours of valuable daylight. Nevertheless, the incident is revealing of the Guards' mindset when faced with limited opposition and supposedly operating to a strict timetable.[23]

Bates argues that Montgomery's plan for MARKET GARDEN put the Guards in a difficult position where they were unable to deploy and fight to their strengths.[24] Major General 'Pip' Roberts, 11th Armoured Division, did not believe his own formation would have fared any better than the Guards if they had led the advance. In today's parlance, we might say that the Guards were set up to fail.[25]

The Guards were certainly not alone in adopting the bludgeoning tactics of calling down artillery and air strikes to deal with even light opposition. Perhaps the Guards' armoured battalions were also more likely to call on artillery and air support because they lacked confidence in their primary weapon system, the M4 Sherman tank. Unfortunately, MARKET GARDEN would only have served to reinforce any anxieties the Guards harboured about the quality of the Sherman. After all, the Guards were forced to proceed on a one-tank front with little opportunity to deploy off-road, making them easy targets for German gunners hidden in the woods and orchards adjacent to the main axis of advance. The Sherman's narrow tracks meant that the tank easily bogged down on the marshy Dutch polder. Of course, German vehicles were also prone to bog, but the heavier Tiger and Panther tanks possessed wider tracks, which distributed their weight more evenly, giving them a slight off-road advantage. The topography of Holland also meant the German defenders simply had to site their guns on the main highway and intersections to continually check the Allied advance.

Operational Character

Operation MARKET GARDEN taught the Guards little more than they already knew about fighting the Germans in terms of tactical deployment and combat. Doherty submits that, despite setbacks, British armoured divisions were working like 'well-oiled machines' by the end of MARKET GARDEN. By this stage of the war, a British infantry division could depend on having an armoured brigade under its control. Similarly, a regiment from one of the armoured divisions might be detached to work alongside units from an infantry division. There was much better co-operation between armour, infantry, artillery, support services and the tactical air force than at the start of the campaign for north-west Europe.[26] On 20 September, for example, the Coldstream Guards Group was placed under the command of the U.S. 82 Airborne Division. The Welsh and Irish Guards were operating with 69th Brigade, 50th Division, 5th East Yorks, and the Green Howards at the end of September.[27] On 1 October, the 1st (Armoured) Battalion, Coldstream Guards, supported the 231st Brigade at Bemmel. The Guards also showed more tactical flexibility, forming small, ad hoc battlegroups to clear villages of enemy troops.[28]

After MARKET GARDEN, W.A. Elliott described how the Scots and Welsh Guards formed the Celtic Battlegroup. Elliott's infantry company, known as Right Flank, was 'married' to 2 Squadron, Welsh Guards, tanks. Elliott explained how they developed a new technique to assault enemy positions, whereby the tanks laid down a smokescreen through which the infantry then attacked. One section of a platoon (eight Guardsmen) would ride on a single tank. The Welsh Guards were equipped with British Cromwell tanks rather than the American M4 Sherman. The Cromwell had several advantages over the Sherman, such as greater speed, a lower profile, and more flat surfaces for infantry to ride on.[29] Lord Carrington believed that the introduction of Regimental Battlegroups, which happened at the end of August, improved the close co-operation of infantry, armour and support services significantly. However, he also thought it imposed its own inflexibility as sometimes an operation required more tanks or infantry.[30]

Sir David Fraser believed that the Division had already established the character of its operations before MARKET GARDEN:

> Henceforth the campaign was going to be a matter of deploying and attacking small parties of the enemy holding, with skill and courage, key points on our route; or, laboriously, of our finding a way around. This was to set the pattern of the advance through northern Belgium, Holland and Western Germany. It is a form of warfare in which small bodies of troops, in defence, can inflict disproportionate casualties and impose disproportionate delay, and the terrain was well suited to it. Much of the ground astride the roads were soft polder in which tanks bogged. Roads were easily covered from woods and banks. Deployment for operations was laborious. Infantry were at a premium, and the enormous mass of vehicles that constituted an armoured division and its logistics train often seemed to impede rather than exploit mobility.[31]

However, although the logistics train was frequently under fire and occasionally halted, the Provost Company of the Division would keep the roads clear and traffic moving most of the time.[32] Moreover, the Corps of Military Police did more than just traffic control. They organised fighting patrols to locate and engage pockets of enemy resistance and helped repulse German attacks along the highway.[33]

MARKET GARDEN revealed some of the shortcomings of a fully mechanised modern army. Operating across a country with limited road space, bisected by numerous water obstacles and marshy terrain unsuitable for off-road deployment, caused traffic congestion and hampered the resupply of the fighting front. Verney believed that had the weather been better, sufficient aircraft made available and the Guards reached Arnhem, it was still doubtful the operation would have succeeded given the tenuous supply situation. Modern vehicles and equipment had given the Allied armies many advantages, such as speed and mobility, but made them highly vulnerable to supply problems.[34] Although logistics and supply problems dogged MARKET GARDEN, even if everything else had gone right with the operation, the Germans' swift response and successful use of ground were likely to have denied the Allies complete success.

An armoured division required 1,000 gallons of petrol to move one mile, and someone had to transport that fuel from tanker to depot to field. Of course, an armoured division required a great deal more than just fuel. It needed a constant supply of casualty replacements, food, ammunition, medical supplies, and countless other sundry items. The complexity of modern warfare meant an ever-increasing service tail to support the teeth arms.[35] Sir David Fraser observed a curious result of what he termed a 'vehicle-bound' army:

Infantry was absolutely necessary for the fighting when it occurred, but nobody marched, although henceforth the distances were not great. A vehicle-bound army generates correspondingly greater demand for fuel – and more fuel-carrying vehicles. Internally and organisationally, the Army, and every unit in it, was wastefully devised and slow and laborious to move. This penalty was insufficiently offset by greater firepower and tactical mobility at the sharp end.[36]

Fraser's observations of a vehicle-bound army stand in stark contrast to Doherty's suggestion that the armoured divisions ran like well-oiled machines. Fraser's assertion that infantry might sit uselessly in the back of lorries when stuck in traffic congestion rather than debouch and march to where they were needed is interesting. Had mechanisation so changed the military mindset that troops had become vehicle-bound? It is likely that with the formation of the Regimental Battlegroup system, the Guards found an operational and tactical formula sufficiently flexible to meet future operational challenges. However, the logistical requirements of Operation MARKET GARDEN created a remarkably complex, cumbersome, and slow formation that was ill-suited to the topography of Holland. As well as the 12,000 vehicles belonging to 30 Corps, the operation required 9,000 sappers of the Royal Engineers, 5,000 vehicles to carry the necessary bridging equipment, and an additional 2,000 vehicles belonging to the Airborne forces administrative tail.[37] For the Guards, having to operate on a one-tank front along a single carriageway without the possibility of deployment off-road only made a bad administrative and tactical situation worse.

The Failure to Relieve Arnhem

Like the Normandy bocage, Holland was a defensive gift to the Germans. The Allies were forced to advance on a one-tank front, enabling the Germans to focus their forces at the point of attack. The marshy Dutch polder meant it was difficult for Allied tracked and wheeled vehicles to deploy off the main highway. Numerous rivers and canals bisected the operation's line of advance. The Germans only had to demolish the bridges over the various waterways and position a couple of well-sighted anti-tank guns to halt the Allied advance temporarily.

The Guards' performance during MARKET GARDEN has been widely criticised over the years and cited as one of the contributory factors of the operation's failure. Hart believed the Guards were over-cautious and lacked the aggressiveness to fight through to 1st Airborne at Arnhem. Furthermore, Hart asserts that the secretary of state for war, James Grigg, had warned the 2nd Army that the Guards might use claims about the inferiority of British armour as a pretext for 'canniness'.[38] As we know, the Guards did possess misgivings about the quality of Allied tanks right from the start of their deployment in Normandy.

There are two main justifications for the accusations of excessive caution against the Guards – first, the failure of the Irish Guards to pass through Valkenswaard and press on toward Eindhoven. Instead, the Guards harboured overnight at Valkenswaard. Buckley explains that the engineers had to bring forward equipment to bridge an unexpected crater and the river at Valkenswaard.[39] According to J.O.E Vandeleur, Irish Guards, Brigadier Norman Gawtkin told him to take his time getting to Eindhoven the next day as the Zon bridge had been destroyed. Vandeleur recalled, 'I think his exact words were "Well, push onto Eindhoven tomorrow, old boy, but take your time. We've lost a bridge."' The following day, the Irish Guards moved out at a leisurely pace between 0800 and 0900hrs.[40] However, the engineers had completed the Bailey Bridge at Zon by 0630hrs.[41]

The Guards' failure to immediately attempt to reach Arnhem after the capture of the Nijmegen road bridge is the second reason often cited as evidence of the Guards' excessive caution during MARKET GARDEN. It is clear from veteran testimonies like Sir Julian Paget that many of the men on the ground believed the Guards should have tried to push on to Arnhem:

> It was felt by many on the spot at that moment, both British and American, that a special task force could and should have been ordered to push forward immediately through the night in a desperate, all-out attempt to reach First Airborne Division, now only eleven miles away, and in desperate trouble. No such move was ordered, and both the Commander of XXX Corps, General Horrocks, and other senior commanders, have written since that the problems involved were just too great.[42]

In hindsight, undoubtedly, a scratch force could have been assembled quickly and pushed on from Nijmegen to Arnhem during the night of 20 September. However, such an improvised and poorly equipped relief force would probably have been quickly isolated and destroyed by the Germans. Paget's assertion, written thirty years after the events, that the Guards were aware of 1st Airborne's desperate situation is misleading. On the contrary, according to an intelligence summary dated 21 September 1944, the Guards had received only 'scanty' information about the airborne troops at Arnhem. Moreover, the report highlights that fierce fighting had been going on in and around Arnhem to control the bridge.

Nevertheless, the report says the situation at Oosterbeek was more promising as the airborne forces had a 'really firm footing here'. The report then mentions the possibility of using a lightly damaged railway bridge and ferry to continue operations north if the Arnhem bridge was unavailable. Overall, the intelligence assessment describes the case for continued operations in the Arnhem area as encouraging. The report's main concern is German forces converging on the Nijmegen bridgehead.[43] Nevertheless, on 21 September the Guards made one last attempt to reach Arnhem but were stopped quickly just short of Elst. Having lost several tanks, the Irish Guards could not deploy off-road due to the carriageway sitting atop a high embankment. Lieutenant Colonel J.O.E. Vandeleur called for artillery and air support, which was not forthcoming due to administrative and logistical problems. According to the Guards mindset and operating procedures, all viable options to continue the advance were now exhausted. The 43rd Infantry Division was brought up to relieve the Guards, but the initiative was lost.[44]

John Gorman described how after the Irish Guards' effort to fight through to Arnhem had failed a troop of tanks from a British Cavalry Regiment appeared. A young lieutenant asked for a briefing for his troop and accompanying platoon of infantry, which was crowded onto the engine covers of the Shermans. Gorman recounted that the young officer had been ordered to simply put his foot down and charge straight through to Arnhem once it got dark. Gorman said that he believed the whole plan was suicidal, but both the troop commander and the infantry officer were determined to 'have a go'. However, just before zero hour this 'kamikaze' mission was called off.[45]

The 2IC (Second in Command), No. 1 Squadron, 2nd Battalion, Irish Guards, provided a first-hand account of the attempt to break through the German lines and relieve the men at Arnhem. He explained they received orders to cross the bridge (Nijmegen) and lead on to the besieged force. The assault force consisted of three squadrons of Irish Guards tanks. The lead squadron was without infantry support, while the following two squadrons each carried a company of infantry riding on the backs of the tanks. The first obstacle was a line of German entrenchments and a battery of 88mm guns on the right of the road and about 2 miles from the start line. The only artillery support available to the Guards was a battery of medium field guns that was supposed to bombard the German positions five minutes before the tanks were due to start their advance. Apparently, no air support was available. However, the officer remarked:

> We were fairly confident and I even asked what to do when we had bounced the Arnhem bridge!

He went on to explain how the recent hard fighting at the Dutch frontier had reduced the number of tanks available to the Irish Guards:

> The Sqn were very depleted after the Break out over the Escaut Canal and consisted of a troop of 3, Sqn HQ of 3, and 2 spare.

The start of the operation was set for 1100hrs. However, when the time arrived to advance, no artillery support had been forthcoming. It proved impossible to raise anyone on the Guards radio net due to heavy radio traffic. The officer explained that while trying to decide what to do next, he heard shells landing some distance away to their front and reasoned that his group was out of position and not as far forward as they had believed. Subsequently, he ordered the tanks to advance. He recalled the tanks went flat out for about a mile until they found themselves unwittingly level with the German gun screen. Suddenly, all three tanks in the leading squadron were hit and brewed up within a matter of seconds. The officer commanding the group was able to pull his tank off the road and behind a cottage before it too became a victim of the enemy guns.

The officer explained how the terrain proved a significant barrier to operating tanks:

> It was obvious from the start that it would be impossible to deploy off the road as it was a raised dyke and there was a ditch on either side, also there were orchards on either side, the trees about the same size as in the Bocage.

Next, one of the Irish Guards' tanks tried to move into the orchard about 10 yards away from the officer's position behind the cottage. The tank was immediately hit and brewed up. At 1500hrs, Lieutenant Colonel G.A.M. Vandeleur, commanding the 2nd (Armoured) Battalion, and cousin of Lieutenant Colonel J.O.E, radioed the group commander to say that his request for air support had been refused and that the troops were to hold where they were. At 2300hrs, with enemy infantry activity becoming bolder and more aggressive, the Irish Guards were ordered to withdraw.

Sometime later, the officer who had commanded the forlorn operation to advance to Arnhem was able to inspect the enemy positions that had blocked his path. He explained that in the woods on the right of the road, he found six long-barrelled 75mm guns and four 88mm guns, which had been moved from the sites originally marked on the overprint of his maps during the operation. He also recalled that there were track marks of a Tiger tank clearly visible and said six of these had taken part in a local counter-attack against the Irish Guards a few days later.

In concluding his testimony, the Irish Guards officer contemplated how things might have turned out with better support for the operation:

> I am fairly certain that with proper arty and air support, we could have got past these positions, but what would have happened if we had got through is a matter of conjecture.[46]

Given the prevailing conditions on the road to Arnhem, could the Irish Guards have done any more to relieve 1st Airborne? The 2nd Household Cavalry Regiment frequently found alternative routes around the opposition during operations, but in this case, they did not find suitable crossing points or bridges for Sherman tanks that would have enabled the Guards to outflank or bypass the Germans. However, the Household Cavalry were equipped with a variety of light reconnaissance vehicles including the AEC (Matador) Armoured Car, which was equipped with a 75mm main gun, and had proved itself very effective against infantry and armour. Could the Irish Guards have progressed beyond Elst if they had worked in concert with the Household Cavalry to threaten the German flanks or rear?[47]

Interviewed in November 1967, Colonel Hans-Peter Knaust described how he had commanded a battlegroup sent south to block the Guards Armoured Division's advance north toward Arnhem. In September 1944, Knaust held the rank of major and commanded 'Kampfgruppe Knaust', which consisted of a Panzergrenadier Battalion reinforced with a company of tanks and a platoon of Sturmgeschütz assault guns. His unit was placed under the command of General Bittrich, 2nd SS-Panzer Corps. Later, Knaust claimed he was reinforced by fifteen to twenty Tiger tanks from the army, and fifteen to twenty Panther tanks from a Waffen-SS unit. Knaust would later receive the Knight's Cross for his actions during the defence of Arnhem and Elst. It is worth recounting at length those sections of Colonel Knaust's testimony that relate to the defence of Elst, and how his battlegroup stopped the Guards' advance north:

> When I finally arrived south of Elst there were already British tanks on the Nijmegen–Arnhem road, heading for Elst. My Tiger tanks had their first brush with the British tanks at this time. I had drawn them up south of Elst so that the British tanks heading north ran straight into them. The Tigers shot at them from all sides and knocked out five Shermans. This must have been on the 23rd or 24th but I do not remember the exact dates. In any case the loss of five tanks seems to have discouraged the British because they were very slow in attacking. They did push back my men off the road to the right but were very slow in taking the offensive. I believe

this was probably the first step in stopping the British here at Elst. It seems to me that a part of the tank column wheeled onto the dike west of the road, probably to try to push through to the Lower Rhine. This must have been the unit (Light Household Cavalry) which you mentioned and which we saw later from Lijnden making their way to Driel.

It was definitely our fire which stopped the British at Elst. After we had been pushed back to Elst I positioned my Tigers around Elst at all roads leading into the town. With the Panther tanks which I now had I attacked west of Elst to take Lijnden, a small town, which seemed to be at the centre of British activity. I was not able to get to Lijnden with my Panthers because the roads could not bear the weight of these tanks. We fought between Elst and Lijnden and it was during this time that I saw an English column heading north on the other side of Lijnden. We shot at the column, but it disappeared in thick fog. I presumed they had thrown up a smokescreen. This column was probably the one which you said reached Driel.

I was not very surprised at my success in stopping the British at Elst because I considered my forces quite adequate. I thought myself very lucky to have received the Tiger and Panther units which gave me about 45 tanks to work with, I drew the Tigers up in position at Elst and tried to use the Panthers in an attack at Lijnden. I did not realize at this time, however, the strength of the British forces moving north. Later when I was a prisoner in Ostend I was interrogated by an Irish captain on the subject of this battle. He asked me whether I had any idea of the number of troops fighting against me. I said that no, I had only the vaguest notion.

Then he gave me the data on the Guards Armoured Division, its fighting strength, number of tanks etc. I laughed. Then I said, 'You should have told me that before. If I had known, I would not have stuck around Elst very long.'

Another reason why I was able to hold off the British was the fact that they could not move off the main road due to the marshy terrain criss-crossed by dikes and water-ditches. I was able to use my tanks to better advantage because I was in a defensive position in Elst. I was worried when I saw the tanks which had somehow left the road to head on a western then northern direction. This meant I had to protect my right flank. When the British reached the southern edge of Elst there was very bitter fighting in this area.

When we were pushed back into Elst there were some British soldiers already positioned as lookouts in the church tower. We tried to pick them off but somehow, they got out and away. We had spotted them because of the telephone wires dangling from the tower. They had already installed their telephones. They disappeared without too much difficulty because at this point there was a fair amount of confusion. The men had to be organized and given their positions.

We fought very hard at Elst to hold back the British and I was in constant fear that we might be encircled. It was a relief when the order finally came from Bittrich to move out.[48]

Confidence or Conceit?

Between the end of August and the start of September, the Guards had covered around 250 miles in six days. As Coble suggests, the intention to advance 60 miles in two days probably seemed achievable to the Guards.[49] General Adair thought the going 'would not be difficult' and 'once we got through (across the start line), I felt our progress should be fairly good'. Adair was so confident that the Guards would achieve their objectives, he said, 'I remember going through Eindhoven and having a feeling of regret that we could not stop and look at the town.'[50]

Over-optimism or arrogance, the Guards' lack of self-awareness during MARKET GARDEN seems to have caused them problems on the ground and made them a target for criticism. The Guards' culture of social superiority and bravado probably conveyed all the wrong messages to the outside world while reinforcing the social norms and attitudes of the group.

On 20 September, Sergeant Charles Murrell, Welsh Guards, reached Grave. Murrell took a very dim view of his unit's security, and believed the Guards were over-confident. Prophetically, he confided to his diary:

> Security is now awful. Map references relating to dispositions given in clear over the radio and maps with localities marked, left carelessly by officers – we are too confident. The 9th SS Panzer Division reported reforming. We might cop it one day.

As well as lamenting his own unit's procedural negligence, Murrell clearly had reservations about the feasibility of the entire MARKET GARDEN enterprise:

> In fact, our 'front' is exactly the width of the main road – no flank protection at all! The attack on the convoy at Eindhoven an example of the vulnerability of our exposed flanks and rear. We're marching in single file – right across the enemy's front.

On 22 September, Murrell wrote:

> This is a crazy battle – we are pushed 60 miles forward with 10,000 Jerries on our left flank, and some 45,000 (admittedly some under military age) on our right. This marching across an enemy front must be unorthodox – if it comes off then it will be a great triumph – if not, then we'll be in a grave position. We're still some 5 miles from the Paratroops at Arnhem – so near and yet so far and they're desperately short of ammunition and supplies. This is, indeed, a battle of bridges, fought, almost exclusively, along a single road, and will, however it goes, cause comment and discussion in military circles for years to come. The fact that our division was chosen to lead it is a compliment, but that's not much of a consolation if we're slumped around here with Jerries eating our rations and smoking our fags.[51]

Following the capture of the Nijmegen road bridge, Colonel Rueben Tucker, U.S. 82nd Airborne Division, was incensed by the Guards' nonchalance. He told General Gavin, 'We have been in this position for over twelve hours, and all they seem to be doing is brewing tea.'[52] Lieutenant Colonel Giles Vandeleur recalled that the Irish Guards were ordered to get through to Arnhem after taking the Nijmegen road bridge. He remarked, 'Our advance, funnily enough, was based on a time program (sic), as though we were on a peacetime march. We were to advance at a normal speed of an approach march, 15 miles in two hours.' Having seen the terrain they would have to advance over, Giles Vandeleur thought the road to Arnhem was 'a ridiculous place to operate tanks'.[53] Rather than an abundance of caution or canniness, on occasions the Guards seem to have allowed over-confidence and conceit to blind them to the operational and tactical realities of MARKET GARDEN.

Chapter Fourteen

Operation AINTREE

After Operation BLUECOAT, the 6th Guards (Tank) Brigade was concentrated between Flers and Tinchebray for a period of rest and maintenance. During this period, the Brigade trained with elements of the 3rd British Infantry Division. It was also during this period that the Brigade attempted to raise a Troop equipped with captured German Panther tanks but were unable to scavenge enough serviceable vehicles from the battlefields around Falaise. While the Brigade rested, the Allied advance continued without them.

All available transport was diverted to support the 2nd Army's rapid advance into Belgium and Holland. Consequently, the 6th Guards (Tank) Brigade, equipped with ponderous Churchill tanks, was left behind. The Brigade eventually moved to the River Seine on its tracks, as no tank transporters were available. The Brigade was still in France when the news broke of Operation MARKET GARDEN. Finally, towards the end of September, the Brigade received its marching orders to move north into Holland.

Having failed to cross the Lower Rhine at Arnhem, Operation MARKET GARDEN had left 2nd Army holding a narrow salient that stretched to Nijmegen. For the next two and a half months, the Brigade would be engaged in operations to expand the flanks of the salient in a prelude to clearing German forces along the western border between the Rivers Maas and Rhine.

In early October, the Brigade supported the 3rd British Infantry Division in an attack towards the River Meuse with the town of Venray (also spelled Venraij) as the objective.[1] The plan, code-named Operation AINTREE, was for 8th British Infantry Brigade Group with the 4th (Tank) Battalion, Coldstream Guards, one squadron of flail tanks of the Westminster Dragoons, 617th Assault Squadron and 42nd Royal Engineers supporting to take Overloon. In phase two of the operation, the 9th British Infantry Brigade Group supported by the 4th (Tank) Battalion, Grenadier Guards, would clear the woods to the east and advance on Venray. Two squadrons of flail tanks and a squadron of Armoured Vehicle Royal Engineers (AVRE) were available, if required. The assault was preceded by an artillery bombardment of enemy positions while air attacks struck at the Maas bridges to cut the enemy's lines of communication. The artillery support was provided by 8th Artillery Group, Royal Artillery (AGRA), and supported from the air by two wings of Hawker Typhoon ground-attack aircraft fitted with rockets and bombs. The artillery and air effort was supplemented by the 2nd Middlesex Regiment firing all its Vickers machine guns and 4.2-inch mortars, who expended over 300,000 rounds of ammunition.[2]

Operation AINTREE began on 12 October 1944. Initially, following the artillery and air barrage, everything went according to plan. However, on reaching the north-west outskirts of Overloon, the infantry divided into two forces: the East Yorks (2nd East Yorkshire Regiment) moving east and the Suffolks (1st Suffolk Regiment) moving south. Unfortunately, this only left the HQ Squadron of the Coldstream Guards to press the centre, and the advance stalled. Soon afterwards, the advance on the flanks also slowed due to extensive minefields and opposition from Panther tanks. The Royal Engineers were called forward to deal with the mines, but by day's end little progress had been made. It was estimated that the Germans had laid a quarter of a million mines around Overloon and Venray. Sergeant Frank Faulkner, 17th Field Squadron, Royal Engineers, believed that during operations in the area his unit lifted about 30,000 mines.[3]

The next day, the plan was for two squadrons of the Grenadiers and three of the Coldstream Guards to push a five-pronged attack into the wooded area south of Overloon. The fighting went on all day, but mines and heavy mortar fire slowed progress to a crawl. On 14 October, No. 3 Squadron, Grenadier Guards, repeatedly had their attack postponed, and did not cross their start line until 1530hrs. Meanwhile, No. 2 Squadron, Coldstream Guards, advanced down the Overloon–Venray road in support of the 1st Norfolks (Royal Norfolk Regiment) with the intention of crossing the Molenbeek waterway and advancing on Venray. As the Guards approached the stream, they were engaged by two Panther tanks while the infantry was pinned down by heavy machine gun fire. The Panthers succeeded in halting the advance, knocking out several tanks. The Guards were dismayed to find repeated strikes using armour-piercing discarding sabot (APDS) ammunition failed to penetrate the frontal armour of one Panther tank. The Panthers proved equally immune to the 25-pounder gun fire from 190th Field Regiment, Royal Artillery. On 15 October, having struggled to make progress during the preceding days, the 3rd Division and Guards (Tank) Brigade paused to regroup.

On day five of the operation, the 185th Infantry Brigade and 4th (Tank) Battalion, Coldstream Guards, and 8th Infantry Brigade and 4th (Tank) Battalion, Grenadier Guards, started an attack on the town of Venray. The 185th Brigade was to advance on the town from the north while 8th Brigade approached from the north-west. However, the Molenbeek proved more of an obstacle than it appeared on British maps. Although the stream was about 10ft wide, it had sloping banks that increased the width to about 25ft. The approaches to the stream were also boggy and liberally sown with mines. Traversing the Molenbeek proved difficult for the engineers, and one of the temporary Kapok pontoon bridges started to collapse after two troops of the

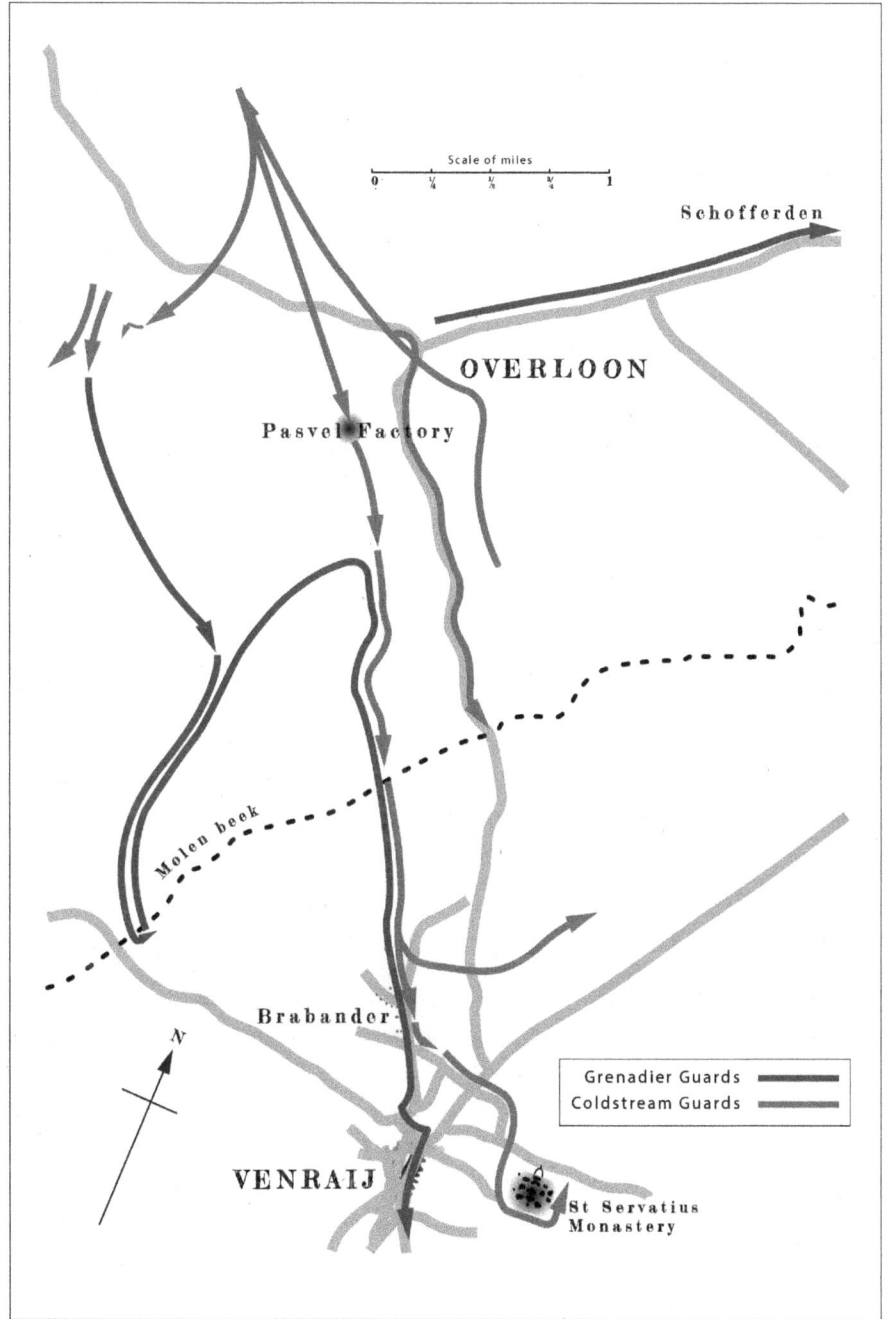

Map 4. Operation AINTREE, Overloon, 12 - 19 October 1944, 6th Guards (Tank) Brigade.

Coldstream Guards had crossed. The German defenders also rained mortar and artillery fire down on the attackers. By nightfall, the British were at the northern outskirts of the town.[4]

According to the war diary of the HQ 6th Guards (Tank) Brigade, the infantry fought house to house for Venray. Operations were hampered by heavy rain, which reduced roads and tracks to quagmires. The fighting was bitter and costly for both sides. On 18 October, the town was reported mostly held but not secure. Nevertheless, the BBC announced Venray captured on 19 October while the infantry continued mopping up pockets of resistance.[5]

The fighting for Venray had been particularly challenging, especially for the infantry, which suffered heavy casualties including three commanding officers and sixteen company commanders. During October 1944, the 3rd British Infantry Division experienced 1,400 casualties. On 20 October, the war diary of the 4th (Tank) Battalion, Grenadier Guards, recorded that the capture of Venray cost them three Guardsmen killed, fifteen wounded and twelve tanks knocked out. In a Special Order of the Day, circulated throughout the 6th Guards (Tank) Brigade, Lieutenant General Richard O'Connor, 8 Corps, congratulated the 3rd British Infantry Division, and remarked on the magnificent performance of 185th Brigade. Similarly, Brigadier Greenacre, 6th Guards (Tank) Brigade, wrote to the 4th (Tank) Battalion, Grenadier Guards:

> I would like to add that I have been much struck by the fine spirit of the Battalion and by the obviously whole-hearted way in which you co-operated with the infantry.
>
> Both the Commander 8 Corps and Commander 3 British Division have personally expressed to me their complete satisfaction with the way in which the Brigade has fought.[6]

A Guardsman's Testimony

When asked to describe his experiences of the fighting at Overloon, Guardsman Bob Dare, 4th (Tank) Battalion, Coldstream Guards, simply said, 'It was absolute hell. A real tank scrap.' In 1999, Dare retold his own harrowing story of the fighting at Overloon to members of the Imperial War Museum's oral history project. After crashing through a hedge, Dare's Churchill tank, named Jackal, struck a mine, which exploded with such force that the vehicle lifted into the air. It was likely that Jackal had struck a German Riegel mine 43 (Sprengriegel/R. Mi. 43) packed with 4kg (8lb 13oz) of TNT explosive. Almost immediately after the detonation, the tank's commander ordered the crew to bail out. Dare, the tank's driver, made good his escape and moved to the back of the vehicle, which was on fire.

Dare quickly realised that his co-driver had failed to escape, so he returned to the driver compartment and managed to pull the stricken man, Lance-Sergeant Johnny Lambert, from the burning tank. Lambert's left leg had been severed below the knee and his right foot detached at the ankle. Dare then dragged Lambert to the rear of the tank, thus providing the wounded man with some protection from further enemy action. According to Bob Dare, the tank was completely ablaze, when the tank commander suddenly emerged from the turret with his uniform on fire. Dare could also hear the screams and shouts from the other members of the crew still trapped inside the tank. Dare managed to clamber onto the back of the tank and pull the burning man clear of the turret. He then dragged the tank commander to the rear of the tank and placed him beside Lambert. Next, Dare returned to the open hatch of the driver's compartment, in the hope of rescuing the men trapped in the turret, but the flames and smoke were too intense for him to gain entry. After a short period, the screams of the men trapped inside the turret subsided, and everything went quiet. Mindful that he and his stricken comrades were still in a minefield, Dare managed to drag his crewmates back to the relative safety of the nearby hedge by walking in the track marks made by Jackal earlier. Dare eventually got the wounded men onto another tank and evacuated to the Regimental Aid Post.

While at the post waiting to be assessed, Dare recalled how his tank commander had thanked him for his life, and told him that there was nothing more he could have done to save the men trapped in the burning tank. Initially, Dare appeared to have suffered nothing more serious than some minor burns to his hands, superficial wounds, and a singed uniform. However, later he developed a series of curious medical symptoms. He found he could no longer use his left leg, suffered from a persistent ringing in the ears and then mutism. Today, Dare would have been diagnosed as suffering from post-traumatic stress disorder (PTSD) due to his battlefield trauma. At the time, he was hospitalised with a diagnosis of battle fatigue, and received hypnotherapy. Eventually, Dare's voice returned, although he retained a stammer for some time. The clinicians who treated Dare also taught him coping mechanisms that he likened to yoga. These techniques enabled him to control his breathing when beset by traumatic flashbacks and panic attacks, which lasted for many years. Hypnotherapy remains an effective treatment for trauma symptoms. Unfortunately, by his own admission, Dare carried an irrational sense of guilt about the loss of his two crewmates that haunted him for the rest of his life. His two friends that were killed on that bleak day in October were Guardsman Robert Silman and Guardsman Gordon Wright. They are buried beside each other at the war cemetery in Overloon.

Many years later, Dare was reunited with his friend and fellow tank driver, Guardsman John Collier, who had witnessed Jackal's demise. Collier had returned to the battlefield sometime after the action hoping to find his friend alive. However, all he found were 'burnt tanks and dead bodies'. Collier fought all the way through the campaign for north-west Europe. Many years later he told his friend that in his opinion the battle for Overloon was the worst action he had experienced during the war.

Dare was to return to Overloon many times to take part in various commemoration ceremonies and to visit the graves of his comrades. After Operation AINTREE, Dare's tank, Jackal, was simply abandoned by the army. Today, it resides at the War Museum Overloon, where it remains on permanent display. Around fifty years after the battle, Dare started to suffer from some mobility issues. After a series of diagnostic tests, an orthopaedic surgeon informed him that his left leg had indeed suffered a fracture, mostly likely due to the mine explosion. Dare passed away in January 2007, aged 82.[7]

A Cuckoo in the Nest

During the fighting around Overloon, the Guards discovered a fully operational Panther tank hidden in a barn. The tank was recovered, repainted in olive drab, and the turret decorated with a five-pointed star on each side to ensure it could be easily identified as an Allied vehicle. The tank joined the 4th Battalion, Coldstream Guards, and was aptly named Cuckoo. Towards the end of November, Cuckoo took part in the reduction of Kasteel Geijsteren, a medieval castle on the River Maas in North Limburg, Holland. The castle had become an enemy redoubt and after the defenders had resisted a direct assault, the fortress was simply reduced to rubble by days of air and artillery bombardment. During the bombardment, it was noted that Cuckoo was repeatedly able to fire shells through the castle's small windows and loopholes. On 1 December 1944, the 4th Battalion received an informal visit from Supreme Allied Commander, General Eisenhower, Lieutenant General Dempsey, and Lieutenant General Ritchie.[8] General Eisenhower inspected Cuckoo and talked to Sergeant Roberts, the tank's commander. As well as the accuracy of the Panther's 75mm gun, Cuckoo also demonstrated superior performance on icy roads. During the winter, where the 4th Battalion's Churchill tanks slid into ditches at every opportunity, Cuckoo, 8 tons heavier, trundled merrily along on frozen roads with no difficulty at all.[9] In February 1945, Cuckoo's fuel pump broke, and the tank had to be abandoned. The Guards had no spares with which to make a repair of an enemy tank. Although it was extremely unusual for a British armoured unit to use a captured German tank, it was not unprecedented. In October 1944, during fighting in Italy, the Canadian Seaforth Highlanders captured an intact Panther and gave it to the 145th Regiment, Royal Armoured Corps, who named it 'Deserter'.

Chapter Fifteen

Operation VERITABLE

Operation VERITABLE was part of a series of battles designed to enable the Allies to break into Germany from the west. The operation's objective was to destroy enemy forces between the Rivers Maas and Rhine. The action was to be quickly followed by the U.S. 9th Army's Operation GRENADE, which would cross the River Roer and move north, linking up with the 1st Canadian Army in a pincer movement. However, an early spring thaw, bad weather and demolition of the Roer dams caused extensive flooding, which delayed the launch of GRENADE until 23 February 1945.[1]

The 6th Guards and the Rhineland Battles

On 1 February 1945, the war diary of the 6th Guards (Tank) Brigade HQ noted that the news from the Eastern Front was extremely good, and that Soviet troops were just 45 miles from Berlin.

Between 2 and 3 February, the Brigade moved from Tilburg to Nijmegen. Around 1,500 tanks, six infantry divisions, 1,000 guns and 300,000 troops concentrated on Nijmegen. Every effort was made to conceal the massive build-up of forces from the enemy. Operation VERITABLE would start with five divisions up and was preceded by a massive air and artillery bombardment. The Brigade came under command of the British 30 Corps for the operation, which consisted of 15th (Scottish) Division, 51st (Highland) Division, 43rd (Wessex) Division, 53rd (Welsh) Division, Guards Armoured Division, 34th (Tank) Brigade, 6th Guards (Tank) Brigade and the 8th (Armoured) Brigade.

The plan for the operation had the Canadians on the extreme left of the advance with the intention to clear the flooded area between the Rhine and the Nijmegen–Cleve Road. In the centre, the 15th (Scottish) with the 6th Guards under command were to breach the Siegfried Line, capture the high ground west of Cleve and then take Cleve itself. Further south, the 53rd Division supported by the 34th (Tank) Brigade was to capture the Reichswald Forest. To the south of them, the 51st (Highland) Division was to clear the area south of the Reichswald between Gennep and Goch. As soon as the 15th Scottish had captured the Matterborn Feature, as the high ground to the west of Cleve was known, the 43rd Division and 8th (Armoured) Brigade were to drive south from Cleve and capture Goch, Weeze, Kevelaer and Geldern. On the fourth day of VERITABLE, if everything went according to plan, the Guards Armoured Division would pass through and take the bridges over the Rhine at Wesel. The American 9th Army was to launch its own offensive, Operation GRENADE, and link up with the British near Geldern.

On 6 February, the Brigade was redesignated and henceforth to be known as the 6th Guards (Armoured) Brigade, Type B. A Standardisation Conference decided to harmonise all British armoured brigades into two types (Type 'A' with an infantry motor battalion within an armoured division, and Type 'B' independently without), all to be equipped with the universal Comet tank in place of Churchills, Cromwells and Shermans. The C.I.G.S. approved this policy on 18 January 1945, although it was not finally authorised until 1 May. However, most brigades continued to use Churchills, Cromwells or Shermans until the end of hostilities.

Under command of the 15th (Scottish) Division, the Guards battalions were assigned to the following brigade groups for the operation: 44th (Lowland) Brigade and the 4th (Tanks) Grenadier Guards, the 46th (Highland) Brigade with the 4th (Tanks) Coldstream Guards and the 227th (Highland) Brigade supported by the 3rd (Tanks) Scots Guards. A brigade group was typically assigned support squadrons of flail tanks, Crocodile flamethrowers, and various AVRE vehicles such as bridge layers. Additionally, the brigade groups could call down considerable artillery and tactical air support.

On 8 February, following a sustained pounding of the enemy defences by concentred artillery fire that lasted five and a half hours, the brigade groups crossed the start line at 1030hrs. The war diary of HQ 6th Guards records that the effect of the artillery barrage on the enemy infantry holding the line was shattering. By 1630hrs, the first objective, the Frasselt road, had been secured and about 400 prisoners taken. Initially, the inclement weather proved the major obstacle to the advance, which reduced visibility and slowed the progress of the tanks. The 3rd Scots Guards, for instance, reported twelve tanks bogged down by 1500hrs.

The next day, the 4th (Tank) Battalion, Grenadier Guards; Left Flank, 3rd (Tank) Scots Guards; the 2nd Gordons; and an Armoured Breaching Group came under command of 44th (Lowland) Brigade. This brigade group was able to force two crossings over a large anti-tank ditch that lay across its line of advance. Many of the flail tanks assigned to clear lanes in the extensive enemy minefields suffered bogging. Nevertheless, after a slow start, the 44th Brigade made rapid progress and by the time it was dark, around 1600hrs, the 15th (Scottish) Division was in striking distance of Cleve.

Operation VERITABLE 109

On 10 February, communication problems became acute on the Division axis. Flood water from the Rhine rapidly encroached on the main northern supply route. After two days of bitter fighting, Cleve was reported cleared of enemy forces. Cleve was the first major German town captured by British forces during the campaign. A week later, the 7th Canadian Infantry Brigade and 3rd (Tank) Battalion, Scots Guards, undertook the clearing of the Cleve–Calcar Road and high ground south of Calcar. German resistance was intense. Units of the 116th Panzer Division and 346th Infantry Division put in a series of counter-attacks to try to halt the Canadian advance. The diarist of HQ 6th Guards (Armoured) Brigade noted that, 'We no longer look for flamboyant armoured dashes but have settled down to a dogged drive South East.'

On 18 February, the 4th (Tank) Battalion, Grenadier Guards were assigned to the attack on Goch, which was heavily defended and partially protected by the natural obstacle of the Niers River and a wide anti-tank ditch. After several failed attempts, the anti-tank ditch was eventually bridged in two places. House by house, the 51st (Highland) Division and the 44th Infantry Brigade systematically cleared the town. In the days that followed, 3rd (Tank) Battalion, Scots Guards, under command of the 46th (Highland) Brigade, cleared the woods

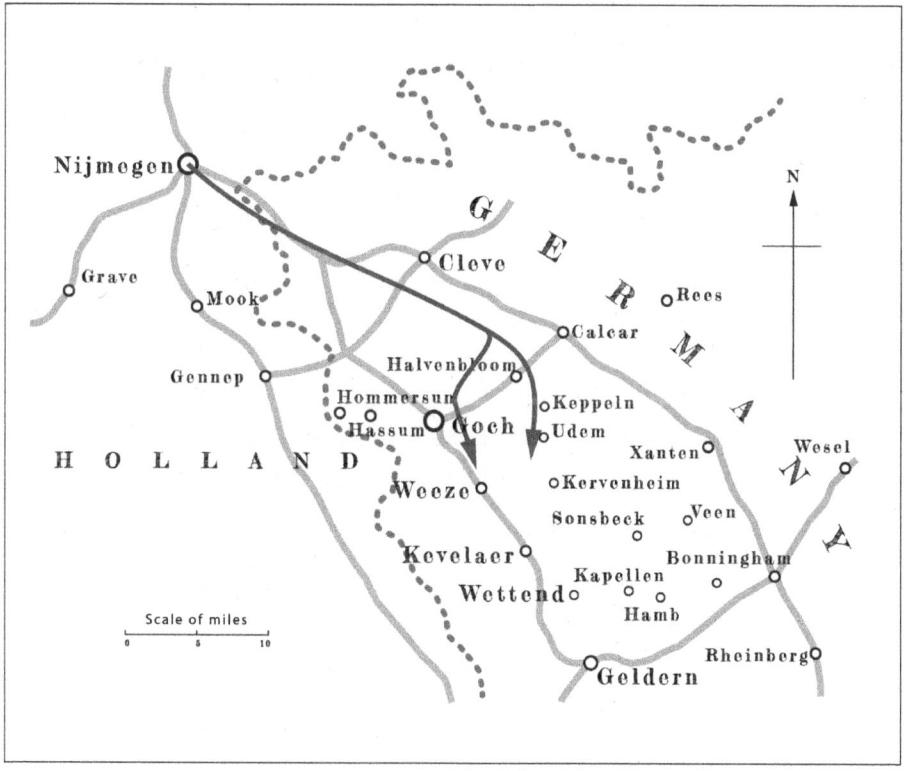

Map 5. Operation VERITABLE, 8 February – 11 March 1945, 6th Guards (Armoured) Brigade.

south of Goch, the infantry suffering many casualties due to enemy mortar and artillery fire. On 24 February, the 15th (Scottish) Division was pulled out of the line and replaced by the 3rd (British) Infantry Division.[2]

Operation BLOCKBUSTER

Operation VERITABLE had failed to reach the Rhine at Wesel in four days as planned. Instead, after more than two weeks of fighting the operation was only halfway towards its final objectives and had run out of momentum. Operation BLOCKBUSTER was the completion of the larger Operation VERITABLE by the 1st Canadian Army, reinforced by the British 30 Corps. The 2nd Canadian Corps, strengthened by another three divisions, planned to push on to Xanten and Wesel through the German last line of defence, the Hochwald 'lay-back' position. The Canadian main effort was against the Hochwald Gap. The German commander, General Schlemm, correctly anticipated the direction of the Canadian effort and concentrated his forces to meet the threat. The British 30 Corps was only given a subsidiary role in the Canadian operation. The 3rd (British) Division was tasked with breaking through south-east of Goch, after which the Guards Armoured Division would pass through and swing east toward Wesel. After being delayed, the American Operation GRENADE was now gathering momentum. Because of this new threat, General Schlemm had no choice but to redeploy some of his forces and shorten his lines, gradually falling back on the vital bridges over the Rhine.

At the end of February, the 3rd (British) Division launched Operation HEATHER. The plan was for two infantry brigades supported by tanks to attack south-east of Goch, through heavily wooded country, and secure the Udem–Weeze road, which lay about 2 miles distant. The 9th Brigade with the Scots Guards would advance on the left to secure the eastern end of the Udem–Weeze road while the 8th Brigade and Grenadier Guards would advance on the right. Next, the 185th Brigade would pass through and capture the town of Kervenheim, a further 2½ miles south-east. On the left was the 11th Armoured Division and, on the right, the 53rd (Welsh) Division, tasked with the capture of Weeze.

The 8th Brigade's principal objective was to capture and hold the vital Muhlen–Fleuth bridge. Once secured, the 53rd (Welsh) Division would use the bridge to attack Weeze, to the south of Goch. Having lost the bridge, the Germans threw in a series of furious counter-attacks, but these were beaten back with the aid of artillery support. The 9th Brigade successfully cut the Udem–Weeze road. The Scots Guards provided close, effective support. Next, the 185th Brigade captured Kervenheim with the support of the Coldstream

Guards. On 2 March 9th Brigade and the Scots Guards cleared Winnekendonk and the woods to its north. The Germans were starting to withdraw towards the Rhine crossings. On 5 March, the Guards Armoured Division passed through the 6th Guards (Armoured) Brigade at Hamb. The Brigade had been in action for twenty-five days without respite. The Brigade was just 8 miles from the west bank of the Rhine. Two days later, news reached the Brigade that General Hodge's 1st U.S. Army was over the Rhine at Remagen. On 10 March, with the collapse of the Wesel pocket and Rhine bridges blown behind the retreating Germans, Operation VERITABLE was over. Two weeks later, the Allies were over the Rhine (Operation PLUNDER) with a secure bridgehead from which to attack the German interior.[3]

Lessons Learned from VERITABLE

In May 1946, the Headquarters of 21st Army Group produced a report on Operation VERITABLE. The report found that VERITABLE and GRENADE achieved their objectives, albeit belatedly, and concluded with 21st Army Group lining the west bank of the Rhine from Düsseldorf to Arnhem. The two operations had direct bearings on one another. The delay in mounting GRENADE, due to the excessive flooding, caused 1st Canadian Army to bear the brunt of the fighting longer than was intended. As a result, however, they attracted several enemy formations from further south. The original enemy garrison in the VERITABLE area of one reinforced infantry division was finally swollen to three infantry, four parachute, two panzer, and one panzer grenadier divisions. On the other hand, the rapid success of the 9th U.S. Army's attack relieved the pressure on the 1st Canadian Army front. By 1 March, the enemy, threatened with encirclement, began to pull out on its southern flank to form the Wesel bridgehead.

It was hoped that after the initial break-in, and again in the BLOCKBUSTER operation, the opportunity would occur for a large-scale breakthrough by Allied armour. Instead, bad weather, extensive flooding, and areas of dense forest made this impossible. The few available roads quickly became traffic congested, and created natural bottlenecks for the German defenders to exploit. Consequently, the enemy turned every town, village, and crossroad into a strongpoint, and made them as tank-proof as possible by digging anti-tank ditches, blowing bridges and cratering roads. On those occasions when armour tried to advance independently, its losses were severe. The effective use of armour was confined to close infantry support, and in this role it proved of great assistance both materially and morally.

The report found that the use of specialised armour such as flail tanks, flamethrowing Crocodiles and AVRE bridge layers were of particular value, especially when operations were planned and co-ordinated carefully. However, the ability of infantry and armour to communicate effectively during actions remained a conundrum. By and large, wireless communications had proven unreliable between the two arms during VERITABLE, as did attempts to use a system of Very lights. The use of smoke generators was found to be the most effective method of rudimentary communication between infantry and tanks once committed to battle. Overall, there were few, mostly minor tactical lessons to be learned from the Rhineland operations. However, the report cautioned that lessons learned from recent operations must be reinforced and applied rigorously in the preparation for upcoming operations otherwise they would be too easily forgotten.[4]

An Infantry Battle for an Armoured Division

Originally, the Guards Armoured Division was selected as the breakout force for Operation VERITABLE. The intention was for the Guards Armoured Division to be held ready to exploit a breach in the German lines and advance swiftly to capture the Wesel bridge over the Rhine. However, the appalling ground conditions meant the 5th Guards (Armoured) Brigade would not be utilised for nearly a month. Instead, the 32nd Guards (Infantry) Brigade under the 51st (Highland) Division went into action on 13 February 1945, attacking eastward toward Goch.[5] The Division did not reform and fight together in its Regimental Battlegroups until 2 March. The Guards helped clear the Bonninghardt Forest and cut the main Xanten Road. Cutting the main highway increased pressure on the Germans who remained within the bridgehead. Finally, on the night of 10 March, the Germans blew the Wesel bridge. By the end of VERITABLE, the 21st Army Group held the west bank of the Rhine from Nijmegen to Neuss.[6] The operation had cost the Division 79 killed, 349 wounded, and 50 missing.[7]

The Application of Lessons Learned in Training

Before Operation VERITABLE, 2nd (Infantry) Battalion, Scots Guards, were at Hougaerde. In preparation for being 'married up' with the 2nd (Armoured) Battalion, Welsh Guards, the Scots Guards received training in how to co-operate with tanks:

> After lunch officers and senior NCOs attended a demonstration by a sqdn of 2 W.G. and 'X' Coy S.G. who showed us how to co-operate with tanks.

The demonstration was a success, and filled in a gap in our trg which everyone felt badly: (through training to become an Inf Bn in the G.A.D. at STOBS we had never co-operated with or even seen a single tank.)[8]

The following day, 4 February, the Scots Guards rifle companies duly practised mounting tanks.

The appendix of the Scots Guards war diary for February 1945 outlines the tank squadron and rifle company group tactics to be demonstrated and practised between 3 and 4 February. Appendix C of the war diary was based on recent lessons learned by the Welsh Guards Group, and stated that all instructional points would be adopted as battle drills in future operations and for training purposes. The detailed instructions on the staging of a deliberate attack, for example, were based on lessons learned from the fighting at Hechtel, northern Belgium, on 12 September 1944.[9]

In preparation for Operation VERITABLE, the 1st (Motor) Battalion, Grenadier Guards, conducted a large-scale, live-fire exercise called ESKIMO, which took place between 26 and 27 January 1945 on an old German firing range south-west of Helchteren. The rifle companies were supported by tanks, machine guns and mortar platoons. On completion of the exercise, the battalion's war diary concluded:

The attack was carried out with dash and the C.O's only criticism was that the liaison between the assaulting infantry and the tanks was not as close as it might have been.[10]

Directly after VERITABLE, the 1st (Motor) Battalion, Grenadier Guards took the opportunity to introduce some new training courses, which had previously been postponed, for officers, corporals, snipers and Wasp units (the flamethrower variant of the Universal Carrier). The battalion also set up a small-arms firing range in the King's Company area.[11]

On 11 March 1945, the 2nd (Armoured) Battalion, Irish Guards, issued Training Instructions No. 3, which stated that many junior officers and NCOs of the battalion had performed well during VERITABLE, despite some months of inaction and a lack of previous battle experience. However, Lieutenant Colonel Giles Vandeleur wrote that several weaknesses and faults were apparent during the battle. For example, in the section on Road Discipline, he highlighted a dangerous tendency for the battalion column to 'telescope' when suddenly halted because vehicles were spaced insufficiently. The subsequent traffic jam caused by the column telescoping denied the leading elements of the battlegroup any room to manoeuvre. Similarly, Vandeleur blamed the inexperience of Troop

Leaders for engaging the enemy too slowly once the battle was joined. However, he was highly critical of the battalion's continued inability to make prompt and accurate shell and mortar reports. These reports were essential to identify and neutralise enemy artillery by counter-battery fire. Vandeleur reminded the battalion that they possessed a complex counter-battery apparatus, and it was 'gross stupidity not to use the support available'.[12]

Toward the end of November 1944, the Division had reorganised its counter-mortar unit based on lessons learned from recent engagements. The revised counter-mortar policy document explained that the unit was equipped with the latest radar location equipment. Nevertheless, it still required timely, accurate shell and mortar reports from front-line units to identify and neutralise enemy mortar fire successfully.[13]

Operation VERITABLE was the Guards Armoured Division's last major battle. Due to poor weather and widespread flooding, VERITABLE quickly assumed the character of a First World War battle with infantry and artillery at a premium. The 32nd Guards Brigade, for example, was organised into three infantry battalions with Welsh Guards tanks and field artillery in support.[14] The 5th Guards Armoured Brigade would be held in reserve for much of February.[15] There is perhaps some small irony that the Guards Armoured Division's contribution to the success of VERITABLE was essentially fighting in its traditional infantry role.

It appears that the Guards training battalions were not adequately preparing replacement troops for battle. As we have seen, infantry replacements arriving from STOBS Camp, on the Scottish Borders, had no experience of operating with tanks. However, the Division itself continued to rapidly analyse, disseminate, and incorporate lessons learned from its most recent battlefield experiences. Additionally, the battlegroups and battalions were adapting tactics and equipment to meet operational objectives.

Chapter Sixteen

The Division as Learning Organisation

All military organisations rely heavily on rules, routines, procedures, and traditions to operate. As discussed earlier, a Guardsman's induction and training at Caterham was little different during the Second World War than the Napoleonic era. Repetition in training, on exercises and during operations reinforced core competencies. However, routine and rigid discipline could also impede change and innovation. Before deployment to Normandy, General Adair remarked how: 'Outsiders would come along and suggest that our whole training was too reminiscent of the barrack square, that the discipline of the Brigade of Guards and the dash required of armour would not combine in battle.'[1] Although Adair refuted these accusations, it is clear that the Division was not as uniformly well trained for combat as it should have been when it arrived in Normandy.

Theo Farrell suggests certain conditions must exist for small-scale, bottom-up, tactical adaptation in war to occur. First, the experience or prospect of defeat is often the catalyst required for change within military organisations. Next, decentralised organisations are more likely to explore alternative methods of operating. Third, a high personnel turnover means old knowledge and norms are quickly replaced by new ideas and perspectives.[2] The Guards Armoured Division met all these conditions during the campaign for north-west Europe. On 28 July 1944, the Division reorganised into battlegroups following its baptism of fire during Operation GOODWOOD.[3] In March 1945, the 1st (Armoured) Battalion, Coldstream Guards, experimented with rockets to supplement its firepower, a purely local initiative.[4] The Brigade of Guards expanded to twenty-one fighting battalions throughout the war, which meant a considerable influx of officers and men who were essentially civilian soldiers, not professionals.[5]

Foley, Griffin, and McCartney argue that it is only recently, during operations in Iraq and Afghanistan (1999 to 2021), that British and U.S. armies have recognised that bottom-up learning is crucial to creating adaptive, flexible forces capable of meeting the challenges of twenty-first-century conflict. Nevertheless, surprisingly, it has taken British and U.S. armies a long time to appreciate the value of front-line feedback and develop new systems capable of capturing and sharing lessons learned throughout their respective organisations.[6]

Foley, Griffin, and McCartney contend that a major barrier to developing a lessons learned culture is the willingness to accept failures. They argue that military organisations do not traditionally tolerate dissent. Additionally, military and political leaders and other vested interests might not want to encourage open and honest debate about strategic, operational, tactical or equipment failures.[7] Visser suggests that the British Army during the Second World War possessed only a moderate learning capability. He argues that officers and men enjoyed little empowerment. The reporting of errors was typically frowned upon by superiors. Lessons learned were censored frequently and only disseminated slowly. The regimental system, decentralised training, a lack of coherent doctrine, and poorly trained combat leaders contributed to Visser's defensive learning cycle.[8]

The deficiencies of British tanks are a good example of where military and political leaders sought to stamp out negative feedback from front-line units rather than address them. The Guards Armoured Division was seen as rocking the establishment boat and was accused of being 'canny' by the secretary of state for war rather than highlighting a genuine concern about the relative capabilities of Allied and German tanks.[9] On 25 June 1944, General Montgomery wrote a personal note to Sir James Grigg about reports of British equipment failures:

> My Dear Secretary of State,
> It has come to my notice that reports are circulating about the value of British equipment, tanks, etc, compared to the Germans. We cannot have anything of that sort at this time. We have got a good lodgement area, we have built up our strength, and tomorrow we will leap on the enemy. Anything that undermines confidence and morale must be stamped on ruthlessly.

Montgomery's note to Grigg was accompanied by a copy of a two-page, typed directive issued to the British 2nd Army, 1st Canadian Army, 79th Division and the chief of staff, 21st Army Group, which explicitly forbid commanders or staff officers from writing or forwarding reports that were critical of operations or equipment to anyone other than their immediate superior.[10]

It is interesting that many of the points cited by Visser as being detrimental to the overall learning capabilities of the British Army, such as the regimental system and decentralised training, seem to have worked in the Guards' favour. Externally, the Guards might have appeared as little more than a socially exclusive boys' club bound by centuries of tradition. Internally, the Guards shared a common ethos and organisational structure that united them and perhaps made disseminating lessons learned easier than the rest of the army. General Adair did not micromanage his division and trusted his brigade and battalion commanders to get the job done. Interestingly, where Adair's preference to devolve responsibility downward had been a distinct failing when training at home, it later appeared a strength when committed to battle.

Bringing the same regiment's infantry and armoured battalions into Regimental Battlegroups was a welcomed operational innovation. General Sir David Fraser explained how two battalions of the Grenadier Guards fought as one group, command exercised jointly between the battalion commanders. They would organise joint Orders Groups and agreed on joint plans to achieve objectives. Fraser described how, 'The arrangement produced remarkably little discord or confusion, largely because personal relationships were so close. We knew each other well, at every level: we were all Grenadiers.' A series of unspoken and informal rules also existed whereby seniority determined command when two officers held the same rank.[11] The war diary of the 2nd (Armoured) Battalion, Irish Guards, described the forming of its battlegroup with the 3rd (Infantry) Battalion as 'a very happy partnership that continued with great success'.[12]

Mad Night Dash

In early April, the Celtic Battlegroup crossed the German frontier and formed a small bridgehead at the town of Nordhorn. The battlegroup's next objective was Lingen and a bridge over the River Ems. In the early hours of 3 April, with Guardsmen riding on the tanks, the Celtic Battlegroup started its 'Mad Night Dash' to the River Ems. The Guards engaged all targets of opportunity along the 12 miles to Lingen, taking the Germans completely by surprise. Erskine contends that 'such an advance, with infantry and tanks working in the closest co-operation in the dark, could be claimed, fairly enough, as an innovation'. However, unfortunately, the Germans destroyed the Ems bridge just as the Scots Guards approached it.[13]

The Guards' night advance was unusual enough to be featured in the press. *The Aberdeen Evening Express* proclaimed the Guards' night advance as possibly the 'most dashing action of the war' in an article entitled 'Great Work by Guards Division, Armoured Charge on Modern Lines'.[14] Several other newspapers, such as *The Scotsman*[15] and *The Nottingham Journal*,[16] also published the story.

Erskine's assertion that the night advance of 3 April was a tactical innovation seems correct. For most of the conflict, it had been a Guards standard operating procedure for tanks to retire from the front line to a relatively safe harbour area before nightfall. However, we can see that operating procedures were evolving gradually based on lessons learned. For example, at the end of January, Lieutenant Colonel J.C. Lewis, Welsh Guards, distributed instructions for operations and training based on lessons learned. In this document, he overturns the accepted procedure of tanks harbouring after dark. Instead, he directs that tanks should not withdraw under any circumstances until a position is entirely consolidated.[17]

In a memorandum entitled, *Tactical Employment of Armour*, Lieutenant Colonel Lewis sets out detailed instructions for the co-operation of tanks and armour in small unit actions, the tactical employment of battlegroups, the deliberate or set-piece attack and overcoming water obstacles. However, point eight, that deals with the subject of capturing large towns and villages, might easily be interpreted as inciting Guardsmen to commit war crimes:

> 8. CAPTURE OF BIG TOWNS/VILLAGES
> (a) When thought to be still containing some enemy, such as BRUSSELS, Tks should enter first at best possible speed, carrying Inf, not hysterical women, upon them, and make straight for the centre of the town, and there establish themselves as quickly as possible, afterwards throwing out small parties of Inf to block roads as established Strong points.
> (b) Tks milling around in such a fashion are liable to cause fear and respect amongst a hostile population and might even in-sight co-operation from workers such as may be met with at places such as ESSEN, DUSSELDORF, and WUPPERTAL.
> (c) On approaching small towns and villages that are hostile and suspected of holding small German garrisons, Tks will immediately destroy a few houses to start with, before they begin to enter the town or village. Some civilian or military hostages should be rounded up at an early stage. 2 or 3 of these will be released and given half an hour to spread the news that if any soldier Inf or Armd, is sniped or shot at during passage through the town or village, then the civilian or military hostages that we are carrying will be immediately put to death, and the town destroyed.
>
> If the slightest opposition is encountered, the leading Sqn of Tks, supported by arty and other Tks within the Group, will set fire to and destroy the whole place.[18]

Lieutenant Colonel Lewis's chillingly expedient instructions to kill hostages and burn villages to overcome enemy resistance in urban areas demonstrates how quickly morals and the rule of law can be eroded by prolonged exposure to combat. Clearly, not all lessons learned, at least by some members of the Division, were positive.

Artillery, Rockets and Tanks

On 30 January, the Guards circulated a report on trials to determine whether Sherman tanks could be employed in an artillery role. The document concluded that there were no technical difficulties to tanks operating as artillery. However, tanks would have to operate *en masse* to be effective partly due to the small calibre of shells. Nevertheless, the trial found the tanks of a division could support the infantry and strengthen the field artillery during deliberate attacks, opposed river crossings, to clear roadblocks and break up enemy troop concentrations. After a bombardment, the tank squadrons would revert quickly to their primary role in supporting the advance.[19] Perhaps prompted by the enemy's defensive tactics and a desire to minimise casualties, this trial and subsequent report helps to illustrate the Guards' growing capacity as a learning organisation and innovator.

By mid-March, elements of the 1st (Armoured) Battalion, Coldstream Guards, started to modify their tanks by adding 60lb rockets usually fired by Hawker Typhoon ground-attack aircraft.[20] According to Robert Boscawen, Captain Dermot Musker got the idea from the Canadians.[21] The Canadians had started to experiment with rockets obtained from the RCAF to increase the firepower of their Staghound armoured cars. However, the Canadian project to use rockets was dropped in February 1945.[22] In mid-March, Boscawen and Musker acquired a supply of rockets from a local RAF airfield. The 5th Brigade's Light Aid Detachment (LAD) fitted the rocket rails (usually suspended under an aircraft's wings) to the sides of some Sherman tanks. By the end of March, Boscawen and Musker had completed a series of demonstrations to the Division. The rockets were given the code name Tulips due to their shape.[23] Although the rockets were wildly inaccurate when fired from a tank, they did prove helpful in clearing woods and enemy roadblocks during the last month of the war.[24] In addition, the rockets supported the Guards attack on the Ems River crossing on 3 and 4 April 1945.[25] The war diary of the 5th Battalion, Coldstream Guards, recorded that the rockets were used with 'great effect'.[26] Originally, Musker and Boscawen got the idea for adding rockets to their tanks from the Canadians. However, the British and Americans were already deploying tank-mounted and lorry-mounted rocket projectors in February 1945.[27]

Action at Ems Bridge

The action fought at the Ems bridge on 3 April 1945 epitomises how far the Division had come and all it had learned both tactically and operationally since arriving in Normandy the year before. First, the artillery fired around the bridge without pre-registering their guns to ensure surprise. Next, the moment the artillery ceased, the tanks opened fire, giving the enemy no chance to recover. Then, just before the infantry rushed the bridge, No. 2 Troop launched a salvo of rockets, which reportedly killed several Germans and 'deafened a great many more'. After that, the company commander, Captain Ian Liddell, single-handedly disabled the demolition charges fitted to the bridge. No. 4 Troop then used its tanks to bulldoze through a German roadblock defending the approach to the bridge. Finally, the infantry captured and consolidated the position. As a result, four 88mm anti-tank guns were seized, forty-five Germans killed and eighty taken prisoner.

The Guards suffered one fatality and eight wounded in taking the Ems bridge. Captain Liddell, who was killed eighteen days later, was posthumously awarded the Victoria Cross for his gallantry. Albeit with some bias, the war diary of the 1st (Armoured) Battalion, Coldstream Guards, described the action at the Ems bridge as 'magnificently planned, perfectly timed and bravely executed'.[28]

By April 1945, the end of the war in Europe was in sight. However, what no one in the Guards Armoured Division knew, as they fought their last battles on the road to the North Sea coast, was that the cessation of hostilities would also mean the end of the formation.

Chapter Seventeen

6th Guards (Armoured) Brigade: From the Rhine to Münster

On 14 April 1945, *The Illustrated London News* featured a full-page photograph, almost certainly staged for the camera, of American paratroopers (mainly medics) grouped around a Churchill tank and its crew. The headline read, 'The Sixth Guards Tank Brigade's capture of Munster, Capital of Westphalia: British Guardsmen and infantry of the U.S. 17th Airborne Division conferring in the heart of the city during a patrol'. The photograph might have been a fake, but the story was true enough.[1] Just two weeks before, on 27 March, the 6th Guards (Armoured) Brigade was ordered to advance at best speed along the axis Wesel–Haltern–Dülmen, breaking out of the Rhine bridgehead and striking at Münster and a crossing over the Dortmund–Ems Canal. The Brigade Group formed for the operation consisted of the 6th Guards (Armoured) Brigade, less the Grenadier Guards, the American 513th Parachute Infantry Regiment, the 3rd Reconnaissance Regiment, the 6th Field Regiment, Royal Artillery, the 77th Medium Regiment, Royal Artillery, and two batteries of the 63rd Anti-Tank Regiment, Royal Artillery.[2]

The Scots Guards were 'married' to the 2nd Battalion, and the Coldstream Guards to the 3rd Battalion, 513th Parachute Infantry Regiment. The war diary of the 4th Battalion, Coldstream Guards mentioned that the Guardsmen and the Americans quickly were on the friendliest of terms; chewing gum and boiled sweets were exchanged, and the paratroopers were shown the chief features of the Churchill tank.[3]

After meeting some opposition, the Scots Guards, leading the Brigade Group, captured Dorsten after a 'lightning dash' through the night. The American paratroopers rode on the tanks, providing protection from the threat of Bazooka Men (enemy troops armed with hand-held anti-tank weapons like the Panzerfaust). Next day, the Coldstream Guards moved to Dorsten. At about 1300hrs a conference was held with the Airborne Corps Commander, General Matthew Ridgway, who explained that it was essential that at least one bridge over the Dortmund-Ems Canal be captured as soon as possible. The 4th Battalion, Coldstream Guards Group was ordered to push on at all speed, passing through the Scots Guards, and advance on Haltern. One of their objectives was to capture intact a bridge over the River Lippe, a tributary of the Rhine, which would enable lateral communication with the U.S. 9th Army, who were on the Battalion's southern flank. However, the advance had barely got under way when it was halted by several batteries of Flak 88 anti-aircraft batteries and enemy infantry. At around 1600hrs, the German gun batteries suddenly increased their rate of fire, which signalled to the Guards that they intended to withdraw. By midnight, the Battalion Group was fighting in Haltern. As ordered, a group of American paratroopers succeeded in capturing intact a bridge over the River Lippe, or so they thought. However, what appeared to be one bridge was two separate structures. Just as the American paratroopers reached the second bridge, the enemy literally blew it up in their faces. While the fighting continued to clear Haltern, a squadron of tanks and accompanying infantry was ordered to bypass the town and press on to Dülmen.

In the early hours of the morning, shortly after leaving Haltern, Lieutenant Stannard, Coldstream Guards, found himself driving just behind what he initially thought was another Churchill tank. However, on closer examination the vehicle was identified as a German Panther tank whose crew were blissfully unaware that they had become the spearhead of the Allied advance. Slowing down slightly, Lieutenant Stannard's tank fired two armour-piercing shells through the back of the Panther, which immediately burst into flames.

On 29 March, the Coldstream Guards reached Dülmen at around 0800hrs. As the town was on a major road intersection, it had received special attention from the RAF's interdiction campaign and had been completely obliterated. The war diarist of the 4th Battalion, Coldstream Guards, remarked that Air Chief Marshall Sir Arthur Harris had indeed done his work so effectively that it delayed the advance of the 4th Coldstream Group for some twelve hours. The delay at Dülmen gave the enemy ample time to prepare good defensive positions around Buldern, which resulted in some bitter hand-to-hand fighting for the American paratroopers. On 30 March, the Scots Guards were ordered to pass through Dülmen, and then bypass the fighting at Buldern, and continue the drive towards Münster. By 2300hrs, the Coldstream Group had reached Appelhülsen, a few miles north-east of Buldern. The speed of the advance was such that some enemy troops were found asleep in their beds, and roused to find themselves prisoners of war. Next day, the Scots Guards Group were ordered to advance to Roxel, where they were to gain a bridgehead over the river Aa and some high ground beyond it. As the Germans withdrew towards Münster, they used a variety of delaying tactics from felling trees and cratering roads to firing on the British and American columns from woods and houses that flanked the roads. Nevertheless, at 1030hrs, on 2 April, No. 3 Squadron, Coldstream Guards, entered the outskirts of Münster.

An additional two battalions of the American 513th Parachute Infantry Regiment were brought forward to clear Münster. Each battalion of infantry was supported by one squadron of tanks. Although Münster was defended by around 3,000 enemy troops, about a third of this force was found to be nothing more than Fire Guards and Air Raid Precautions (ARP) wardens. By 4 April, Münster was cleared. The Coldstream and Scots Guards were settled into billets, working on vehicle maintenance, and preparing for the next operation.[4]

On 3 April, the war diary for the HQ 6th Guards (Armoured) Brigade noted:

> The clearing of Munster is being completed by the infantry. The task of the 6th Guards Armoured Brigade Group is now virtually complete. We have opened up the road to Hanover and Berlin from the Rhine bridgehead and captured the most important rail, road and canal communication centre on the 2nd Army front. Perhaps the most outstanding feature of this operation has been the entirely successful and happy co-operation with our American allies and both we and they have learned mutual respect in the course of the last two week's fighting.[5]

The war diarist of the Coldstream Guards summarised the advance on Münster and the partnership between Guardsmen and paratroopers as follows:

> In less than a week the Bn. Group had advanced over 50 miles meeting very stiff opposition on at least two occasions, finally capturing the capital of Westphalia. The co-operation between the men of the Bn. and those of the 17th Airborne Division was of the highest order and the mutual feeling of respect could not have been greater. The Americans fought with a dash that had to be seen to be appreciated. Whatever the odds against them (on one occasion five paratroopers took on 60 Germans) they took on any task with the greatest of enthusiasm and loved getting to close quarters with those 'filthy Krauts'. The phrase by which they will always be remembered is 'Come on, boys, let's go.'

During the advance the Coldstream Group took around 2,000 prisoners and killed several hundred enemy troops. The 4th Battalion suffered seven killed, twenty-six wounded and seven missing. They had one Churchill tank knocked out and five damaged. The Battalion also lost one Honey M3 Stuart light tank destroyed and another damaged.[6]

Interviewed for the Imperial War Museum's oral history project, Major Charles Farrell, 3rd Battalion, Scots Guards, remarked on how different it was operating with American paratroopers than British infantry. Typically, Guards

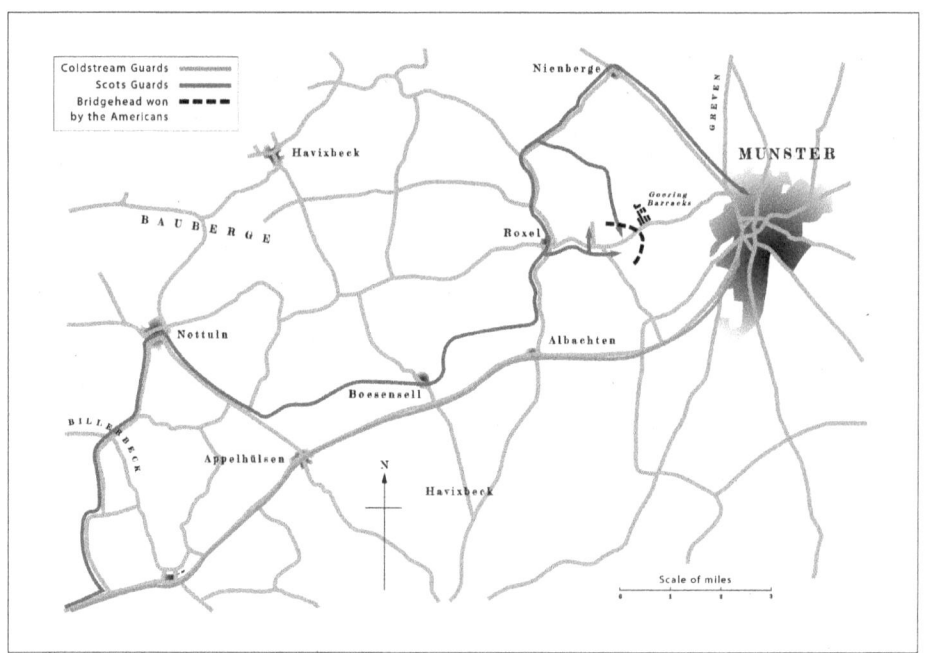

Map 6. Advanced to Munster, 27 March-2 April 1945, 6th Guards (Armoured) Brigade.

tank battalions were always subordinate to whatever British infantry formation they were attached. During the breakout to Münster, the roles were reversed. In Farrell's opinion, as the tank squadrons were equipped with good wireless communications compared with those of the infantry, it made more sense to have the tanks control the battle. As we have seen elsewhere, once battle was joined, it was often difficult to maintain communications between the infantry and the tanks tasked to support them.[7] Patrick Forbes believed that constantly moving the Brigade between Divisions, Corps and Armies did not make for efficient co-operation in battle. He believed that where staffs and units got to know one another intimately, planning for operations was easier, quicker, and surer. This was certainly true for the Brigade's close association with the 15th (Scottish) Division, where the two units were familiar with each other down to the infantry platoon and tank troop. It seems clear that familiarisation between units was a key determinant in the successful outcome of operations. As Forbes observed, the British soldier fights best among his friends.[8]

The Grenadier Guards and British Airborne

When the BBC's one o'clock news announced that the 6th Guards (Armoured) Brigade, carrying American paratroopers on their tanks, had captured Dorsten, the 4th Battalion, Grenadier Guards, found themselves sitting on the sidelines, but not for long. On 28 March, the Battalion received move orders to join the British 6th Airborne Division. The newly formed battlegroup's first objective was the industrial town of Coesfeld. By day's end, the Guardsmen and paratroopers had advanced around 28 miles and secured their objective. Although never designed for fast-moving armoured operations, the Churchill tank appears to have coped remarkably well with its new exploitation role.

Coesfeld, like Dülmen, had been reduced to rubble by the RAF, which delayed the Grenadier Guards Group for about an hour. The next objective was to capture a vital bridge over the River Ems at Graven, about 35 miles distant. After sweeping aside sporadic resistance, the Grenadiers Group reached Graven. When about 500 yards from the bridge, the paratroopers leapt off the tanks and rushed forward to secure their objective. However, in a remarkably similar situation to that which faced the American paratroopers at Haltern, there were two bridges at Graven. The first bridge led to an island in the middle of the Ems. The second bridge, about 300 yards upstream, was blown by the Germans about twenty minutes later.

The River Ems was the first of three water barriers that had to be crossed as the British 2nd Army advanced across northern Germany. Although delayed until the Sappers of the Royal Engineers had constructed a bridge across the Ems, the advance continued to the Dortmund–Ems Canal, which also required bridging. On 3 April, the Grenadiers and paratroopers advanced towards Osnabrück, and the next water obstacle, the River Weser. By 7 April, the Grenadiers Group was over the Weser, although delayed for nearly two days. Three days later, the battlegroup was just 10 miles from Hanover when they were halted while the U.S. 84th Infantry Division captured the city. By the time they had reached Hanover, the Grenadier's Churchill tanks had carried them around 250 miles.[9]

The Final Push

By mid-April, the 6th Guards (Armoured) Brigade had been reunited with its old friends, the 15th (Scottish) Division. Together, they advanced to the River Elbe. Two weeks later, the Brigade was over the Elbe pushing north-east towards Lübeck. On VE Day, 8 May 1945, the Brigade entered Kiel on the Baltic coast. In June, the Brigade lost its tanks and reverted to its traditional infantry role. Alongside the Guards Armoured Division, the 6th Guards (Armoured) Brigade held its last parade as an independent formation on Rothenburg Airfield before being incorporated into the ranks of the Guards Division. Towards the end of April 1945, Lieutenant General W.H. Simpson, commanding the U.S. 9th Army, wrote a letter of commendation to General Dempsey, British 2nd Army, about the 6th Guards (Armoured) Brigade. In the final paragraph of his letter, General Simpson, referring to the advance on Münster, concludes:

> Officers and men of the 17th Airborne Division are unanimous in their commendatory remarks regarding the work of the Brigade during their period of close association. It is noteworthy that this association began during the planning phase of the operation, and culminated in a successful combined operation on the battlefield. I need hardly state that I am most appreciative of the fine spirit of co-operation evident on the part of both units. I feel that it represents one of the finest examples of team work, spontaneous co-operation, and effective co-ordination that has been brought to light during the entire campaign. May I request that you transmit my personal commendation to the Officers and men of this fine organization for their splendid performance.

The Brigade had come a long way since the dark days of June 1943 and 1944 when it had been threatened with disbandment. As the 6th Guards (Tank) Brigade, the unit had proved to be an entirely dependable partner to whichever infantry unit it had been tasked to support. As an armoured brigade, the Guards had shown determination, flexibility and elan as the spearhead of 2nd Army. Patrick Forbes believed that the formation of the 6th Guards (Tank/Armoured) Brigade proved two things. First, that any infantry unit, well officered, disciplined and properly equipped, could make the conversion to armour in about a year. Second, that there was value to having infantry trained officers in a tank unit. Most of the senior officers in the unit had experience of tackling infantry problems. Therefore, they could appreciate the challenges faced by the infantry units they supported and help to solve them. This co-operative spirit of mutual respect and understanding had often proved vital on the battlefield.[10]

The End of the Guards Armoured Experiment

The Guards Armoured Division was conceived during the dark days of late 1940 and early 1941, when the British Army feared the very real threat of a German invasion of the British Isles. Nevertheless, by 1943 it was clear that the army would need more infantrymen than tanks to meet its commitments in the Mediterranean and forthcoming campaign in north-west Europe. As we have seen, without the personal intervention of the prime minister, both the Guards Armoured Division and 6th Guards (Tank) Brigade would have been broken up and the Guardsmen returned to infantry duties by early 1944.

6th Guards (Armoured) Brigade: From the Rhine to Münster

On 14 August 1943, the secretary of state for war, Sir James Grigg, wrote to Sir Alan 'Tommy' Lascelles, private secretary to King George VI, to explain the proposed reorganisation of the Brigade of Guards to ensure it could meet its expected wartime commitments going into 1944:

My dear Tommy,
You are only too painfully aware of all the troubles we are in because of the reduced allotment of manpower to the Army. I send you a note showing in broad outline what we are being forced to do to meet this horrible situation. The Prime Minister has approved this plan so I must now let you know what it looks like involving for the Brigade of Guards. These proposals are being sent to Arthur Smith[11] for his concurrence, but I thought that His Majesty would like to know at once what is going on without my waiting for Arthur Smith's reactions.

You probably know that Alex proposed to break up one of the Guards Brigades in North Africa to be able to fill up and keep filled the other two. We thought, however, that whatever was done, we must (a) keep these three brigades going and up to strength (b) do the same for the Guards Armoured Division and the 6th Guards Tank Brigade. To have a reasonable chance of doing this it will be necessary

(i) to reduce the number of training battalions from five to two and holding battalions from three to one, and

(ii) to break up the Headquarters and one battalion of 33 Guards Brigade and convert the other battalion into a 'duties' battalion in London District, which would be mainly men of the lower medical categories.

I am certain that, although it will no longer be possible to keep separate training battalions for each regiment, it will be found practicable to maintain regimental identity on a company basis.

Oh dear! What a horrible game this is of getting a quart out of a pint pot. However, it doesn't get any pleasanter by delaying facing it.

Yours sincerely,
P.J. GRIGG.[12]

By the end of the war in Europe, the Guards Armoured Division had suffered 5,447 casualties.[13] However, planning had already started to ensure the Brigade of Guards could meet its commitments for the second phase of the war, the one being fought in the Far East. In Germany, Major General Allan Adair, GOC, Guards Armoured Division, suddenly found himself inundated by requests from officers and men wishing to volunteer for service in the Far East either by posting or transfer to Commando and Special Service Units. However, as the question of the Brigade of Guards' commitment in the Far East remained classified, Adair was placed in a difficult position of not being able to answer requests for transfers or postings.

On 19 May 1945, Lieutenant General Sir H. Charles Loyd, Major General Commanding the Brigade of Guards, wrote to Major General J.S. Steele, Director of Staff Duties (DSD), asking that Adair be given permission to reveal the basic plan for the Guards deployment to the Far East, which earmarked battalions from the Grenadier, Coldstream, and Welsh Guards for service. As a result, officers and men from those battalions selected for Far East service would be refused permission to transfer to other units. However, members of the Scots and Irish Guards would be allowed to volunteer for Far East service, on the proviso that those individuals could be spared by their regiments. In closing, Loyd remarked:

> I think you will agree that it is a healthy sign that officers and men want to fight the Japanese and one to be encouraged.[14]

On 21 May, Major General Steele agreed that Allan Adair could make a statement to his commanding officers about the likely plans for various Guards regiments in the war against Japan. However, the war in the Far East also reopened the debate about the practicality of retaining Guards battalions in an armoured role.[15]

On 25 May 1945, a report by the Deputy Chief of the Imperial General Staff (DCIGS) entitled 'The Organisation of the Brigade of Guards in the Second Stage of the War' questioned whether the Guards should retain their tanks.

With the support of the Major General Commanding the Brigade of Guards, the report recommended that the Guards should revert to an entirely infantry role. The report cited three main factors that enabled the authors to reach their conclusion. First, the army possessed sufficient armoured units for future operations in the Far East, so Guards armoured formations were surplus to requirements. Second, the production of 'Armoured' Guardsmen was lengthier and more expensive in overheads than that of normal Royal Armoured Corps (RAC) troopers, as Guardsmen were given comprehensive infantry training before being passed on to armoured training. Third, it had already been decided that the Guards' commitment in the Far East would be on an infantry-only basis.

To expedite matters, the Major General Commanding the Brigade of Guards had already consulted the king, unofficially, to seek his approval to disband the armoured formations. Additionally, the Brigade of Guards' new organisational structure was proposed at twelve infantry battalions, which might be further reduced to ten after the war's end. It is possible some horse trading was done with the War Office, the Guards agreeing to relinquish its armoured role to obtain an agreement on a peacetime establishment of twelve battalions, something the king was eager to secure.[16]

Just as the Brigade of Guards and War Office arrived at a decision to return all armoured battalions to an infantry role, effectively disbanding the Guards Armoured Division and 6th Guards (Armoured) Brigade, Field Marshal Montgomery and 21st Army Group muddied the waters of a smooth transition. It appears that 21st Army Group Headquarters issued a directive that several armoured formations would be broken up, losing their tanks, and the surplus troops assigned to occupation duties. However, it is clear from a letter written by Lieutenant General Loyd, Major General Commanding the Brigade of Guards, to Major General Steele that 21st Army Group's decision to 'unhorse' its armoured formations without consultation was viewed with suspicion.

In a letter dated 28 May 1945, Lieutenant General Loyd complained to Major General Steele that because the Guards Armoured Division and 6th Guards (Armoured) Brigade had arranged a 'Farewell to Armour' parade on 9 June, he was now forced to explain to the king what was happening about post-war policy with the War Office and the 'unhorsing' programme within 21st Army Group. He continued:

> I can quite see Adair's point of view: he realised that in fact the handing in of his tanks is the end of armour for them whatever the 21 Army Group 'unhorsing' programme really is, and he sees quite clearly too that he can have no sort of parade once his tanks have gone.
>
> I think it would have been better, in view of all the business that occurred with the King, when the Guards Division went over to armour in 1941, if I had been officially informed of what was happening in 21 Army Group: at present I know nothing except what I have heard privately.[17]

Clearly, the lieutenant general was annoyed that he had not been consulted prior to 21st Army Group beginning its unhorsing programme. In response, Major General Steele tried to placate Loyd, writing:

> As I explained to Adair when I saw him recently, the orders which 21 Army Group are issuing for the reduction of armoured units to a Foot basis is purely a local and temporary expedient which applies to nearly all armour in 21 Army Group, and which is a necessity to affect the most economical organisation for an occupational role.[18]

In a memorandum dated 9 June 1945, the day the Guards armoured formations were officially disbanded, Major General Steele wrote:

> The formal approval of His Majesty The King to the reversion of the armoured units of the Brigade of Guards to Infantry has now been received.
>
> Reorganisation of such units onto the appropriate War Establishment will take place forthwith, and the necessary adjustments to the training machine will be made.
>
> The Major General Commanding the Brigade of Guards has been notified to this effect in a separate communication.[19]

It seems likely that the prime minister, Winston Churchill, was purposely kept in the dark about the agreement between the War Office and Brigade of Guards to disband its armoured formations so that he could not interfere in the matter. The day after the Farewell to Armour parade had taken place, the prime minister wrote a curt note to the secretary of state for war, Sir James Grigg, which read:

> Please explain why you have destroyed the Guards Armoured Division. Are you doing anything else like this without making any report to me or to the Cabinet?[20]

On 11 June 1945, Grigg responded to Churchill's note about the disbandment of the Division, first, with an apology for not informing him about the plans to return the Guards to an infantry role. However, Grigg then goes on to justify his actions, writing:

> The Guards themselves want this change; the King wants it: and I think a good many people are now of the opinion that it was a mistake ever to have made the Guards into an Armoured Division.[21]

A draft, unsigned note, probably written by the secretary of state for war, Sir James Grigg, and intended for the prime minister, explains that all Guards armoured units would revert to infantry to fulfil their role in the next stage of the war. The second paragraph of the note has a diagonal line running through it, suggesting that it was removed from the final draft, which says Field Marshal Montgomery found it necessary to 'take the division off its tanks' to provide more men for occupation duties in Germany. Montgomery's decision seems to have pre-empted any final decision made at home about the Guards' fate, but there can be little doubt the result would have been the same.

Major General Allan Adair seems to have taken it upon himself to organise the Farewell to Armour parade, which appeared to have wrong-footed officialdom.

Assuming the author of the note was Grigg, he was concerned that any press coverage of the parade would make the disbandment of the Guards Armoured Division and 6th Guards (Armoured) Brigade public knowledge before any official decision had been made or a suitable press statement prepared. Nevertheless, thanks to Major General Adair, the Guards Armoured Division was able to have its parade and recognise the hard work and sacrifice of so many, rather than simply fade into obscurity without remark as some would have preferred.[22]

On 9 June 1945, the Guards Armoured Division was formally disbanded at the Farewell to Armour parade, Rothenburg Airfield, Germany. A group of Royal Engineers assisted by some German prisoners-of-war (POWs) built a saluting stand and roofed enclosure for dignitaries attending the parade. The Division's tanks were stripped of their machine guns and any other extraneous items such as spare track links. Tank crews often welded sections of tank track to the hulls and turrets of their vehicles as a form of improvised armoured protection. The tanks were painted battleship grey courtesy of the German navy, and finally paraded in front of the viewing stand before disappearing over a ridge while the massed bands of the Brigade of Guards played *Auld Lang Syne*. The crews dismounted their tanks, formed up by battalions and marched back over the ridge, as Foot Guards once again.[23]

Field Marshal Montgomery addressed the parade and congratulated the Division on its achievements.[24] However, one can only speculate as to the sincerity of his speech. In May 1945, Lieutenant General Ritchie, 12 Corps, wrote to Major General Allan Adair:

> This is to wish you all good fortune, and to say how much we all in 12 Corps admire the great fighting qualities of your Division. It has been a great honour to have had the GAD in battle. You have always carried through everything asked of you, and I do congratulate you all.[25]

Perhaps the biggest tribute paid to the Division came from its old nemesis, the German 7th Parachute Division, who refused to surrender to any troops other than the Guards Armoured Division.[26] Recalling his own memories of the Farewell to Armour parade, General Sir David Fraser wrote:

> We owed everything to these men, our Guardsmen – to their patience, their sense of humour, their endurance.[27]

And, so, the short life of the Guards Armoured Division and 6th Guards (Armoured) Brigade came to an end.

Conclusions

Currently, there is no universally accepted method to determine the military performance and effectiveness of formations like the Guards Armoured Division and the 6th Guards (Tank) Brigade. According to Millett, Murray, and Watman the basic characteristics of military effectiveness cannot be measured with precision. Instead, any examination must rely on more concrete indicators of effectiveness at the political, strategic, operational, and tactical levels. To determine the overall military effectiveness of the Guards armoured formations I have adopted the Millett, Murray, and Watman method.[1]

Political Effectiveness

As we have seen, the British Army entered a period of experimentation in tank design after the First World War. However, the economic crisis of 1929 severely curtailed British military spending on tank development. The British Army of the inter-war years had to meet its operational objectives on an extremely tight budget. Reduced in size and with limited resources, the army focused on policing the British Empire rather than preparing for another European war. Political unwillingness to rearm from the mid-1930s and the British Army's failure to establish an explicit doctrine of armoured warfare created its own set of problems. When the war started, the British Army's adoption of a dual approach to armoured doctrine required role-based Infantry and Cruiser tanks, which placed an additional burden on an already over-stretched industrial sector. Having to design, test and build several different types of tanks added extra cost and complexity at every step of the supply chain. Consequently, British-designed and built tanks suffered from numerous deficiencies, from poor mechanical reliability to inadequate firepower until 1943, after which the situation improved steadily.[2]

After the Dunkirk evacuation and fall of France in 1940, the hastily compiled Bartholomew report placed too much emphasis on the role of the tank and German panzer division as war-winners. In something of a knee-jerk reaction to both the Bartholomew report and the threat of a German invasion, the British Army rushed to create new armoured formations.[3] However, by 1942

Conclusions 133

the army had started to re-evaluate its operational priorities and a need for more infantry, not armour, to achieve its strategic aims. By 1943, the Guards Armoured Division and the 6th Guards (Tank) Brigade faced the prospect of being broken up to provide infantry replacements for units fighting in Italy. Only the personal intervention of the Prime Minister prevented the Guards armoured formations being disbanded in 1943 and again in 1944.[4]

Once committed to operations in Normandy, the Guards Armoured Division became something of a political embarrassment after hectoring the government about the inferiority of British tanks and equipment when compared with the Germans. Nevertheless, Operational Research reports found that nearly 70 per cent of tank crews escaped unhurt from their vehicle after being hit. The reports also found that half of all casualties sustained by tank crews occurred while they were outside of the protection of their armoured vehicles.[5]

The formation of the Guards Armoured Division had been something of a contentious issue between the Brigade of Guards and the War Office. However, once victory in Europe had been secured in May 1945, the two sides finally found something they could agree upon, and that was the unhorsing of Guards armoured formations and their return to an infantry role. In 1945, the idea of training Guardsmen for tank crews was regarded as needlessly time-consuming, expensive, and unnecessary. After all, the British Army possessed a Royal Armoured Corps dedicated to the purpose of recruiting and training tank crews. By divesting the Guards of their tanks, the War Office got the infantrymen they needed for occupation duties in Europe, and to help prosecute the war against Japan. The Brigade of Guards was able to secure its peacetime establishment at twelve battalions.[6] Overall, the political establishment and military authorities performed ineffectively from the mid-1930s to the end of the war in terms of the development of armoured doctrine, the provision of equipment, training, and manpower management. The decision to form a Guards Armoured Division was taken in haste, and not without justifiable resistance. Once established, the Guards armoured formations were able to repeatedly exert enough political influence to prevent their own disbandment until such time that it suited the Brigade of Guards to return its Guardsmen to an infantry role.

Strategic Effectiveness

In 1940, the British Army's strategic imperatives were to survive, and then to resist a German invasion of the British Isles. As the threat of invasion receded at home, the government determined to resist Axis forces across the Middle East, Mediterranean and Far East. However, between 1941 and 1942 British and Commonwealth forces suffered a succession of military disasters including the fall of Malaya, the loss of Crete and surrender of Singapore. At the start of 1941, Churchill's determination to resist aggression might have appeared as hubris. Nevertheless, by the end of 1941 Britain had gained two strategic partners in the United States of America and the Soviet Union. By the end of 1942, partly due to the materiel resources of the United States, the British Army started to celebrate victories such as the Second Battle of El-Alamein. Certainly, Churchill's government had assumed a huge risk by refusing to capitulate to Nazi Germany after the fall of France. For Britain, the strategic gamble to keep fighting had paid off when America and the Soviet Union entered the war, but the effort to stand alone against German aggression had come at an unsustainable cost in resources and manpower. By 6 June 1944, when the Western Allies landed in Normandy, the British Army was facing a manpower crisis that would affect its ability to conduct operations, and make it increasingly risk averse.

In 1943 and 1944, Montgomery tried and failed to have the Guards armoured formations broken up as a source of replacement manpower. In a petty act of malice, not uncommon to his character, Montgomery removed the 6th Guards (Tank) Brigade from his original order of battle for OVERLORD. Therefore, the Brigade did not land in Normandy until mid-July. However, it was the 15th (Scottish) Division who would suffer for Montgomery's snubbing of the Brigade. During Operation EPSOM, the 15th (Scottish) Division was supported by the 31st Tank Brigade, but the two formations had not worked together before, and so infantry and armoured co-operation was poor.[7] In fact, wireless communications between the tanks and infantry had broken down before the two formations had crossed the start line. During the fighting, the tanks and infantry frequently lost touch with one another, and on occasion the supporting tanks mistakenly fired on their own troops. As a result of Operation EPSOM, the 15th (Scottish) Division suffered grievous casualties. In contrast, when the 15th (Scottish) Division was reunited with the 6th Guards (Tank) Brigade during Operation BLUECOAT, the two were able to achieve great success. Although on occasions, the Guards tanks advanced without infantry support to exploit opportunities on the battlefield, the two formations never lost contact with one another. Inadvertently, the decision to place the 6th Guards in Army reserve for OVERLORD provided the Brigade with an opportunity to learn some valuable lessons from the early fighting in Normandy.[8]

It is possible that the OVERLORD plan placed too much emphasis on the initial seaborne landings and not enough on subsequent operations once the Allied forces were ashore in Normandy. Original D-Day objectives such as the capture of Caen failed to materialise, and German resistance to the invasion quickly achieved a stalemate during June 1944. Montgomery, as commander of land forces during the Normandy campaign, determined to fight an attritional campaign to denude the German defenders of the means to resist. Montgomery sought to place the Allies' strength in airpower, tanks, artillery firepower and logistics against the enemy's inability to replace its losses. However, Montgomery's preference for set-piece battles often sacrificed operational flexibility, mobility, and tempo.

In Normandy, as Allied casualties mounted, but without corresponding progress on the ground, Montgomery's strategy of war by attrition was increasingly questioned by General Dwight D. Eisenhower, SHAEF, politicians, and the press. Under pressure to increase the tempo of operations, and achieve a decisive breakthrough around Caen, Montgomery sanctioned Miles Dempsey's GOODWOOD plan. The intention of Operation GOODWOOD was to launch three armoured divisions from the Orne bridgehead to capture the rest of Caen and the Bourguébus Ridge. GOODWOOD was the Guards Armoured Division's first major battle. The operation revealed failures in the Guards training and confirmed flaws in British armoured doctrine that had already been exposed during Operation EPSOM. According to doctrine, the Division should have been used for exploitation and pursuit following a breakthrough of the enemy's line rather than being employed to make the break-in itself. Furthermore, the experience of the GOODWOOD battle had a negative psychological effect on the Division's armoured battalions, who discovered just how vulnerable their vehicles were to German anti-tank gunfire. The failure of GOODWOOD to achieve a decisive breakthrough of the German defences around Caen also widened the chasm that already existed in relations between Eisenhower and Montgomery. Eisenhower felt that Montgomery had misled him over GOODWOOD's objectives and likely results.[9]

In September 1944, Montgomery once again proposed an ambitious plan that would deviate from his standard operating procedures. The intention of Operation MARKET GARDEN was for Allied forces to push north into Holland, outflank the German Siegfried Line, turn right and drive into the important industrial region of the Ruhr, and so hasten the end of the war. Instead, MARKET GARDEN proved to be a costly strategic gamble that failed to deliver. Following the failure of MARKET GARDEN, Eisenhower rejected the narrow front strategy preferred by generals Montgomery, Bradley, and Patton, who sought to concentrate combat power and increase the tempo of operations. Instead, Eisenhower chose to pursue a more cautious, methodical broad front strategy. MARKET GARDEN had deviated from British armoured doctrine and Montgomery's own preference for carefully planned, lavishly supported, set-piece battles. Consequently, the Guards Armoured Division found its combat power and operational flexibility dissipated by the constraints of terrain, weather, logistics and administration. It can be argued that the strategic decisions that gave rise to Operations GOODWOOD and MARKET GARDEN placed the Guards Armoured Division in operational situations for which they were neither properly prepared nor well suited to perform. Similarly, the questionable strategic decision to remove the 6th Guards (Tank) Brigade from the original order of battle for Operation OVERLORD proved detrimental to the 15th (Scottish) Division during Operation EPSOM. However, the same decision also offered the 6th Guards (Tank) Brigade an opportunity to benefit from lessons learned about fighting in Normandy, which they were able to apply during Operation BLUECOAT.

Operational Effectiveness

The Guards Armoured Division was formed in the spring of 1941 under the command of Major General Oliver Leese. The Division spent the first six months of its existence learning how to operate and maintain its tanks. However, Leese would only remain in post for a year before being replaced by Major General Allan Adair, a Grenadier Guardsman without any operational experience of armoured warfare. In the Guards, tradition and regimental parochialism trumped common sense and dictated that only a Guards officer could command a Guards formation rather than selecting the best candidate for the job.

Harrison Place[10] and Murray[11] cite the paucity of coherent armoured doctrine and numerous decentralised training programmes across the British Army as significant obstacles to curriculum development. Harrison Place was also highly critical of Major General Adair's reluctance to impose a uniform training programme on his subordinates after taking command of the Division. His criticism of Adair seems justified as a Guards Armoured training directive issued in August 1941 states:

> There is no desire at Divisional H.Q. to interfere with Brigade and Unit Commanders' responsibilities in the training and preparations of their commands for war.[12]

Doherty contends that by 1943 the army had assimilated many lessons learned from North Africa. Consequently, the Division's order of battle went through several changes to improve its balance of forces. Simultaneously, the War Office published new training pamphlets that emphasised close infantry and armoured co-operation in battle. Nevertheless, the Guards Armoured remained wedded to outdated, cavalry-styled, massed armoured charges without infantry support. Moreover, several primary source testimonies indicate that infantry and armour seldom trained together before the Division was deployed to Normandy.[13]

As part of the force restructure of the Guards Armoured Division towards the end of 1942, the 6th Guards (Armoured) Brigade was replaced by the 32nd Guards (Infantry) Brigade. The 6th Guards (Armoured) Brigade joined the 15th (Scottish) Division, which was a mixed division at that time. The 6th Guards was redesignated a Tank Brigade, equipped with Churchill tanks, and cast in an infantry support role. The war diaries of the 2nd Battalion Glasgow Highlanders and the 6th Battalion King's Own Scottish Borderers (KOSB) show that the 6th Guards (Tank) Brigade and 15th (Scottish) Division undertook an intensive schedule of joint training with close co-operation between infantry and tanks as its focal point. During large-scale exercises, the Brigade also demonstrated a newfound capacity for tactical flexibility, switching from its prescribed infantry support role to one of armoured exploitation when opportunities presented themselves. Before the Brigade deployed to Normandy, Charles Farrell, Scots Guards, was attached to 30 Corps as an observer of the early fighting. Following his secondment, Farrell prepared a series of lectures for the Brigade on lessons learned in Normandy. Farrell warned his comrades that they must forget everything they had previously learned about tank warfare from the North Africa campaign and training manoeuvres on Salisbury Plain. Instead, Farrell believed the Brigade should focus on working closely with its infantry partners and on gaining a tactical advantage over the enemy by exploiting the Churchill tank's excellent cross-country performance. During the fighting south of Caumont, the 6th Guards (Tank) Brigade showed that it could apply its accumulated knowledge imaginatively to achieve its battlefield objectives.[14]

As we have seen, after an inauspicious start to operations in Normandy, the Guards Armoured Division improved infantry and armoured co-operation and tactics rapidly, as evidenced by the 'Fighting in the Bocage' directive. Before the liberation of Brussels, the Division reorganised into Regimental Battlegroups, marrying infantry and armour of the same regiments, which appeared to improve operational performance and morale. The war diary of the 2nd (Armoured) Battalion, Irish Guards, described the formation of its battlegroup as 'a very happy partnership that continued with great success'.[15]

During Operation MARKET GARDEN, the Guards' persona of panache appears to have been misinterpreted by many involved. For example, Colonel Rueben Tucker, U.S. 82nd Airborne Division, was incensed by the Guards' nonchalance. He told General Gavin, 'We have been in this position for over twelve hours, and all they seem to be doing is brewing tea.'[16] Regrettably, when urgency was required to reach the beleaguered paratroopers at Arnhem, the Guards were often perceived as arrogant, inflexible, and lethargic. However, the MARKET GARDEN plan and its administrative execution robbed the Division of its operational flexibility and tempo. The Division was forced to advance on a single tank front, unable to deploy off-road due to the marshy nature of the Dutch polder, which proved a gift to the German defenders who were able to concentrate their combat power on the Guards centre line. The failure of airborne forces to capture and secure all the bridges intact from Valkenswaard to Arnhem, most notably the Nijmegen bridge, which the Guards had to take themselves, also proved a boon to the German defenders as it gave them time to recover their composure after the initial shock of the landings. As well as being the centre line of the advance, the single highway to Arnhem was also the main line of communication for the operation, which made it an essential thoroughfare. If the planner's intention was that the Guards should reach Arnhem with all speed, then why was part of the Division's combat power dissipated by guarding the Grave bridge? Later, instead of fighting north toward Arnhem the Grenadier and Coldstream Guards Groups were ordered south to reopen the highway that had been cut behind them. It seems that during MARKET GARDEN rather than place the Guards' strength against German weakness, the opposite occurred. Certainly, the operational concept for MARKET GARDEN fell short of its strategic objectives.

Following Operation VERITABLE, the Division entered a period of innovation. The Division experimented with tanks in an artillery support role, started to conduct bold night operations, and fitted 60lb rocket projectiles to tanks of the Coldstream Guards. The successful action fought at the Ems bridge on 3 April 1945 was a practical demonstration of all the Guards had learned. Overall, during its ten months in combat, the Division demonstrated a capacity to assimilate lessons learned and adapt its battlefield operating procedures. In addition, the formation of Regimental Battlegroups helped to facilitate internal communications, raise morale, and improve operational effectiveness.

Between 6 June and 10 July, Brigadier James Hargest, New Zealand Army, observed operations in the Normandy bridgehead. In his subsequent report, Brigadier Hargest was scathing about the British Army's use of armour. He wrote that British tanks were badly led and fought. He believed that only a numerical superiority in tanks and over-reliance on artillery kept British armoured formations in the field. He criticised British tank crews for bunching up, timidity, an unwillingness to operate after dark, and an inability to exploit opportunities when they presented themselves on the battlefield. Hargest believed that a large proportion of the blame for the failures of British armoured forces was due to 'the retention of the absurd regimental system'. He was particularly scornful of British cavalry regiments, who had been forced to trade their horses for tanks. In such regiments, Hargest believed tradition and a 'we've always done things this way' attitude was a barrier to change and innovation.[17] Similarly, military historian Max Hastings has written that a reasonable level of understanding between British infantry and tank commanders was often absent in Normandy. Like Hargest, Hastings blamed the parochialism of the British Army's regimental system for the inability of infantry and armour to co-operate on the battlefield.[18]

In the Guards Armoured Division, the size of the formation and its force structure probably proved more of a barrier to speedy battlefield adaptation than anything to do with regimental elitism. As an independent tank brigade, the 6th Guards did not appear to have been hampered by regimental petty-mindedness in any way. On the contrary, the 6th Guards successfully partnered with numerous brigades and divisions during operations in north-west Europe. Of course, the Brigade had a very different role from the Guards Armoured Division. In fact, until the last weeks of the war, the Brigade's tank squadrons operated separately from their parent battalions, and in support of infantry battalions. In battle, the infantry battalion commander and tank squadron commander formed a partnership to co-ordinate operations. For all practical purposes, each of the 6th Guards tank squadrons was an independent command. Having been redesignated as an armoured brigade in February 1945, the 6th Guards showed remarkable operational flexibility in adapting to its new role during the advance on Münster. For the first time, the Brigade's battalions operated as integrated battlegroups with command resting on the tank formation instead of the infantry. The new system worked well.[19] According to the war diary of the 4th Battalion, Coldstream Guards, the Battalion Group advanced over 50 miles in less than a week, sweeping aside enemy opposition, captured the capital of Westphalia, and formed a tight bond of mutual respect and co-operation with the paratroopers of the U.S. 17th Airborne Division.[20]

Tactical Effectiveness

Although the British Army mechanised during the inter-war period, its development of armoured forces and doctrine left much to be desired. In the early years of the war, British industry struggled to produce tanks of the quality or quantity the army required. However, British tank production improved steadily from 1943. After the hasty conversion of Guards infantry battalions to armour, the newly formed Guards Armoured Division made slow progress in its development. Initially, a lack of vehicles, equipment and suitable training areas retarded the Division's operational and tactical development. However, the British Army's preference to devolve training responsibilities down to individual regiments and battalions seems to have been the most retrograde action. As a result of decentralised training, the tactical proficiency of battalions varied considerably. Typically, Guards battalions trained largely in isolation, only occasionally working together with sister battalions and support services. Consequently, the Division was neither skilled in infantry and armour co-operation nor all-arms collaboration when it deployed to Normandy. In contrast, once redesignated as an independent tank brigade and moved out of the Division, the 6th Guards quickly adapted to its new role of infantry support. Working in partnership with the 15th (Scottish) Division, the 6th Guards developed a very effective training template for infantry and tank co-operation that delivered consistent results.

By 1944, British and American manufactured tanks like the Cromwell and M4 Sherman were a match for most German tanks and assault guns. The German Tiger and Panther tanks were generally considered superior to Allied tanks in terms of armoured protection and firepower. However, Tiger and Panther tanks were produced in relatively low numbers compared with Allied tank production. The Tiger and Panther also suffered from several shortcomings such as poor mechanical reliability, heavy fuel consumption, and lack of range and mobility. In Normandy, the Allies enjoyed more than a three-to-one advantage in tanks.[21] Nevertheless, the Guards Armoured Division complained vociferously about the inferiority of British tanks and equipment to such an extent that General Montgomery forbade any criticism of operations and equipment. Analysis by Operational Research found that although some criticism of the M4 Sherman's combustibility was justified, overall, the tank provided sufficient armoured protection for its crew. Nevertheless, the perception that the Sherman was inferior to most German tanks and a 'death trap' persisted.

The Guards Armoured Division was accused of being slow and methodical in operations, and concerns about the perceived quality of their tanks probably resulted in unnecessary tactical caution.[22] The 6th Guards (Tank) Brigade had similar misgivings about some features of the Churchill tank when compared with the Tiger and Panther, especially its lack of firepower. However, the Churchill tank also possessed some advantages such as outstanding cross-country performance, an ability to climb steep gradients, and thick frontal armour. The Churchill also appeared to be less likely to catch fire immediately after being hit, giving the crew vital seconds to bail out of a stricken vehicle. In his report on the early fighting in Normandy, Brigadier Hargest remarked that none of the wrecked Churchill tanks he had examined showed any signs of fire damage. In contrast, he noted that most Sherman and German tanks burned after being hit. Although not fast, the Churchill was regarded as reliable, versatile, and an effective tank. Perhaps most importantly, the Guardsmen had confidence in the Churchill. Once committed to battle, the crews learned quickly how to gain maximum tactical advantage from their tanks.[23]

Overall, British troops seem to have lacked the tactical skill of their German counterparts. The British in north-west Europe fought to Montgomery's functional doctrine, using bludgeoning material superiority and firepower to conserve manpower. However, on occasions, such as Operation GOODWOOD, Montgomery's strategy proved a false economy. His reliance on set-piece attacks with limited objectives appears to have frequently stifled the initiative of junior leaders, and meant that opportunities for exploitation were often missed. A report by the Director of Military Training, 15th Army Group, Italy, 1943, stated:

> Our tactical methods are thorough and methodical, but slow and cumbersome. In consequence our troops fight well in defence and our set-piece attacks are usually successful, but it is not unfair to say that through lack of enterprise in exploitation, we seldom reap the full benefit of them.[24]

A year later, a German Army intelligence report, dated November 1944, assessed British tactical ability thus:

> The British soldier is a little slow-witted. The NCO is for the most part very good. Junior officers are full of theoretical knowledge, but in practice are generally clumsy ... not really trained to be independent.[25]

As we have seen, on several occasions the Guards Armoured Division found itself placed in situations where operational concepts and strategic objectives were misaligned, most notably during GOODWOOD and MARKET GARDEN. Immediately after GOODWOOD, the Guards abandoned the tactical principles they had learned in training, which required armour and infantry to operate separately. Instead, the Division hastily reorganised into battlegroups that sought to combine infantry, armour, artillery, and engineers for mutual support. However, Guards battlegroups created their own self-imposed rigidity, dictating that the same infantry and armoured battalions operated together regardless of operational or tactical requirements.

Overall, the Guards Armoured benefited tactically from the close grouping of infantry and armour, but the Guards system or ethos generally promoted orthodoxy over innovation. Once committed to battle, the Guards Armoured Division was in the line for ten months, which gave it few opportunities to make in-depth analysis of what it had learned on the ground. Nevertheless, the Division was able to translate some of what it had learned into new or refined operational and tactical methods. Although bound by Montgomery's strategic doctrine, the Guards did occasionally demonstrate flashes of tactical innovation, such as operating at night, and an ability to capitalise on lessons learned.

On leaving the Guards Armoured Division, the 6th Guards (Tank) Brigade followed a very different trajectory. As we have seen, once cast in an infantry support role, the Brigade was able to develop an effective training template for infantry and tank co-operation. Considering the number of different formations the Brigade fought under during the campaign for north-west Europe, it is perhaps surprising that it was able to achieve such consistently good results in terms of force integration. Unlike the somewhat monolithic Guards Armoured Division, where its size and force structure sometimes worked against it, the 6th Guards operated quite differently. Typically, a tank squadron would operate independently of its own battalion headquarters in support of an infantry battalion. Patrick Forbes theorised that the 6th Guards had a distinct advantage over other independent tank brigades that enabled them to work so effectively with many different infantry units. As infantrymen who had converted to armour, the 6th Guards tended to be more sympathetic and appreciative of the challenges faced by the infantry they were tasked to support. Having enough time for the infantry and armour to get to know one another and prepare a mutually supportive plan also seems to have been a determinant in the positive outcome of most operations. In February 1945, the 6th Guards was once again designated an armoured brigade. Montgomery chose the Brigade to spearhead the 2nd Army's advance into north-east Germany following the Rhine crossing. Unlike the Guards Armoured Division during Operation MARKET GARDEN, the Brigade was able to rendezvous swiftly with the airborne forces. Within a week, the Coldstream and Scots Guards and paratroopers of the U.S. 17th Airborne Division had advanced around 50 miles and taken Münster. Similarly, the Grenadier Guards and the British 6th Airborne Division had reached Minden. It was the first time during the campaign that the 6th Guards had formed integrated battlegroups with command resting on the tank brigade, not the infantry. The new system worked well. A few weeks later, and the war in Europe was over. The Brigade had come full circle, from narrowly avoiding disbandment and being removed from the order of battle for Operation OVERLORD to making news headlines with daring night-time advances and the capture of Münster.

Final Assessment

The primary focus of this book was to examine whether the expedient of transforming Guards battalions into an armoured division was successful, or should they have been retained in their infantry role? As the war progressed, the British Army found it had an abundance of armoured formations and a chronic shortage of trained infantrymen. This lack of infantrymen inevitably raises a series of secondary questions. For example, would the Guards Armoured Division and 6th Guards (Tank) Brigade have contributed more to the war effort if they had remained riflemen?

Of course, one can only speculate about what the Guards battalions might have achieved in the Mediterranean or elsewhere had they not been formed into armoured formations. As we have seen, there was resistance to the formation of a Guards Armoured Division. Some believed that Guardsmen were physically, intellectually, and psychologically unsuitable to meet the challenges of armoured warfare. According to Forbes, many responsible persons predicated that Guardsmen would never be successful in tanks.[26] Additionally, the Guards ethos and the 'dash required of armour would not combine in battle'.[27]

It certainly appears that the army and War Office misjudged the relative importance of German panzer divisions in the battle for France, and the primacy of the tank on the battlefield in 1940. Along with the Guards Armoured, the 9th, 11th, 42nd and 79th Armoured Divisions were raised between 1940 and 1942.[28] However, the British Army started to reduce its armoured formations by the following year due to lessons learned about unit composition and manpower shortages. As a result, the 8th and 42nd Armoured Divisions were disbanded in 1943. The 9th and 10th Armoured Divisions were broken up in the summer of 1944.[29]

My research shows that the formation of the Guards Armoured did not have a significant impact on available infantry resources during 1941. Furthermore, the creation of the Division did not prevent it from performing its primary task of protecting London and the south coast against a potential German invasion during 1941 and into 1942. Furthermore, contrary to what some believed at the time, this study has found that Guardsmen were perfectly capable of retraining in technical roles such as fitters.[30] Finally, the Brigade of Guards expanded considerably between 1939 and 1945. By September 1944, the Foot Guards numbered twenty-one fighting battalions, with 28,750 Guardsmen retained in an infantry role. This expansion of fighting battalions surely offset the 2,664 officers and rankers converted initially to armour. However, when the British Army and the Guards were critically short of infantrymen, almost half of the Foot Guards' available strength was in training and holding battalions at home.[31]

The Guards Armoured Division: A Short History explains how the formation of the Division caused reinforcement problems in 1943 after the three Guards Brigades fighting in Italy sustained heavy losses.[32] Similarly, the regimental history of the Scots Guards describes how in June and July 1944, 1,500 men from the RAF Regiment were transferred to the Brigade of Guards for retraining as Guardsmen due to a lack of available casualty replacements. However, the question of why thousands of Guardsmen remained in training and holding battalions instead of being deployed overseas remains unanswered.[33]

It was probably unnecessary to have raised an armoured division from the Brigade of Guards in 1941. However, having decided to do so, the number of Guardsmen converted to an armoured role was relatively insignificant and quickly offset by the subsequent expansion of Guards rifle battalions. Moreover, Guardsmen proved themselves technically capable of an armoured role. Nevertheless, the Guards manpower crisis of 1943 was probably the right moment to disband the two formations and return them to an infantry role. In fact, without the personal intervention of the Prime Minister, both the Guards Armoured Division and the 6th Guards (Tank) Brigade would have been disbanded to provide the required casualty replacements. Once the decision was made to retain the Guards armoured units, it is only possible to assess what they did during the campaign for north-west Europe, not what they might have done in Italy.

The performance of the Guards Armoured Division and the 6th Guards (Tank) Brigade cannot be quantified in absolute terms. Once deployed to Normandy, the Division's first major engagement during Operation GOODWOOD revealed the inadequacy of its training to prepare it for battle. In response to lessons learned, the Division reorganised and adapted operationally and tactically to meet the realities of fighting in Normandy. Nevertheless, Montgomery's strategic doctrine of attritional warfare, which utilised set-piece battles supported by overwhelming airpower, artillery, and tanks, frequently robbed British armoured divisions of their ability to conduct high-tempo, mobile operations. There was a tension between Montgomery's grand strategy and the operational ability of formations like the Guards Armoured to achieve results. When used in its pursuit and exploitation role, the Division performed well operationally and tactically, as exemplified by the long advances of late August and early September 1944 that culminated in the liberation of Brussels. In contrast, unorthodox operations like MARKET GARDEN, for example, denuded the Division of its tactical flexibility, forcing it to fight along a single highway with few opportunities to deploy off-road. Once over the Rhine, the Guards pursued a disintegrating but stubborn enemy with operational flexibility and tactical novelty until the cessation of hostilities.

In summary, the Division was tactically and operationally effective when performing its pursuit and exploitation role. However, it can be argued that as an all-arms formation the Guards Armoured Division should have been more flexible and adaptable to the changing strategic and operational demands of 21st Army Group. Montgomery refuted the dual-approach to armoured doctrine that required Infantry and Cruiser tanks to perform specific roles. Instead, he believed that the tank on the spot should have been capable of tackling whatever challenge was in front of it. Although assigned to an infantry support role for most of its time in action, the 6th Guards (Tank) Brigade showed that the delineation between units equipped with slow-moving, heavily armoured Infantry tanks and fast-moving Cruiser tanks was a false one. From Operation BLUECOAT to the Elbe, the Brigade demonstrated operational and tactical flexibility, working with numerous different formations. During its first battle, the Brigade was able to secure vital high ground south of Caumont by utilising the Churchill tanks' impressive cross-country performance. In the same action, the Brigade also showed itself willing to ignore doctrine to exploit a tactical opportunity by advancing without infantry support. Similarly, once over the Rhine, the 6th Guards adapted successfully to a new armoured exploitation role as the spearhead of 2nd Army. Of course, unit size, force structure, training, and operational requirements meant that the Guards Armoured Division and 6th Guards (Tank) Brigade fought very different wars. Nevertheless, the two formations shared a common origin and ethos, but when the Guards Armoured Division was faced with unorthodox operational and tactical situations its leadership, administration, and sheer size meant that it was slow to adapt, and struggled to meet its objectives.

Postscript

On 9 June 1945, the Guards Armoured Division and the 6th Guards (Tank) Brigade officially ceased to exist. Nevertheless, that was not quite the end of the story. The Guards Armoured Division would be cast in the central role of two post-war feature films. A bitter dispute between Major General G.L. Verney and the Brigade of Guards would prevent the publication of the official history of the Division for a decade. Finally, the Division's reputation would be tarnished by the Hollywood movie adaptation of the book *A Bridge Too Far*.

They Were Not Divided

In 1946, the Brigade of Guards hoped that an official history of the Division could be written quickly. However, it would take ten years and much controversy before *The Story of the Guards Armoured Division* by Rosse and Hill would eventually be published. Instead of a book, the story of the Guards Armoured Division would first be told on the cinema screen.

During the war, all three of the armed services had co-operated with the British film industry to produce films for propaganda, recruitment, and morale purposes. In 1946, the services agreed upon a new definition of what constituted useful film publicity, which differed from the narrow pre-war emphasis mainly on propaganda. Instead, the services wanted to harness the power of cinema to promote themselves to the widest possible audience.

The British film industry had a good war. Cinema attendances rose between 1939 and 1946 from 990 million annual cinema admissions to a staggering 1.8 billion during the period. The production qualities of British films also improved considerably until they could rival Hollywood in some respects.

During the late 1940s and early 1950s a series of popular war stories were published, which quickly transferred to the cinema screen. It is unclear what prompted this bout of wartime nostalgia. Nevertheless, the armed services were keen to take advantage of the public appetite for 'war films' and were willing to assist commercial filmmakers in telling these stories. Immediately after the war, for example, the British Army helped Ealing Studios produce

The Captive Heart, a romantic film set in a German PoW camp. Similarly, the British Army provided considerable assistance in the making of the war film *They Were Not Divided*.

Released in 1950, *They Were Not Divided* was written and directed by Terence Young and produced by the Two Cities film company. The picture was advertised as telling the story of the Guards Armoured Division. In short, the film chronicles the lives of three raw recruits who join the Welsh Guards. It follows the Division from its long period of training with the Home Army to its eventual embarkation to the battlefields of Normandy, Belgium, and Holland. The film reaches its rather sombre climax with the German Ardennes offensive, commonly referred to as the Battle of the Bulge.[1]

Although *They Were Not Divided* received mediocre reviews from film critics, it did well at the UK box office, grossing £167,000, which would be around £6.4 million today.[2] Writing for *The Sketch*, the critic C.A. LeJeune believed the filmmakers had dealt capably with the military aspects of the picture, but 'the bits of sentiment and domestic chit-chat' were handled amateurishly.[3] To coincide with the film's release in 1950, *They Were Not Divided* was also serialised by writer Peter Burdett for several regional newspapers such as the *Leven Mail*[4] and *Coatbridge Leader*.[5]

The film is most noteworthy for its sense of authenticity. *The Brechin Advertiser* claimed:

> 'They Were Not Divided' is not an ordinary film. It is a gripping war story of the Guards Armoured Division sweeping across Europe in the fight for liberation. It is above all a realistic film made almost entirely on location in England and Western Germany. It has no stars – the male cast was entirely composed of ex-service men and serving soldiers. It includes some of the most exciting tank battle scenes ever filmed.[6]

The army's Directorate of Public Relations arranged for filming to take place at the Guards Depot, Caterham, with serving Guardsmen assuming minor roles.[7] Terence Young had served with the Irish Guards in the Guards Armoured Division. Similarly, most of the cast were ex-servicemen. Young's screenplay clearly drew on his own experiences at Caterham and with the Irish Guards, giving the film an authentic feel. Young's script also acknowledges Gerald Kersh's popular novel *They Die With Their Boots Clean* based on the author's experiences of joining the Guards. Released in 1946, Young had co-written the screenplay of *Theirs is the Glory*, a film about the battle of Arnhem, which featured hundreds of veterans of Operation MARKET GARDEN. He went on to make a trio of James Bond spy movies: *Dr. No*, *From Russia with Love*, and *Thunderball*.

One of the more memorable performances in *They Were Not Divided* was delivered by Regimental Sergeant Major Ronald 'Tubby' Brittain, Coldstream Guards, who played himself. In a career that spanned thirty-eight years in the army, Brittain reportedly drilled some 40,000 cadets. As the most senior NCO in the army, he presided over many state occasions. Brittain would continue to play the bawling sergeant major on film and television and became known as the loudest voice in the British Army.

Although promoted as the story of the Guards Armoured Division, *They Were Not Divided* does contain some historical inaccuracies. The 2nd Battalion, Welsh Guards, for example, served with the Guards Armoured Division. However, Young created the fictional 4th Battalion as the unit at the centre of his film. Another of the production's anomalies was that the 2nd Battalion, Welsh Guards, went to war in British Cromwell tanks, but the film's 4th Battalion is equipped with Sherman tanks. Nevertheless, overall, the film does achieve a high standard of historical authenticity. Some of the film's exterior sequences were shot on location in France, Belgium, and Germany. The picture also contains many original armoured vehicles from scout cars to tanks. Where original vehicles were not available, the filmmakers used archive footage neatly spliced into the film to create a sense of realism, such as the scenes that feature Covenanter and A13 Cruiser tanks during training exercises in England.

The British Army of the Rhine (BAOR) provided nine Sherman tanks for the film, some reportedly rescued from scrapyards and restored to working order. A couple of non-running Sherman hulks were used to represent tanks that had been hit and 'brewed up'. Additionally, most of the tanks were crewed by Guardsmen. The film also features several German tanks. Some of the sequences that feature German armour were taken from Young's earlier production of *Theirs is the Glory*. However, at least one genuine Tiger tank was used, albeit briefly, during the filming. Cinema audiences would have to wait until 2014 and David Ayer's war movie *Fury* to see another genuine Tiger tank appear on screen.[8]

They Were Not Divided proved such a success that the film was re-released at British cinemas in 1961.[9] Since then, it has been released on DVD and is shown regularly on British daytime television.[10]

The Book Dispute

Eight months after the war in Europe concluded, the Guards Division found itself part of the BAOR, helping to administer the British zone of Allied occupation. Captain Michael Parsons, 6th Earl of Rosse, had served with the Irish Guards, Guards Armoured Division, during the war. On 5 January 1946, someone only identified as Adrian wrote to Michael, Lord Rosse, from

Postscript 149

Headquarters, Guards Division, BAOR, about preparing a history of the Guards Armoured Division. Adrian explained that the history must be written quickly, 'something readable and snappy' that would appeal to everyone rather than a book filled with details and the length of *Gone with the Wind*. Adrian requested that Lord Rosse come to Germany to help co-ordinate the collection of battalion and brigade histories and to compile the book.[11]

On 3 June 1946, GOC Guards Division, Major General John C.O. Marriott wrote to Lord Rosse confessing that he was in a quandary to get someone to complete the history of the Guards Armoured Division. He explained how a Captain D.A. Pryce-Jones had collected much of the required information about the Division's formation in England in 1941 until its departure for Normandy in 1944 and all the necessary material concerning the fighting in north-west Europe. However, Captain Pryce-Jones was under contract to a film company and not in a position to complete the project. In his letter, Major General Marriott asked Lord Rosse if he would take on the task of completing the book as quickly as possible.[12]

Rosse and Verney

Sometime after the summer of 1946, Lord Rosse started to collaborate with Major General G.L. Verney on writing a history of the Guards Armoured Division. Major General Verney was commissioned in the Grenadier Guards in 1919. He transferred to the Irish Guards in 1939. He commanded the 2nd (Armoured) Battalion, Irish Guards, while training in the United Kingdom. He later commanded 32nd Guards Brigade, Guards Armoured Division.[13] In August 1944, Major General Verney was appointed GOC 7th Armoured Division. However, like his predecessor, he was sacked in November 1944 having failed to stiffen the resolve of the war-weary formation.[14] According to Peter Verney, General Verney's son, by late November, his father was worn out and medically rested after the 7th Armoured Division liberated Ghent.[15]

Initially, the Rosse and Verney collaboration proceeded favourably enough that a notice appeared in the autumn edition of *The Guards Magazine* confidently promoting the book's publication the following spring:

> The History of the Guards Armoured Division, written by the Earl of Rosse in conjunction with Major General G. Verney, containing over 300 pages, maps and photographs, will be published in the spring of 1952 by William Collins & Sons Ltd. The price will be about 20s. if bought through Regimental Headquarters or Headquarters Brigade of Guards.[16]

Of course, in the autumn of 1951 no one could have foreseen the many troubles ahead and ultimate tragedy that would blight the publication of *The Story of the Guards Armoured Division*.

In April 1952, Major General J.A. Gascoigne sent Lord Rosse a copy of a letter originally written to General Verney plus a request to send amended maps and a middle-length version of the book's epilogue to Collins publishers. General Gascoigne explained to General Verney that he had unwillingly been put into the position of arbiter on certain points about the book on the Guards divisional history, although he had had little to do with the Division himself.

General Gascoigne instructed Mark Bonham Carter, abbreviated in the correspondence as MBC, to try to rectify all the confusion and technical difficulties delaying the book's publication. Bonham Carter, later Lord Bonham-Carter, served with the Grenadier Guards during the war, and worked for William Collins publishers, where he later became a director.[17]

General Gascoigne instructed that a new dedication and foreword, both written by Major General Allan Adair, go into the book. He also wanted mistakes on certain maps corrected and a nine-page epilogue, written by Lord Rosse, to go into the book. General Gascoigne concluded that if everything was sent to Collins on time, MBC believed the book would be published by the latter half of June. However, MBC's confidence that the book's publication was imminent was to be misplaced.[18]

More than five years had elapsed since the idea of writing a history of the Guards Armoured Division had first been suggested. It seems part of the reason for the long delay in publication was because the Brigade of Guards had run foul of the Net Book Agreement (NBA). The NBA was a piece of legislation that fixed the price of books sold in the United Kingdom and Ireland except for educational titles. The NBA was finally revoked in the 1990s.[19]

On 24 April 1952, General Verney wrote to Lord Rosse about a letter he had received from Major General Julian Gascoigne asking him to clarify if he had withdrawn his objections to the original text of the dedication for the book. Unfortunately, we do not currently know what was in that earlier draft of the dedication that General Verney found so objectionable, but a copy may well exist among the Rosse Papers. However, a new dedication was prepared, written by Major General Adair. Verney also complained that it was confusing for the publisher, Collins, to know who they were dealing with when representatives of the Brigade of Guards interfered in the book's editing and approval process. He closed his letter, telling Lord Rosse that he hoped all outstanding matters had been cleared up and the book's proofs were back at the printers. Finally, he enquired when MBC would announce a firm publication date.[20]

In 1952, General Verney and Lord Rosse believed the publication of their book was imminent. Nonetheless, another two and a half years would elapse without any meaningful progress. On 9 December 1954, Lord Rosse wrote optimistically to General Verney about a meeting he had attended with the publisher William Clowes and Son that might offer a solution to all their problems. Sammy Clowes confirmed that military histories were not subject to the NBA. According to Lord Rosse, Clowes was not surprised that Collins had been uncertain about whether a divisional history was exempt from the NBA, as they did not usually publish military histories.

Sammy Clowes apparently told Lord Rosse that after a slump in the popularity of military histories, the market had recovered, and it would be an opportune time to publish. Clowes went on to say that he would write to Hunters Solicitors to confirm the legal point regarding the NBA. Clowes also expressed his company's own interest in publishing the book.[21]

It seems Lord Rosse's optimism about resolving the outstanding issues concerning the book were to be short-lived. On 18 December 1954, Lord Rosse wrote to General Verney that he was disappointed by Verney's rejection of Clowes as an alternative publisher to Collins. Verney's objections seem to have centred around the apparent interference of Major General Sir George Frederick Johnson with the book project, and his desire to close the business with Collins. Johnson was Major General commanding the Household Brigade and General Officer Commanding London District. General Verney's later point must have been frustrating for Lord Rosse as Collins had agreed to let Clowes publish the book and was happy to do so. Rosse expressed his frustrations thus: 'I am surprised and seriously disturbed at some of what you write.'

It appears that Lord Rosse had believed the two men were working together amicably to overcome the various difficulties that had delayed publication of the book. Rosse continued, quoting part of Verney's letter back to him:

> Certainly I have been acting all along on the assumption that we were in partnership, but you now suddenly tell me 'I am not prepared to go into partnership with you again because of the claim of the Major General to interfere in the contents or the production, or both, of our book. If he is prepared to give us, in writing before Christmas, fully satisfactory answers to the questions I sent you last week, then I will consider drawing up a new agreement with you.'

General Verney appeared concerned about Major General Johnson's editorial control over the final contents of the book. He was also unhappy with the business relationship with the publisher, Collins. Finally, he disputed that the book project was initiated by Major General John Marriott, who was GOC of the Guards Division in Germany in 1945, and later Major General commanding the Brigade of Guards and GOC London District.

In response to Verney's accusations, Lord Rosse wrote that he believed the book was always to some extent subject to the approval of the Brigade. Additionally, Lord Rosse confirmed that Major General Marriott did indeed commission the book and asked him to take it on. Lord Rosse was most emphatic on this point of the book's origin. He dismissed Verney's assertion that the book was not Marriott's idea as ridiculous. In closing, Lord Rosse asked Verney to reconsider his position and allow them to deal with Clowes in the hope of a speedy publication.[22]

Between the end of December 1954 and January 1955, it appears General Verney and Lord Rosse continued to correspond about the division history. However, it is clear from a brief note written by Verney to Lord Rosse that the relationship between the two men had soured markedly. Verney was evidently troubled by what he regarded as the censorship of his work by the Brigade of Guards. He demanded to know the identity of the person to be appointed censor by the Brigade and what powers they would hold. General Verney was emphatic that he would not renew his writing partnership with Lord Rosse until matters were clarified to his personal satisfaction.[23]

On 9 February 1955, General Verney wrote to Lord Rosse setting out in detail all his allegations against the Brigade of Guards for what he regarded as undue interference in the editing of their book, the misappropriation of Brigade funds, and copyright infringement. Additionally, he repeatedly admonished Lord Rosse for dishonesty, a lack of moral courage when dealing with the Brigade and tardiness over fact checking. General Verney's letter is reproduced below in its entirety:

Dear Michael,
A variety of circumstances have prevented me from answering your letter of Dec 18th and 31st and Jan 12th. I also had to go to London and while there I took the opportunity of initiating further steps to prevent the misappropriation of Brigade Funds. I expect you will be hearing about these later on.

1. After you received my letter of Dec 13th you wrote and protested against my 'sudden decision' and said you were 'Amazed'.
   Why don't you bother to read my letters?
   On Nov 16th I wrote and told you that under the circumstances then prevailing there could be no other conclusion than that our

partnership must cease and that it could not be renewed until outside interference ceased.

In your reply you made no comment, but I thought it as well in my next letter, of Nov 25th, to draw your attention to the fact that you had apparently accepted the position. Again, you made no comment, nor did you do so when the matter was mentioned in our short conversation of Dec 7th.

I have no doubt you have gone round saying that I made a 'sudden decision', and you had no business to do so. I suppose it is too much to expect you to put right this misinformation that you have circulated.

There are, of course, numerous other reasons why I do not wish to renew our partnership. Here are some more.

2. You have been making the astounding statement that our book was initiated by Marriott.

    If this were true, I would not be concerned in the matter.

    In fact you failed in your task and were faced with the alternative of abandoning the book or, obtaining a collaborator.

    Our book was initiated by me here at the end of 1950, and some months later you accepted my terms for collaboration. Had this not been so, there would have been no History.

3. There was, however, a consideration attached to our partnership.

    This you broke by going behind my back and taking a copy of the Proofs to London District <u>after</u> you had passed and approved the contents of the book.

4. Both you and Gascoigne refused to answer my questions as to why the book 'had to be approved' by him and why nothing was said either before we went into partnership or when the script was submitted for official approval or for Gascoigne's private perusal.

5. You did not have the decency or honesty or moral courage to stand up to Gascoigne and tell him of the agreement by which you were bound.

    That you were afraid to do so is no surprise, but you might at least have had the sense to leave the matter to me instead of saying things that were not true and behaving in such a contemptible manner.

6. In writing that you 'have more than once recorded' your view that the book has always been to some extent subject to the 'approval of the Brigade' you are again behaving most dishonestly, for you well know that you said nothing until after I had finished the book and after you had passed the Proofs.

7. I am aware that you have denied passing the Proofs, but unfortunately for you I still have your copy here together with your covering letter.

8. It is also untrue to say that we agreed to differ over the matter of the Major General's interference.

    You well know that I refused throughout to accept any interference, for it is both morally and legally unjustified.

9. There were no reasons why Johnson should not withdraw his falsehoods concerning his acceptance of Collins' claim. As I have already said, this book was not initiated by Marriott.

    I am glad to see that you agree that Collins were neither introduced to nor accepted by the Brigade.

10. It is quite untrue to say that we have worked amicably together.

    Times without number I have complained at untrue statements made by you, and you have always refused to take any notice. Have a look in your file – if you have the courage to do so.

11. To say that you have done your utmost to help is a blatant lie.

    You have ignored our agreements, you have ignored the undertakings given us by Johnson and Collins, and you have 'carted' the Brigade and me in a way that must be unique.

12. I was wisely advised to hold up the letter to Colonels, Lieut. Colonels etc. until I found out the reason Collins gave for making a claim on the Brigade.

    This, at last, I have been able to do, and, as you are probably aware, they are completely untrue and can be contradicted from letters in my files.

    This of course, immensely strengthens the case against Johnson, who, in any case, behaved most dishonourably in not telling us about Collins' claim and in making a bargain that he tried to keep secret.

    Have you ever protested? Of course not, you didn't dare.

13. Although you know that Collins have gone back on every single undertaking they have given us, without exception, you are still fool enough to accept what they say about letting us take the Proofs to some other publisher etc.

14. You know quite well that Collins' admission that the sole rights were vested in us precluded them from making any claim on the Brigade, and makes all their dealings with Johnson illegal.

    Have you ever had the guts to protest?

15. The same applies to Johnson's recognition of our copyright, for you will recollect that he tried to obtain it from us. All his dealings with Collins are illegal, but you have never dared to protest,

16. It is not accurate to say that Johnson has given us an undertaking of non-interference. You know quite well that a few months ago he

instructed his solicitors to write and say that they could not advise him to give any undertaking.

That was a real twister's letter.

17. You will know that Collins have neither moral nor legal claim on the Brigade, and that Johnson's actions have been immoral and illegal, but you appear quite content to have the Brigade robbed – and you an ex-officer of the Brigade; your former brother-officers may well be ashamed of you. Fancy doing nothing to prevent the 'obtaining money by false pretences'.

18. There are numerous reasons why you were not free to approach another publisher. I have had to write to Clowes and tell them so.
    a) Johnson has now disputed our copyright
    b) He has refused to give an undertaking not to interfere
    c) Certain inaccuracies in the book remain to be corrected
    d) More credit has to be given to the Household Cavalry
    e) As it stands now the book has not had the approval of the highest military authority; it cannot be published until alteration is made. It is as well that I checked it.
    f) You have written that the book has to have the approval of the Major General, but you have refused to tell me why or in what respects. You have forgotten that I hold guarantees in writing from you in this matter, particularly one that says the book is to be shown to no one, either in type or in print.

19. It seems to have escaped your notice that in my various drafts for the information of the Colonels etc. I omitted any mention of your behaviour. I am advised that the letter ought to include mention of this.

20. You cannot expect me, or anyone else, to desire to go into partnership with an individual to whom agreements even in writing mean nothing, who has no regard for the truth, who refuses to answer letters and who lacks the decency and ordinary moral courage to stand up against lying, deceit and dishonesty.

    If you consider this judgement unfair or unjustified in any way, do please write and say so. I would always be willing to withdraw what I have said.

21. There is now only one matter outstanding between you and me. Thanks solely to your breach of contract with me and to your not having the strength of character to stick to it, I have been put to much expense to defend my copyright. I therefore look to you to meet these expenses.

I hope this matter may not lead to further difficulty and publicity – of the latter, there is an increasing amount already.

Signed:

G. Verney

P.S. Pray be good enough to obtain from London District the Proof Copy that was so improperly given to them by you, and kindly let Hunters know when you have done so. I object to property which is partly mine being in the wrong hands.

FINALLY

You have forgotten the most important point of all. Johnson himself killed the book when he instructed his solicitors to write on Oct 20th last that 'all arrangements made with reference to the book, ... 'including those for the Regiments to be given a 'number of copies, fall through'.

What a vicious and vindictive thing to do.

I am now preparing a report of this for the information of senior officers, pending the issue of a full statement after further consultation with higher authority.

It is only right that they should know that it has been made impossible for us to produce cheap copies for the benefit of former members of the Division, for whom the Major General has no thought or consideration.

I take it that you are agreeable to having your name associated with this interim report.

GV[24]

Rosse and Hill

Toward the end of February 1955, following an exchange of solicitors' letters, the Brigade officially abandoned the Verney and Rosse book collaboration. Having severed the relationship with General Verney, the Brigade sent Lord Rosse and Colonel E.R. Hill a commissioning letter asking that they jointly undertake to write a history of the Guards Armoured Division. The letter emphasised that it was of the upmost importance that none of General Verney's work be included in the new book. The letter went on to say that the co-authors would be given every assistance by Brigade Headquarters, and the book was to be published on a not-for-profit basis. The regiments of the Brigade would be asked how many copies of the new book they were prepared to take. Finally, the letter made it clear that the book was being commissioned by Headquarters and copyright would remain the property of the Brigade. The manuscript would have to be submitted to Brigade Headquarters for final approval before being committed to a publisher.[25]

On 9 June 1955, General Verney wrote to General Johnson accusing him of cancelling the book deal with Collins behind his back and then lying about the reasons. He alleged General Johnson misused Brigade funds contrary to the Copyright Act. General Verney claimed that on 10 July 1953, General Johnson had given him a verbal and written undertaking of non-interference with the book project, but never stuck to the agreement. He accused General Johnson of being duplicitous, stating that he, Johnson, had no rights in the book while all the time acting as if he had been the sole owner of the project. General Verney blamed Johnson for intriguing with the publisher, preventing changes being made to the manuscript, attempting to dictate the terms of the contract, and then killing the book by cancelling the arrangement for the sale of copies through Regimental Headquarters despite a written promise to do so.

Referring to his own book, *The Guards Armoured Division: A Short History*, written independently of the Brigade and without Lord Rosse, General Verney asked General Johnson to let him know if there were any special facts he did not wish disclosed, and to say why he wanted them withheld. Rather mysteriously, General Verney wrote that if he did not hear from Johnson on this matter, he would assume the Brigade had nothing to hide, and he would provide information to anyone concerned or interested.

General Verney wrote that he was happy to forgo any royalties that he made from publishing his own book on the Guards Armoured Division and suggested the monies could be used to offset the costs incurred by the improper use of Brigade funds. Apparently, this was an offer he had made more than once without reply or thanks from General Johnson. Finally, he closed with a stinging rebuke and observation:

> I resent your continued rudeness. I suggest the time has now come for you to behave in a less ill-mannered and dictatorial fashion.[26]

During the summer of 1955, General Verney's book, *The Guards Armoured Division: A Short History*, went to press. Simultaneously, the Brigade of Guards commissioned Lord Rosse and Colonel Hill to write the 'official' history of the Division. In an act of sophistry, General Verney continued to extend his offer to transfer the royalties from the sale of his book to help recoup the alleged loss of Brigade funds from the failed book project, of which his own actions were a prime cause.[27] In July, Lord Rosse corresponded with the publisher, Collins, who had decided to withdraw from the fracas altogether. Lord Rosse had to concede that as General Verney had published his book first, and with the possibility of more litigation on the horizon, he could understand why the publisher was reluctant to continue its relationship with the Brigade even after Major General Johnson had made an offer of compensation.[28]

On 3 January 1956, Major V.F. Erskine Crum, Headquarters, Scots Guards, wrote a confidential note to Lord Rosse and Colonel Hill informing them that Mr. Murray, solicitor, would send them a Memorandum of Agreement in about a fortnight. It appears that the Brigade was in search of a means to circumvent the Net Book Agreement. This would enable them to sell copies of the Rosse and Hill book through Headquarters, Household Brigade, at trade price. The details are set out below:

CONFIDENTIAL

Note – The Story of the Guards Armoured Division

1. At a meeting held on 14th November, 1955, by the Major General with Colonel Hill and Mr. Gibb, it had been decided that, in order to avoid possible infringement of the Net Book Agreement with regard to those copies of the Story of the Guards Armoured Division which are to be sold through Headquarters Household Brigade, the latter should become Publishers and Guarantors, with Geoffrey Bles Ltd acting as Producers and Distributors.
2. Accordingly a draft Memorandum of Agreement was produced setting out this arrangement. When, however, this was sent to Mr. Murray, he pointed out that as Headquarters, not being a legal entity, could neither enter into such an Agreement nor act as Publishers. Nor would it be practicable for the Major General in his official capacity to do so.
3. Accordingly a further meeting was held by the Chief of Staff on 2nd January, 1956, with Mr. Murray and Mr. Gibb. At this it was made clear that the previous proposition was unworkable, and the conclusion was reached that there was no alternative to Geoffrey Bles Ltd acting as Publishers, and entering into a normal Memorandum of Agreement with the authors, Lord Rosse and Colonel Hill. As, however, the authors had been 'commissioned' by Headquarters Household Brigade to write the book, it was further agreed that their position both financially in reference to the guarantee, and legally in reference to any possible violation of copyright, should be safeguarded by Headquarters Household Brigade by means of an exchange of letters.
4. Mr. Gibb undertook to prepare a new Memorandum of Agreement, and Mr. Murray undertook to draft the necessary letters setting out the

'Gentlemen's Agreement' between Headquarters Household Brigade and the authors.
5. Various alternative courses were considered with a view to circumventing the terms of the Net Book Agreement in order to allow Headquarters Household Brigade to obtain limitless copies at trade price for direct sale to ex-members of the Division. It was finally agreed that Sefton Praed Ltd should be approached to act as agent for this purpose, on the basis of their allowing Headquarters Household Brigade the difference between trade price and sale price, less 5% of sale price, for each copy sold in this manner. Mr. Gibb undertook to approach Mr. Loyd with this suggestion, and the Chief of Staff said that he would also take an opportunity of speaking to Mr. Loyd.[29]

In August and September 1956, General Verney launched an attack on the publication of *The Story of the Guards Armoured Division* by Rosse and Hill. On 14 August, General Verney wrote to the Brigade Major, Household Brigade, to protest that he believed some passages that appeared in the Rosse and Hill book infringed his copyright. He went on to demand that the book's publication be postponed until the matter was dealt with.[30] The next day, Colonel Hill refuted General Verney's accusations of copyright infringement. Colonel Hill insisted the manuscript he and Lord Rosse had worked on predated the one General Verney had later worked on.[31] Nevertheless, on 21 August, Major Erskine Crum wrote to Lord Rosse from Headquarters, Household Brigade with the following news:

> I am afraid that this is a bitter pill. It was only after the strongest legal advice, and the deepest consideration, that Brigadier Billy decided on the course adopted.

Attached to Major Erskine Crum's letter was the wording for an acknowledgement slip that would be inserted into every copy of *The Story of the Guards Armoured Division*, which stated:

ACKNOWLEDGEMENT

In writing this book use was made, in error, of certain material which also appeared in *The Guards Armoured Division: A Short History* (Hutchinson, 1955) by Major General G.L. Verney, DSO, MVO. The authors and publishers make full acknowledgement to Major General Verney and to Messrs Hutchinson and wish to express regret for the inadvertent inclusion of this material which appears on pp. 199 and 200.

Major Erskine Crum's letter also contained a copy of a situation report on the book dispute:

CONFIDENTIAL

GUARDS ARMOURED DIVISION HISTORY

Situation – 21st August 1956
1. At the same time as he wrote his letter of 14th August to the Brigade Major, General Verney instructed his solicitors, Rubinstein, Nash and Co, in connection with alleged violations of his copyright.
2. Mr. Rubinstein also acts for Geoffrey Bles on frequent occasions, and therefore contacted Mr. Gibb. He gave his opinion as a friend, and not as a rival's solicitor, that definite breaches of copyright had undoubtedly taken place, and drew attention in particular to the almost identical extracts from both books which appear at Appendix 'A'.
3. Mr. Rubinstein has informed General Verney that he will make available his good offices to endeavour to secure an amicable settlement, but that, if General Verney wishes to resort to legal action, he would no longer be willing to represent him.
4. The origins of the extracts at Appendix 'A' are obscure. (At Appendix 'B' is an extract from the original draft by Lord Rosse, corresponding to these paragraphs.) They may have been written by Lord Rosse, by General Verney, by an officer from the Battalion concerned, or jointly by any of these. Lord Rosse may be able to ascertain this. The legal position in copyright, however, as set out by Mr. Rubinstein and confirmed by Mr. Murray and Mr. Gibb, is that the fact that they were first published by General Verney indubitably, and whatever their origin, vests a copyright in them in General Verney; and that it is a definite and serious breach of copyright for them to have been repeated, in almost identical words, in the book by Lord Rosse and and (sic) Colonel Hill.
5. This situation having come to light, a meeting was held by the Chief of Staff on 21st August, at which Mr. Gibb, Mr. Murray and the Brigade Major were present.
6. It was decided to proceed with the publication of 'The Story of the Guards Armoured Division', unless legally restrained by injunction.
7. The question of whether or not to offer any apology or acknowledgment to General Verney was considered. A possible course was to take no such action, but to go ahead and 'publish and be damned'. The

advantage of this was that, if the whole matter was to come up before a court of law, General Verney could hardly fail to come out of it in a most unfavourable light, and because of this the damages awarded might be insignificant.

8. On the other hand, the following were considered to be overriding arguments: -
   (a) According to all available legal advice, a definite breach of copyright had been made, and the hope of proving the contrary was almost non-existent.
   (b) Although it was impossible to estimate damages, it was not inconceivable that these would amount to £200/300 apart from costs.
   (c) The judge would almost certainly order the indemnity to be produced which would inevitably bring the Major General, both personally and by office, into the case.
   (d) It was much to be feared that the Press in the resulting publicity, would take the side of the individual against the representative of authority, despite the previous history of the case. Indeed the outside danger existed that the office of the Major General might be held up to ridicule.
   (e) Headquarters Household Brigade had hitherto invariably acted legally and correctly in this business. Now it appeared that a mistake had been made. The correct course was to acknowledge that mistake.
9. In view of these considerations and the strong advice of both Mr. Murray and Mr. Gibb, the Chief of Staff therefore reluctantly agreed to associate Headquarters Household Brigade in an offer to General Verney of the inclusion of an acknowledgment in such copies of the History as have not yet been distributed.
10. It was agreed that Mr. Gibb should write to Mr. Rubinstein the letter attached as Appendix 'C', with the draft proposed acknowledgment at Appendix 'D'.
11. In order to allow time to insert the necessary acknowledgment slips before publication date, it was also reluctantly agreed that this letter and the enclosure would have to be despatched at once, without the opportunity for further consultation with those concerned.
12. It was also agreed that the Brigade Major should send General Verney a brief acknowledgment of his letter of 14th August.
13. Mr. Rubinstein will strongly recommend General Verney to accept these terms. In any case the offer of them has put the authors, the

publisher and Headquarters Household Brigade on a sounder legal footing. They may be sufficient to soothe the Verney vanity. If he does not accept them, Mr. Rubinstein will represent him no more. But the possibility of another change of lawyers, and an injunction to stop publication still exists.[32]

Toward the end of August 1956, and after some additional legal wrangling, General Verney decided to drop his threat of an injunction and a copyright action against the Brigade on the understanding that he would be acknowledged as the author of certain passages that appeared in the Rosse and Hill book. Lord Rosse and Colonel Hill agreed to the terms of the acknowledgment.[33] Geoffrey Bles placed an advertisement in the summer edition of *The Guards Magazine*, publicising the forthcoming release of *The Story of the Guards Armoured Division*, which emphasised that this was the 'official' history and claimed the book would be indispensable to both the amateur and professional student of the recent war.[34] On 3 September, as advertised, *The Story of the Guards Armoured Division* was published. Two weeks later, Mr Gibb of Geoffrey Bles Ltd., publishers, wrote to Lord Rosse on the successful launch of the book:

> The book really has had a very good press indeed – and I think it will have more in due course. We were completely sold out by the day of publication but more copies will be along here in a few weeks and I see and am told by the travellers that there are still copies about in the shops so that I think we can tide over the gap sufficiently and indeed a slight gap never does any harm as it stimulates want.[35]

On 22 September, *The Irish Times* published a scathing review of the Rosse and Hill book by General Verney.

In the first three paragraphs of his review, General Verney disparages the combat record of the Guards Armoured Division as distinctly mediocre. He then turns his attention to the authors of *The Story of the Guards Armoured Division*:

> This extremely long book is most inaccurate, and it would appear that the authors have made no use of the several admirable regimental and other histories available – there is certainly no acknowledgement of any of them. The maps are inadequate and, worst of all, many of the names of persons, some of them very senior officers, and of places mentioned in the text are not included in the index. There are mis-statements about the distance the division covered in the advance to Brussels, and absurd exaggerations concerning the speed of tanks; there are several contradictions, various

technical terms are not explained, and much of the story is confused and hard to follow.

Misleadingly, the book is described as 'official', and one can only regret that the authorities responsible have not taken more care to produce a history worthy of the splendid fighting qualities of the regimental officers and men, and of the high traditions of the Brigade of Guards.[36]

Even after the publication of the Rosse and Hill book, General Verney persisted with his accusations about the authors. On 20 November 1956, Erskine Crum, promoted to lieutenant colonel, wrote to Lord Rosse warning that 'various other documents are doubtless circulating above his signature or at his instigation, containing various degrees of stigmatism, down to the obviously libellous'. However, Erskine Crum was convinced that any action taken on behalf of the Brigade of Guards and the book's authors would simply give General Verney an opportunity for further self-expression. The lieutenant colonel confessed that the Brigade fund could not afford any more solicitors' fees and suggested that everyone concerned now adopted a policy of remaining aloof in any action toward General Verney.[37]

The book dispute was effectively over by Christmas 1956. We do know that General Verney was able to wring certain concessions out of the Brigade of Guards over his claims of copyright infringement, although Colonel Hill was adamant that these were baseless. General Verney also repeatedly accused certain senior Guards officers such as Major General Johnson of the misappropriation of Brigade funds. The validity of General Verney's accusations of financial wrongdoing remains somewhat opaque. However, we do know that the Brigade did indeed seek to circumvent the Net Book Agreement. We also know that General Verney's letters became increasingly vitriolic in tone and substance, perhaps understandably, as the Brigade of Guards closed ranks against him. Nevertheless, it is the obvious enmity that appeared to exist between General Verney and the Brigade's major generals that is incongruous. After all, Generals Verney, Gascoigne and Johnson had all been battalion commanders at the formation of the Guards Armoured Division. Later, Generals Verney, Johnson and Marriott had each commanded 32nd Guards Brigade.[38] Clearly, these men knew each other well, regardless of how cordial their individual relationships, which begs the question why select General Verney to co-author the history of the Division if his abilities, talents, or temperament were ever in doubt? If, on the contrary, General Verney was seen as a safe pair of hands to help complete the division history then what went wrong? Tragically, the potential source of the protracted book dispute was revealed when General Verney died in the spring of 1957.

Published in *The Guards Magazine*, Major General J.C. Haydon, formerly Irish Guards, explained the circumstances of General Verney's death in his obituary:

> GERRY VERNEY died of a brain tumour on 3rd April, 1957, a few months before his fifty-seventh birthday. His illness was mercifully short, but the root cause of it had been building up within him for some years and, without doubt, increasingly coloured and affected his whole approach to life and people as it neared its climax.[39]

One can only speculate as to the extent General Verney's illness changed his true nature, behaviour, and powers of reasoning. As we have seen, there was more than a grain of truth to many of his accusations. Although Major General Haydon's obituary recounts General Verney's successful career as a military historian and author, it regrettably, but notably, fails to mention his book *The Guards Armoured Division: A Short History*. It seems, even in death, and with the truth of General Verney's illness laid bare, the Brigade of Guards could not bring itself to forgive him.

A Bridge Too Far

Released in 1977, *A Bridge Too Far* is an epic war movie in every sense of the word. Based on the book by Cornelius Ryan, *A Bridge Too Far* tells the story of Operation MARKET GARDEN, the Allies' ill-fated attempt to shorten the war by using airborne troops to pave the way for an advance into Germany's industrial heartland, the Ruhr. Like its subject matter, the film was to generate much controversy and is regarded by many as a dramatic and commercial failure.[40]

A Bridge Too Far had an estimated production budget of $17 million but would eventually cost over $26 million to make. To ensure the film recouped its costs, the producer Joseph E. Levine promoted it extensively in the press. However, the ostentatious marketing and publicity campaign attracted criticism as being inappropriate for the subject matter. Among the film's many critics was Viscount Montgomery, the son of Field Marshal Montgomery, who complained that his father was absent from the screenplay altogether. Similarly, the famous novelist Daphne Du Maurier, the widow of General 'Boy' Browning, commander of the 1st Airborne Corps, was upset by the portrayal of her husband as a cold, arrogant careerist who was determined to launch the operation regardless of the evident risks.[41]

In 1974, Du Maurier was sent a copy of *A Bridge Too Far* and found the description of her husband and assessment of General Browning's role in MARKET GARDEN as balanced and fair. In the spring of 1976, Du Maurier asked Richard Attenborough for a copy of the film's screenplay, which he sent to her. However, she was horrified by what she read, as it was clear that General Browning was to be cast in a very unflattering light. Additionally, William Goldman, the screenwriter, had edited out many of the senior commanders originally involved in MARKET GARDEN such as Montgomery, Dempsey, Brereton, and Adair. Du Maurier wrote to Attenborough about her concerns, which he seems to have ignored.[42]

About a month before the film's premiere, Du Maurier learned from a journalist that the filmmakers had cast Browning as a villain. In response, Du Maurier requested that Earl Louis Mountbatten of Burma boycott the film's London opening, which he refused to do as the premiere was a charity event. After seeing the film, Mountbatten informed Du Maurier that he saw nothing detrimental in Dirk Bogarde's portrayal of Browning. General Sir John (Shan) Hackett wrote to *The Times* newspaper complaining that the film's portrayal of General Browning was both untruthful and unkind. However, once the film went on general release Browning's reputation was irrevocably tarnished.[43]

Cornelius Ryan's book and the subsequent film take their title from a comment attributed to General Browning, who reportedly told Montgomery during a planning meeting seven days prior to the start of MARKET GARDEN that he feared the operation might be going a bridge too far.[44] However, the filmmakers radically changed the context of the famous line by placing it in the penultimate scene of the movie. In the film, immediately after the Arnhem debacle, Major General 'Roy' Urquhart, played by actor Sean Connery, arrives at General Browning's Headquarters to determine what went wrong with the operation. General Browning, portrayed as an unsympathetic automaton by Bogarde, tells the incredulous Urquhart that Montgomery believed the operation to have been 90 per cent successful. When Urquhart presses General Browning for his own opinion of the failed operation, he replies with cold indifference, 'Well, as you know, I always felt we tried to go a bridge too far.'[45]

As well as upsetting many MARKET GARDEN veterans, the film also managed to attract the criticism of the Household Division for its portrayal of the capture of the Nijmegen road bridge. In the film, Robert Redford's Major Julian Cook and his paratroopers heroically capture the bridge. However, it was the Grenadier Guards who seized the bridge, not the Americans. Viscount Montgomery suggested the film was another example of how American filmmakers liked to peddle the myth that America won the war without the assistance of her allies.[46]

The historical errors evident in Levine's film caused so much consternation among former and serving Guardsmen that the editor of *The Guards Magazine* felt compelled to highlight the matter in the 1978 spring edition:

Many letters have been received from all ranks within the Household Division, expressing strong feelings about alleged inaccuracies in the film now showing, called 'A Bridge Too Far', about the Arnhem operation in 1944.

The criticisms centre on three points. First, an inaccurate and derogatory portrayal of Lieutenant General Sir Frederick Browning, Grenadier Guards, as Commander 1st Airborne Corps. Second, a false impression given that the Nijmegen road bridge was captured by American paratroops, rather than by the Grenadier Guards. Third, the impression given that the Guards Armoured Division could, and should, have broken through to Arnhem, immediately after capturing the bridge.

It is not our intention to stir up controversy, but, in view of the widespread feeling that history is not being accurately portrayed, it is essential that the record is put straight.[47]

In response to the concerns of *The Guards Magazine*'s readership about the authenticity of *A Bridge Too Far*, Lieutenant Colonel Sir Julian Paget, Coldstream Guards, wrote an eight-page article. In his article, Paget re-examined the MARKET GARDEN plan, the capture of the Nijmegen road bridge and the decision to temporarily halt the advance thereafter. Paget is emphatic that General Browning told Montgomery during a meeting seven days prior to the start of the operation that he thought the plan might be going a bridge too far. However, the filmmakers chose to pervert the truth for dramatic affect. As we have seen, the filmmakers also decided to cast General Browning as the villain. Paget rejected the filmmakers' view of Browning.

Major General Allan Adair, GOC Guards Armoured Division, and General Browning were old friends who had served together in France during the First World War. In Paget's article, Adair described Browning as a first-rate commander, with a striking presence and strong personality. General Adair also recalled how he had expected the Nijmegen bridge to already be in airborne hands by the time the Guards reached it. Instead, Nijmegen and its bridges remained firmly in German hands. Consequently, the Guards had to fight to secure the town and the road bridge, which further delayed the operational timetable.

In regard to the taking of the Nijmegen road bridge, Paget is clear about the sequence of events. The bridge was captured by the Grenadier Guards Group of the Guards Armoured Division. After crossing the River Waal, men of the American 82nd Airborne advanced along the riverbank to the north end of the railway bridge and captured it. They remained about 1,000 yards short of the road bridge, which the enemy controlled until dislodged by the Guards.[48]

In the film, immediately after the capture of the Nijmegen road bridge, an unco-operative Guards officer refuses the pleas of Robert Redford's Major Julian Cook to drive on and attempt to relieve the besieged men at Arnhem. In Paget's article, he describes the situation differently:

> The Irish Guards tanks and infantry followed the Grenadiers over the bridge in the evening and a precarious defensive position was established for the night. It was felt by many on the spot at that moment, both British and American, that a special task force could and should have been ordered to push forward immediately through the night in a desperate, all-out attempt to reach First Airborne Division, now only eleven miles away, and in desperate trouble. No such move was ordered, and both the Commander of XXX Corps, General Horrocks, and other senior commanders have written since that the problems involved were just too great.[49]

Some film critics condemned *A Bridge Too Far* as a piece of theatrical entertainment. They thought the film was overly long at three hours' running time and lacked a satisfactory plot resolution. The film does not end with a climactic battle where the heroes prevail. In fact, quite the opposite. Perhaps the filmmakers misjudged the appetites of the cinema-going public in Britain and America at the time. In 1977, audiences wanted to lose themselves in 'feel good' science-fiction films such as *Star Wars* and *Close Encounters of the Third Kind*.[50] After a decade of war in Vietnam, it seems curious that Hollywood producer Joseph E. Levine believed the American public was ready for a war film about defeat and failure. Daphne Du Maurier refused to see the film that had sullied her husband's reputation and eclipsed his many years of distinguished service to the British establishment.[51]

Of course, *A Bridge Too Far* was never meant to be a historical documentary. The film was created as a piece of commercial entertainment, and that is how it must be judged. It cost around $27 million to make and grossed $50,750,000 at the box office.[52] However, it is unclear how much Levine spent on advertising, marketing, and public relations. Roger Ebert, the Pulitzer Prize-winning film critic of the *Chicago Sun-Times*, described the film as the longest B-grade war movie ever made.[53] In 1979, *The Economist* labelled *A Bridge Too Far* as one of cinema's most costly mistakes.[54]

Notes

Introduction
1. Richard Doherty, *British Armoured Divisions and Their Commanders, 1939–1945* (Barnsley: Pen & Sword, 2013), pp.140–141.
2. Major General G.L. Verney, *The Guards Armoured Division: A Short History* (London: Hutchinson & Co. (Publishers) Ltd, 1955), p.16.
3. Peter Alexander Rupert Carrington, *Reflect on Things Past: The Memoirs of Lord Carrington* (London: Collins, 1988), p.39.
4. London, The British Newspaper Archive (TBNA), A.B. Austin, 'The Guards Snap Into Tanks', *Daily Herald*, 6 March 1942, p.2.
5. Verney, *The Guards Armoured Division*.
6. Captain the Earl of Rosse and Colonel E.R. Hill, *The Story of the Guards Armoured Division 1941–1945* (London: Geoffrey Bles Ltd, 1956).
7. John Sandars and Michael Chappell, *British Guards Armoured Division 1941–45* (Oxford: Osprey Publishing, 1979).
8. Patrick Forbes, *6th Guards Tank Brigade: The Story of Guardsmen in Churchhill Tanks*, (London: Sampson, Low, Marston & Co., 1946).
9. Lionel Frederic Ellis, *Welsh Guards at War* (Aldershot: Gale and Polden, 1946; repr. 2002).
10. Patrick Forbes, *The Grenadier Guards in the War of 1939–1945: The Campaigns in North-West Europe* (Aldershot: Gale and Polden Limited, 1949).
11. Desmond J.L. Fitzgerald, *History of the Irish Guards in the Second World War* (Aldershot: Gale & Polden, 1949).
12. Michael Eliot Howard and John Hanbury Angus Sparrow, *The Coldstream Guards: 1920–1946* (London: Oxford University Press, 1951).
13. Roden Orde, *The Household Cavalry at War: Second Household Cavalry Regiment* (Aldershot: Gale & Polden, 1953).
14. David Erskine, *The Scots Guards, 1919–1955* (London: William Clowes and Sons Ltd, 1956; repr. 2020).
15. Exact Editions Ltd, *The Guards Magazine*, 2020, https://shop.exacteditions.com/the-guards-magazine [accessed 10 June 2021].
16. General Sir Michael Gow, 'Churchill and the Foot Guards in World War Two', *The Guards Magazine*, Spring 1984, pp.2–5.
17. Timothy Harrison Place, *Military Training in the British Army, 1940–1944: From Dunkirk to D-Day* (London: Frank Cass Publishers, 2000).
18. J.P. Harris, *Men, Ideas and Tanks: British Military Thought and Armoured Forces, 1903–1939* (Manchester: Manchester University Press, 1995; repr. 2015).
19. Harold R. Winton, *To Change an Army: General Sir John Burnett-Stuart and British Armored Doctrine, 1927–1938* (Lawrence: University Press of Kansas, 1988).
20. David French, *Raising Churchill's Army: The British Army and the War against Germany, 1919–1945* (New York: Oxford University Press, 2000).

21. John Buckley, *Monty's Men: The British Army and the Liberation of Europe* (New Haven and London: Yale University Press, 2013; repr. 2014).
22. John Buckley, *British Armour in the Normandy Campaign 1944* (London: Routledge, 2004).
23. John Ellis, *The Sharp End: The Fighting Man in World War II* (Newton Abbot: David & Charles, 1980; repr. 2011).
24. Alan Allport, *Browned Off and Bloody-Minded: The British Soldier Goes to War, 1939–1945* (New Haven and London: Yale University Press, 2015; repr. 2017).
25. Carrington, *Reflect on Things Past*.
26. Carrington, *Reflect on Things Past*, p.51.
27. Ian Daglish, *Operation Goodwood: Attack by Three British Armoured Divisions* (Barnsley: Pen & Sword Books Limited, 2004; repr. 2018).
28. Rosse and Hill, *The Story of the Guards Armoured Division*, p.38.
29. John Nelson Rickard, 'The Test of Command: McNaughton and Exercise 'Spartan,' 4–12 March 1943', *Canadian Military History*, 8/3 (Summer 1999), pp.22–38.
30. Ian Daglish, *Operation Bluecoat (Battleground Europe)* (South Yorkshire: Pen & Sword, 2003).
31. Major J.J. How, *Normandy: The British Breakout* (London: William Kimber and Co. Ltd, 1981).
32. John Buckley, *Monty's Men: The British Army and the Liberation of Europe* (New Haven and London: Yale University Press, 2013).
33. John Peaty, 'Operation MARKET GARDEN: The Manpower Factor', in *Operation Market-Garden: The Campaign for the Low Countries, Autumn 1944: Seventy Years On*, ed. by John Buckley & Peter Preston-Hough (Solihull: Helion and Company Ltd, 2016), pp.58–73.
34. William F. Buckingham, *Arnhem 1944* (Stroud: Tempus Publishing Ltd, 2002, repr. 2004).
35. Antony Beevor, *Arnhem: The Battle for the Bridges, 1944* (London: Penguin Random House UK, 2018).
36. W.D. & S. Whitaker, *Rhineland: The Battle to End the War* (London: Mandarin Paperbacks, 1989).
37. R.W. Thompson, *The Battle for the Rhineland* (London: Hutchinson & Co. (Publishers) Ltd, 1958).
38. Patrick Delaforce, *Monty's Iron Sides: From the Normandy Beaches to Bremen with the 3rd Division* (London: Chancellor Press, 1995).
39. Robin McNish, *The Iron Division: The History of the 3rd Division 1809–1989* (London: 3rd Armoured Division, HM Stationery Office, 1978).
40. Allan Adair, *A Guards' General: The Memoirs of Major General Sir Allan Adair* (London: Hamish Hamilton, 1986).
41. W.A. Elliott, *Esprit de Corps: A Scots Guards Officer on Active Service 1943–1945* (Norwich: Michael Russell (Publishing) Ltd, 1996).
42. Carrington, *Reflect on Things Past*.
43. William Arthur Eager, *Beyond the Rhine – The Sacrificial Lamb* (Amazon, 1995, repr. 2013).
44. Robert Boscawen, *Armoured Guardsmen: A War Diary, June 1944–April 1945* (Barnsley: Leo Cooper, 2001, repr. 2010).
45. B.D. Wilson, *The Ever Open Eye* (Cambridge: Melrose Books, 2014).
46. David Fraser, *Wars and Shadows: Memoirs of General Sir David Fraser* (London: ALLEN LANE, Penguin Press, 2002).
47. Sir John Gorman, *Times of My Life: An Autobiography* (Leo Cooper, 2002).

48. William Whitelaw, *The Whitelaw Memoirs* (London: Aurum Press Ltd, 1989).
49. Charles Farrell, *Reflections 1939–1945: A Scots Guards Officer in Training and War* (Bishop Auckland: Pentland Press, 2000).

Chapter One
1. J.P. Harris, *Men, Ideas and Tanks: British Military Thought and Armoured Forces, 1903–1939* (Manchester: Manchester University Press, 1995; repr. 2015), p.65.
2. Andrew Salmon, *To the Last Round: The Epic British Stand on the Imjin River, Korea 1951* (London: Aurum Press Ltd, 2009; repr. 2010), pp.34–36.
3. David Fletcher, *British Battle Tanks: British-Made Tanks of World War II* (Oxford: Osprey Publishing, 2017), pp.6–20.
4. Harold R Winton, *To Change an Army: General Sir John Burnett-Stuart and British Armored Doctrine, 1927–1938* (Lawrence: University Press of Kansas, 1988), p.24.
5. Harris, *Men, Ideas and Tanks*, p.197.
6. Harris, *Men, Ideas and Tanks*, pp.195–236.
7. Alaric Searle, 'The Birth of an Idea: "Plan 1919"' in *The Military Papers and Correspondence of Major General J.F.C. Fuller, 1916–1933*, ed. by Alaric Searle (Stroud: The History Press for the Army Records Society, 2017, pp.93–138 (pp.110–125).
8. Alaric Searle, *Armoured Warfare: A Military, Political and Global History* (London: Bloomsbury Publishing, 2017), pp.30–33.
9. Harris, *Men, Ideas and Tanks*, pp.210–219.
10. Harris, *Men, Ideas and Tanks*, p.278.
11. Jonathan Fennell, *Fighting the People's War: The British and Commonwealth Armies and the Second World War* (Cambridge: Cambridge University Press, 2019), pp.25–38.
12. Williamson Murray, 'British Military Effectiveness in the Second World War', in *Military Effectiveness: Volume 3 The Second World War New Edition*, ed. by Allan R. Millett and Williamson Murray (Cambridge: Cambridge University Press), pp.110–128.
13. Murray, *Military Effectiveness*, p.128.
14. Harrison Place, *Military Training in the British Army*, pp.95–102.
15. I. Daglish, *Operation Goodwood: Attack by Three British Armoured Divisions* (Barnsley: Pen & Sword Books Limited, 2004), Chapter 4. The Goodwood Plan, Kindle eBook, Location 581–600.
16. David Fletcher, *The Universal Tank: British Armour in the Second World War Part 2* (London: Stationery Office Books, 1989; repr. 1993), p.121.
17. Lt. General Sir Giffard Le Q. Martel, *Our Armoured Forces* (London: Faber and Faber Limited, 1945), pp.219–220.
18. Fennell, *Fighting the People's War*, pp.23–31.

Chapter Two
1. Verney, *The Guards Armoured Division*, p.15.
2. Rosse and Hill, *The Story of the Guards Armoured Division*, p.17.
3. *War Diaries, 1939–1945: Field Marshal Lord Alanbrooke*, ed. by Alex Danchev and Daniel Todman (London: Weidenfeld & Nicolson, 2001), p.160.
4. Forbes, *The Grenadier Guards in the War of 1939–1945*, I, 57.
5. Fraser, *Wars and Shadows*, pp.166–168.
6. Fraser, *Wars and Shadows*, p.166.
7. Adair, *A Guards' General*, pp.127–128.
8. Rowland Ryder, *Oliver Leese* (London: Hamish Hamilton Ltd, 1987), p.89.

9. London, The National Archives (TNA), WO 166/8569, Letter from Sergison-Brooke to Brigade of Guards, War Diaries, 1st (Motor) Battalion, Grenadier Guards, Battalion Orders, Part 1, 4 June 1942.
10. Danchev and Todman, *War Diaries,* pp.155–160.
11. Martel, *Our Armoured Forces,* pp.106–107.
12. Major R.J.R Trefusis, 'The First Days of the Guards Armoured Division', *The Guards Magazine* summer edition 1996, pp.76–77.

Chapter Three
1. Forbes, *The Grenadier Guards in the War of 1939–1945,* p.57.
2. Buckley, *British Armour in the Normandy Campaign 1944,* pp.72–85.
3. Fitzgerald, *History of the Irish Guards in the Second World War,* pp.106–107.
4. Martin Samuels, *Piercing the Fog of War: The Theory and Practice of Command in the British and German Armies, 1918–1940* (Warwick: Helion and Company Ltd, 2019), pp.286–287.
5. TNA, CAB 106/220, Final Report of the Bartholomew Committee on Lessons to Be Learnt from the Operations in Flanders, July 1940.
6. Samuels, *Piercing the Fog of War,* p.288.
7. Carrington, *Reflect on Things Past,* p.41.
8. Fraser, *Wars and Shadows,* pp.166–168.
9. George Forty, *Companion to the British Army 1939–1945* (Port Stroud: The History Press, 1998; repr. 2009), pp.65–66.
10. Howard and Sparrow, *The Coldstream Guards,* pp.558–559.
11. H. Hanning, *The British Grenadiers: Three Hundred and Fifty Years of the First Regiment of Foot Guards 1656–2006* (Barnsley: Pen & Sword Military, 2006), p.197.
12. John Robert Peaty, 'British Army Manpower Crisis, 1944' (unpublished doctoral thesis, King's College, University of London, 2000), pp.143–145.
13. Verney, *The Guards Armoured Division,* p.17.
14. Delaforce, *The Black Bull,* pp.12–13.
15. Forbes, *The Grenadier Guards in the War of 1939–1945,* p.57.
16. TBNA, A.B. Austin, 'THE GUARDS SNAP INTO TANKS', *Daily Herald,* 6 March 1942, p.2.
17. TNA WO 166/4091, War Diary, 1st Battalion, Coldstream Guards, Appendix 2, Reorganisation, General Instructions, 19 June 1941.
18. TNA, WO 166/4091, War Diary, 1st (Armoured) Battalion, Coldstream Guards, Appendix C. Battalion Reorganisation, Instruction No. 2.
19. Peaty, 'British Army Manpower Crisis 1944', p.143.
20. Howard and Sparrow, *The Coldstream Guards,* p.55.
21. Peaty, 'British Army Manpower Crisis 1944', p.143.

Chapter Four
1. Michael Craster, 'Cunningham, Ritchie and Leese', in *Churchill's Generals,* ed. by John Keegan (London: George Weidenfeld & Nicolson Ltd, 1991), pp.200–224 (p.220).
2. TNA, WO 166/879, Training Directive No. 10: Amendment of Training for Armoured Brigades and Bns, Guards Armoured Division, General Staff (GS), August–December 1941.
3. TNA, WO 166/8566, War Diary, 4th Battalion, Coldstream Guards, 6th Brigade, Guards Armoured Division, 12 November 1942.
4. TNA, WO 166/6656, War Diary, HQ 6th Guards (Armoured) Brigade, 23 September 1942.

5. Adair, *A Guards' General*, p.130.
6. TNA, WO 166/879 Guards Armoured Division, Training Directive No.1; Crew Training of an Armoured Brigade; Notes on Tank Fire, 1941.
7. Harrison Place, *Military Training in the British Army*, pp.111–114.
8. Murray, *Military Effectiveness*, p.112.
9. TNA, WO 166/879, Guards Armoured Division, Training Directive No.1. Detailed Notes on Individual and Crew Training for Armoured Brigades, Home Forces, 21 August 1941.
10. Julian Paget, *The Crusading General: The Life of General Sir Bernard Paget, GCB, DSO, MC* (Barnsley: Pen & Sword Books Limited, 2008), pp.78–81.
11. Harrison Place, *Military Training in the British Army*, pp.50–51.
12. Paget, *The Crusading General*, pp.82–87.
13. TBNA, The New Army, *The Scotsman*, Wednesday 1 April 1942, p.4.
14. Wellington Barracks, London, Welsh Guards Archive (WGA), Sergeant Charles Murrell, Box Folder 123, Hand-Written Diaries, Volume 11, Guards Armoured Division (ii), 1942–1944, Monday 7 December 1942, p.70.
15. Robert Murphy, 'First Official Recognition for Wartime Tragedy', *ITV News Website*, 2012, www.itv.com/news/westcountry/2012-04-13/first-official-recognition-for-wartime-tragedy [accessed 26 March 2022].
16. London, Imperial War Museum (IWM) Sound Archive, Interview with George Ernest Teal, 1st (Armoured) Battalion, Coldstream Guards, Catalogue number 18698, REEL 3, recorded by Conrad Wood, March 1999.
17. TBNA, '14 Killed on War Exercise', *Daily Mirror*, Tuesday 14 April 1942, front page.
18. TBNA, 'Army Manoeuvres – M.P.s to Ask About Casualties', *The Daily Mail*, Thursday 16 April 1942, front page.
19. TBNA, 'Casualties in Manoeuvres – M.P.s Questions', *The Coventry Evening Telegraph*, Thursday 16 April 1942, front page.
20. The Regimental Archivist, Regimental Headquarters, Coldstream Guards, Wellington Barracks, London, War Diary, 1st (Armoured) Battalion Coldstream Guards, 13 April 1942.
21. Harrison Place, *Military Training in the British Army*, pp.50–62.
22. WGA, 2nd Battalion, Welsh Guards, Box File: Training, 1944–1945, five-page assessment of the organisation and training of 2nd Battalion Welsh Guards, the author is anonymous, pp.3–4.
23. Farrell, *Reflections 1939–1945*, p.45.
24. Harrison Place, *Military in the British Army*, pp.126–127.
25. TNA, WO 166/8576, War Diary, 2nd (Armoured) Battalion, Irish Guards, 22 May 1942, Exercise on Salisbury Plain.
26. TNA, WO 166/8576 War Diary, 2nd (Armoured) Battalion, Irish Guards, 22 June 1942.
27. Martel, *Our Armoured Forces*, p.150.
28. TNA, WO 166/8576, War Diary, 2nd (Armoured) Battalion, Irish Guards, 19 October 1942.
29. TNA, WO 166/12469, War Diary, 3rd (Infantry) Battalion, Irish Guards, Northwood, 1–4 February 1943.
30. Gorman, *Times of My Life*, p.555, Kindle eBook.
31. Gorman, *Times of My Life*, p.616, Kindle eBook.
32. Boscawen, *Armoured Guardsmen*, p.8.
33. Wilson, *The Ever Open Eye*, p.88.

34. IWM, Interview with William Hugh Griffiths, 2nd Battalion, Welsh Guards, Guards Armoured Division, Catalogue No. 17506, REEL 1, Recorded 1997.
35. A.C. Reynolds, *Grandad's War: A Coldstream Guards Frontline Experiences During WWII* (Self-published on Amazon, 2021), Kindle eBook, Location 253.
36. Harrison Place, *Military Training in the British Army*, pp.102–110.
37. Harrison Place, *Military Training in the British Army*, pp.128–152.
38. Verney, *The Guards Armoured Division*, pp.18–25.
39. Doherty, *British Armoured Divisions and Their Commanders*, pp.118–121.
40. WGA, 2nd Battalion, Welsh Guards, Box File: Training, 1944–1945, five-page assessment of the organisation and training of 2nd Battalion, Welsh Guards, pp.4–5.
41. The Regimental Archivist, Regimental Headquarters, Coldstream Guards, Wellington Barracks, London, War Diary, 1st (Armoured) Battalion Coldstream Guards, March 1943.
42. TNA, WO 166/12473, War Diary, 2nd Battalion, Welsh Guards, March 1943.
43. TNA, WO 166/12468, War Diary, 2nd (Armoured) Battalion, Irish Guards, 16 March 1943.
44. TNA, WO 166/10733, War Diary, H.Q. 5th Guards Armoured Brigade, 5 May 1943.
45. Adair, *A Guards' General*, p.135.
46. John Nelson Rickard, 'The Test of Command: McNaughton and Exercise 'Spartan,' 4–12 March 1943', *Canadian Military History*, Vol.8, No.3, Summer 1999, pp.22–38.
47. WGA, Sergeant Charles Murrell, Box Folder 123, Hand-Written Diaries, Volume 11, Guards Armoured Division (ii), 1942–1944, Thursday 10 June 1943, p.119.
48. WGA, Sergeant Charles Murrell, Box Folder 123, Hand-Written Diaries, Volume 11, Guards Armoured Division (ii), 1942–1944, sixth day of Exercise BLACKCOCK, Thursday 30 September 1943, p.171.
49. War Office, Military Training Pamphlet No. 41, Part 2, The Tactical Handling of the Armoured Division and Its Components: The Armoured Regiment, 1943.
50. Fraser, *Wars and Shadows*, pp.205–206.

Chapter Five
1. TNA, WO 166/6656, War Diary, Headquarters, 6th Guards (Armoured) Brigade, Appendix B, Exercise CRUISER, 5–6 June 1942.
2. Lieutenant General H.G. Martin, *The Fifteenth Scottish Division 1939–1945*, (William Blackwood and Sons Ltd, 1948; repr. 2022), p.17.
3. Harrison Place, *Military Training in the British Army*, pp.141–144.
4. TNA, WO 166/12469, War Diary, 3rd (Infantry) Battalion, Irish Guards, Northwood, 1–4 February 1943.
5. TNA, WO 166/12546, War Diary, 2nd Battalion, Glasgow Highlanders, Appendix A, Training Programme, 15 June–2 July 1943. Appendix H, Training Instructions No. 4 with 4th (Tank) Battalion, Coldstream Guards, 1943. WO 166/12597, War Diary, 6th Battalion, King's Own Scottish Borderers, May–July 1943.
6. TNA, WO 166/12470, War Diary, 3rd (Tank) Battalion, Scots Guards, 14–15 June 1943.
7. TNA, WO 166/12466, War Diary, 4th (Tank) Battalion, Grenadier Guards, Brigade Exercise ALEXANDER, 23–26 July 1943.
8. TNA, WO 166/12470, War Diary, 3rd (Tank) Battalion, Scots Guards, Exercise BLACKCOCK, August–October 1943.
9. IWM, Interview with Kenneth Banks Ohlson, 531st Battery, 190 Field Regiment, Royal Artillery, 15th (Scottish) Division, 1943–1944, Catalogue No. 33890, REEL 4, Recorded 2013.

10. TNA, WO 166/12461, War Diary, 4th (Tank) Battalion, Coldstream Guards, 6–26 March 1943.
11. IWM, Interview with Gordon Thomas Calthrop Campbell, 131st Field Regt, Royal Artillery, 15th (Scottish) Infantry Division, 1943, Catalogue No. 11955, REEL 4, Recorded 1991.
12. TNA, WO 291/399, Army Operational Research Group, A.O.R.G. Memorandum No. 45, Casualties to Churchill Tanks in 25 PDR H.E. Concentrations, 9 July 1943.
13. TNA, WO 291/399, Army Operational Research Group, A.O.R.G. Memorandum No. 45, Casualties to Churchill Tanks in 25 PDR H.E. Concentrations, Appendix C – Short Account of the Trials at Larkhill, 5 June 1943.

Chapter Six
1. Gregory Blaxland, *Destination Dunkirk: The Story of Gort's Army* (London: William Kimber and Co. Ltd, 1973), p.266.
2. Richard Collier, *The Sands of Dunkirk* (Glasgow: William Collins Sons & Co. Ltd., 1961; repr. 1974), pp.65–70.
3. Adair, *A Guards' General*, p.129.
4. TNA, WO 166/879, Guards Armoured Division, Training Directive No. 1, 21 August 1941.
5. WGA, 2nd Battalion, Welsh Guards, Box File: Training, 1944–1945, five-page assessment of the organisation and training of 2nd Battalion, Welsh Guards, pp.3–4.
6. John Christopher Malcolm Baynes, *The Forgotten Victor: General Sir Richard O'Connor, KT, GCB, DSO, MC* (London: Brassey's (UK) Ltd, 1989), p.186.
7. Harrison Place, *Military Training in the British Army*, pp.126–127.
8. Liddell Hart Centre for Military Archives (LHCMA), King's College London, O'CONNOR, Gen Sir Richard, (1889–1981), OCONNOR: 8, Appraisal of the careers of selected senior military personnel, 1971, Major General Sir Allan Adair.
9. Stephen Ashley Hart, *Colossal Cracks: Montgomery's 21st Army Group in Northwest Europe, 1944–45* (Stackpole Books, 2007), p.137.
10. Peter Rostron, *The Life and Times of General Sir Miles Dempsey: Monty's Army Commander*, (Pen & Sword Military, 2010), p.141.
11. LHCMA, O'CONNOR, Gen Sir Richard, (1889–1981), OCONNOR: 8, Appraisal of the careers of celected senior military personnel, 1971, Major J.K. Nairne recollections of Major General Sir Allan Adair.
12. David French, 'Colonel Blimp and the British Army: British Divisional Commanders in the War against Germany, 1939–1945', *The English Historical Review*, 111.444 (1996), 1182–1201.
13. Fraser, *Wars and Shadows*, p.195.
14. Rosse and Hill, *The Story of the Guards Armoured Division*, p.303.
15. Adair, *A Guards' General*, p.150.
16. Stephen Ashley Hart, *Colossal Cracks*, p.137.
17. Duncan Stone, 'Deconstructing the Gentleman Amateur', *Cultural and Social History*, (2019), 1–22 (pp.1–4).

Chapter Seven
1. Hanning, *The British Grenadiers*, pp.9–20.
2. Adair, *A Guards' General*, p.132.
3. Russell A. Hart, *Clash of Arms: How the Allies Won in Normandy* (Boulder, USA: Lynne Rienner Publishers, 2001), p.150.

4. Michael Eliot Howard, *Captain Professor: A Life in War and Peace* (London: Continuum UK, 2006), p.53.
5. Reynolds, *Grandad's War*, Kindle eBook, Location 106.
6. Howard, *Captain Professor*, p.56.
7. Ronald Melvin, *The Guards and Caterham: The Soldier's Story* (Old Coulsdon: Guardroom Publications, 1999; repr.2020), pp.196–202.
8. Keith Briant, *Fighting with the Guards*, (London: Evans Bros. Ltd, 1958), pp.14–22.
9. Melvin, *The Guards and Caterham*, p.200.
10. TBNA, 'An Irish Guardsman tells how the Army's No. 1 fighting man is made. To the 'Telegraph's' military correspondent he reveals that Guardsmen are human under the bearskin', *Ballymena Weekly Telegraph*, Saturday, 19 April 1941, p.6.
11. Gerald Kersh, *They Die with Their Boots Clean*, (London: William Heinemann Ltd, 1941; repr. 1943), p.8.
12. Carrington, *Reflect on Things Past*, p.32.
13. Howard, *Captain Professor*, pp.57–58.
14. Gorman, *Times of My Life*, Kindle eBook, Location 499.
15. *Dig or Die: The Memoirs of Guardsman John Elliott, The Second Battalion Coldstream Guards in Tunisia and Italy 1943–1944*, ed. by Margaret Robson, (Amazon: Adam Robson, 2016), Kindle eBook, Location 379.
16. WGA, Sergeant Charles Murrell, Box Folder 123, Hand-Written Diaries, Volume 11, Guards Armoured Division (ii), 1942–1944, Thursday 19 November 1942, p.56.
17. WGA, Sergeant Charles Murrell, Box Folder 123, Hand-Written Diaries, Volume 11, Guards Armoured Division (ii), 1942–1944, Thursday 25 May 1944, Visit by General Eisenhower and Speech, pp.245–246.
18. Martel, *Our Armoured Forces*, p.104.
19. Allport, *Browned Off and Bloody-Minded*, pp.97–112.
20. Allport, *Browned Off and Bloody-Minded*, p.29.
21. Christopher Bulteel, *Something About a Soldier: The Wartime Memoirs of Christopher Bulteel, MC* (Shrewsbury: Airlife Publishing Ltd, 2000), p.27.
22. Howard, *Captain Professor*, p.57.
23. Sarah Katharina Kayss, *'Competent, Assertive, Athletic and Privileged? Britain's Future Army Officers'*, Website, Wavell Room: Contemporary British Military Thought, 11 September 2018, https://wavellroom.com/2018/09/11/competent-assertive-athletic-and-privileged-britains-future-army-officers [accessed 31 May 2022].
24. TNA, WO 166/4091, War Diary, 1st (Armoured) Battalion, Coldstream Guards, Appendix C, September 1941, Battalion Reorganisation, Instruction No. 2.
25. 'Raven's Progressive Matrices', Online Encyclopaedia, Wikipedia, 27 March 2022, https://en.wikipedia.org/wiki/Raven%27s_Progressive_Matrices [accessed 31 May 2022].
26. TNA, WO 166/8576, War Diary, 2nd (Armoured) Battalion, Irish Guards, 12 June 1942.
27. WGA, Sergeant Charles Murrell, Box Folder 123, Hand-Written Diaries, Volume 11, Guards Armoured Division (ii), 1942–1944, Sunday, 13 December 1942, p.71.
28. Allport, *Browned Off and Bloody-Minded*, pp.11–12.
29. WGA, 2nd Battalion, Welsh Guards, Box File: Training, 1944–1945, five-page assessment of the organisation and training of 2nd Battalion, Welsh Guards, p.1.
30. Charles Murrell, *Dunkirk to the RhineLand: Diaries and Sketches of Sergeant C S Murrell, Welsh Guards*, ed. by Nick Murrell (Barnsley: Pen & Sword Military, 2011; repr. 2020), p.131.
31. Allport, *Browned Off and Bloody-Minded*, p.75.

32. Allport, *Browned Off and Bloody-Minded*, p.218.
33. TBNA, A.B. Austin, THE GUARDS SNAP INTO TANKS, *Daily Herald*, 6 March 1942, p.2.
34. Murrell, *Dunkirk to the RhineLand*, p.172.
35. Lieutenant General Sir Brian Horrocks, *A Full Life* (London: Collins, 1960), p.198.
36. Patrick Forbes, *6th Guards Tank Brigade: The Story of Guardsmen in Churchhill Tanks*, The Naval (London: Sampson, Low, Marston & Co., 1946), pp.8–12.
37. TNA, PREM 3/55/10, Prime Minister's Office: Operational Correspondence and Papers, Army Manpower Requirements and Distribution, 1944–1945.
38. TNA, PREM 3/55/10, Prime Minister's Office: Army Manpower Requirements, 1944–1945.
39. TNA, PREM 3/55/10, Prime Minister's Office: Army Manpower Requirements, 1944–1945.
40. TNA, PREM 3/55/10, Prime Minister's Office: Army Manpower Requirements, 1944–1945.
41. Elliott, *Esprit de Corps*, pp.104–107.
42. Farrell, *Reflections*, pp.56–57.

Chapter Eight
1. Adair, *A Guards' General*, p.131.
2. WGA, 2nd Battalion, Welsh Guards, Box File: Training, 1944–1945, five-page assessment of the organisation and training of 2nd Battalion, Welsh Guards, p.3.
3. Boscawen, *Armoured Guardsmen*, p.7.
4. Boscawen, *Armoured Guardsmen*, pp.8–9.
5. Searle, *Armoured Warfare*, Chapter Two, Kindle eBook, Location 76.
6. Steven J Zaloga, *Armored Thunderbolt: The U.S. Army Sherman in World War II* (Merchanicsburg: Stackpole Books, 2008), pp.22–31.
7. Zaloga, *Armored Thunderbolt*, pp.46–48.
8. Belton Y. Cooper, *Death Traps: The Survival of an American Armoured Division in World War II* (New York: The Random House Publishing Group, 1998; repr. 2003), pp.321–322.
9. Jeremy Black, *Tank Warfare* (Indiana: Indiana University Press, 2020), Kindle eBook, pp.55–56.
10. Mark Anthony Beer, 'The Evolution of Operational Doctrine of U.S. Armored Forces, 1917–1942' (unpublished masters thesis, Kansas State University, 1988), pp.108–112.
11. Major Bryan E. Denny, 'The Evolution and Demise of U.S. Tank Destroyer Doctrine in the Second World War' (unpublished masters thesis, Faculty of the U.S. Army Command and General Staff College, 1990), pp.9–18.
12. Roger Ford, *The Sherman Tank* (Staplehurst: Brown Packaging Books Ltd, 1999), pp.55–56.
13. Harrison Place, *Military Training in the British Army*, pp.118–127.
14. Boscawen, *Armoured Guardsmen*, p.18.
15. Fitzgerald, *A History of the Irish Guards*, pp.393–398.
16. Hart, *Clash of Arms*, p.111.
17. Patrick Delaforce, *The Black Bull: From Normandy to the Baltic with the 11th Armoured Division*, (Stroud: Sutton Publishing Ltd, 1993; repr. 2002), p.11.
18. Michael Carver, *Out of Step: Memoirs of a Field Marshal* (London: Hutchinson, 1989), p.180.
19. Doherty, *British Armoured Divisions and their Commanders 1939–1945*, p.145.
20. TNA, WO 194/845, Fighting Vehicle Proving Establishment, F.T. 1553, Field Trials Report on Comparative Trials of Various A.F.V's in Soft Ground Conditions, December 1944.
21. David Fletcher, *Churchill Tank: Vehicle History and Specification* (London: HMSO, 1983; repr. 2020), pp.6–21.

22. David Erskine, *The Scots Guards, 1919–1955* (London: William Clowes and Sons Ltd, 1956), pp.330–331.
23. Buckley, *British Armour in the Normandy Campaign 1944*, pp.113–115.

Chapter Nine
1. Robin Neillands, *The Battle of Normandy 1944* (London: Cassell Military Paperbacks, 2002; repr. 2003), p.143.
2. Charles Forrester, *Monty's Functional Doctrine: Combined Arms Doctrine in British 21st Army Group in Northwest Europe, 1944–45* (Helion and Company, 2015; repr. 2018), pp.73–74.
3. Alexander McKee, *Caen: Anvil of Victory* (London: Souvenir Press, 1964; repr. 2000), p.247.
4. Daglish, *Operation Goodwood*, Kindle eBook.
5. Buckley, *Monty's Men*, pp.93–95.
6. Daglish, *Operation Goodwood*, Kindle eBook.
7. McKee, *CAEN*, pp.250–252.
8. Jackson, *OPERATIONS OF EIGHTH CORPS*, p.74.
9. Jackson, *OPERATIONS OF EIGHTH CORPS*, p.83.
10. Verney, *The Guards Armoured Division*, pp.39–45.
11. Stephen Napier, *The Armoured Campaign in Normandy: June–August 1944* (Stroud: The History Press, 2015), p.45.
12. Verney, *The Guards Armoured Division*, p.46.
13. General Sir William Scotter, 'A Role for Non-Mechanised Infantry', *The RUSI Journal*, 125.4 (1980), 59–62.
14. Charles J. Dick, 'The Goodwood Concept – Situating the Appreciation', *The RUSI Journal*, 127.1 (1982), pp.22–28.
15. Christopher Dunphie, *The Pendulum of Battle: Operation GOODWOOD – July 1944* (Barnsley: Pen & Sword Books Limited, 2004), Kindle eBook, pp.4–10.
16. Daglish, *Operation Goodwood*, Kindle eBook, Location 581.
17. Forrester, *Monty's Functional Doctrine*, pp.75–78.
18. Buckley, *Monty's Men*, pp.111–112.
19. Daglish, *Operation Goodwood*, Kindle eBook, Location 2940–2963.
20. Buckley, *Monty's Men*, p.111.
21. TNA, CAB 106/1061, N.W. Europe Campaign, OPERATION 'GOODWOOD', 18 July 1944, Notes of Conversation between General Dempsey Commander Second British Army and (a) Lt Col G.S. Jackson, 8 March 1951 (b) Capt. B.H. Liddell-Hart, 28 March 1952, p.13.
22. Rostron, *The Life and Times of General Sir Miles Dempsey*, p.118.
23. Stephen Napier, *The Armoured Campaign in Normandy: June–August 1944* (The History Press, 2015), pp.228–230.
24. Napier, *The Armoured Campaign in Normandy*, p.409.
25. Napier, *The Armoured Campaign in Normandy*, p.231.
26. Adair, *A Guards' General*, p.147.
27. Rosse and Hill, *The Story of the Guards Armoured Division*, p.46.
28. TNA, WO 171/1252, War Diary, 5 Battalion, Coldstream Guards, 13 July 1944.
29. TNA, WO 171/1256, War Diary, 2nd (Armoured) Battalion, Irish Guards, 10 July 1944.
30. TNA, WO 171/638, War Diary, HQ 32 Guards Brigade, 13 July 1944.
31. TNA, WO 171/1253, War Diary, 1st (Motor) Battalion, Grenadier Guards, 13 July 1944.
32. Erskine, *The Scots Guards*, p.351.

33. Adair, *A Guards' General,* p.147.
34. Roberts, *From the Desert to the Baltic,* p.184.
35. Adair, *A Guards' General,* p.147.
36. Napier, *The Armoured Campaign in Normandy,* p.273.
37. Buckley, *British Armour in the Normandy Campaign 1944,* p.98.
38. Rosse and Hill, *The Story of the Guards Armoured Division,* p.190.
39. Jocelyn Pereira, *A Distant Drum: War Memories of the Intelligence Officer of the 5 Bn Coldstream Guards: 1944–45* (Gale & Polden, 1948; repr. 2020), p.68.
40. Carrington, *Reflect on Things Past,* p.51.
41. Fraser, *Wars and Shadows,* pp.205–206.
42. TNA, WO 171/605, 5 Guards Armoured Brigade, War Diaries, Appendix J., Memorandum Entitled Fighting in Bocage Country, 15 August 1944.
43. TNA, WO 171/377, HQ Guards Armoured Division, October to November 1944, GDS ARMD DIV REVISED COMPOSITION OF BRIGADES, 30 November 1944.
44. TNA, WO 166/12469, War Diary, 3rd (Infantry) Battalion, Irish Guards, Northwood, 1–4 February 1943.

Chapter Ten
1. TNA, WO 171/605, 5 Guards Armoured Brigade, Fighting in Bocage Country, 15 August 1944, p.1.
2. TNA, WO 171/605, 5 Guards Armoured Brigade, Fighting in Bocage Country, 15 August 1944, p.1.
3. TNA, WO 171/605, 5 Guards Armoured Brigade, Fighting in Bocage Country, 15 August 1944, p.1.
4. TNA, WO 171/605, 5 Guards Armoured Brigade, Fighting in Bocage Country, 15 August 1944, p.2.
5. Murray, *Military Effectiveness,* p.125.
6. TNA, WO 166/879, Guards Armoured Division, Training Directive No.1, 1941.
7. Murray, *Military Effectiveness,* p.128.
8. Forrester, *Monty's Functional Doctrine,* pp.78–79.
9. Buckley, *British Armour in the Normandy Campaign 1944,* p.96.
10. Carver, *Out of Step,* p.180.
11. TNA, WO 166/12469, War Diary, 3rd (Infantry) Battalion, Irish Guards, Northwood, 1–4 February 1943.
12. War Office, Military Training Pamphlet No. 41, Part 2, The Tactical Handling of the Armoured Division and Its Components: The Armoured Regiment, 1943.
13. War Office, Military Training Pamphlet No. 41, Part 2, The Tactical Handling of the Armoured Division and Its Components, 1943, p.4.
14. War Office, Military Training Pamphlet No. 63, The Co-Operation of Tanks and Infantry Divisions, May 1944.
15. TNA, WO 171/1253, War Diary, 1st (Motor) Battalion, Grenadier Guards, August 1944, Appendix A, Account of Clearing DROUET WOODS and Battle of DROUET HILL, p.3.
16. Pereira, *A Distant Drum,* p.26.
17. TBNA, L Marsland Gander, '8th Battling Ahead in 'Quagmire' More Minefields and Demolitions, 1000 Prisoners Taken, Germans Rush Reinforcements from North Italy', *The Scotsman,* December 1943, p.5.
18. Roberts, *From the Desert to the Baltic,* p.171.
19. Rickard, 'The Test of Command', pp.23–38.

Chapter Eleven

1. Rostron, *The Life and Times of General Sir Miles Dempsey*, p.120.
2. Murrell, *From Dunkirk to the Rhineland*, pp.101–102.
3. Hugh Darby and Marcus Cunliffe, *A Short Story of 21 Army Group: The British and Canadian Armies in the Campaigns in North-West Europe, 1944–1945* (Aldershot: Gale & Polden Limited, 1949), pp.46–55.
4. Buckley, *Monty's Men*, pp.158–160.
5. Daglish, *Operation Bluecoat*, pp.30–46.
6. Forbes, *6th Guards Tank Brigade*, pp.16–18.
7. Daglish, *Operation Bluecoat*, pp.32–40.
8. Martin, *The Fifteenth Scottish Division*, pp.85–86.
9. Whitelaw, *The Whitelaw Memoirs*, pp.15–16.
10. Forbes, *6th Guards Tank Brigade*, p.26.
11. Forbes, *6th Guards Tank Brigade*, pp.35–37.
12. Forbes, *6th Guards Tank Brigade*, pp.26–38.
13. IWM, Interview with Ronald Buckland, Intelligence Officer, 4th (Tank) Battalion, Coldstream Guards, Catalogue No. 22369, REEL 1, Recorded 10 January 2002.
14. TNA, WO 171/1258, War Diary, 3rd (Tank) Battalion, Scots Guards, Appendix K1, Account of 3rd (Tank) Battalion, Scots Guards Action at CAUMONT, 30 July 1944, Sheet Six.
15. TNA, WO 171/1258, War Diary, 3rd (Tank) Battalion, Scots Guards, Appendix K3, Account of Action Fought by 32nd Guards Brigade and 3rd (Tank) Battalion, Scots Guards at Chenedolle, Sheet 7, p.13.
16. IWM Archive, Documents. 12309, Private Papers of Lieutenant General Sir Giffard Martel KCB, Box No: Con Shelf (Volume 14), 8/3 Miscellaneous Correspondence Files, 1936–1955, B. Liddell Hart, Lessons from Normandy, February 1953, pp.1–3.
17. Buckley, *British Armour in the Normandy Campaign 1944*, p.178.
18. TNA, WO 171/1253, 1st (Motor) Battalion, Grenadier Guards, Appendix A, Account of the Clearing of DROUET WOODS and Battle of DROUET HILL, 2 to 4 August 1944, pp.3–5.
19. How, *Normandy*, pp.217–223.

Chapter Twelve

1. Boscawen, *Armoured Guardsmen*, pp.40–48.
2. Peter Verney, *The Micks: The Story of the Irish Guards*, Abridged edition (London: Pan Books Ltd, 1970; repr. 1973), p.172.
3. TNA, W0 291/2385, Analysis of 75mm Sherman Tank Casualties between 6 June and 10 July 1944. No. 2 Operational Research Section, 3 April 1945, Sheet 2.
4. TNA, W0 291/2385, Analysis of 75mm Sherman Tank Casualties, Sheet 2.
5. TNA, W0 291/2385, Analysis of 75mm Sherman Tank Casualties, Sheet 3.
6. Steven J Zaloga, *Sherman Medium Tank 1942–1945* (Oxford: Osprey Publishing, 1993; repr. 2010), p.16.
7. Zaloga, *Sherman Medium Tank 1942–1945*, pp.10–19.
8. James Holland, *Brothers in Arms: One Legendary Tank Regiment's Bloody War from D-Day to VE-Day* (London: Bantam Press, 2021), p.151.
9. TNA, W0 291/2385, Analysis of 75mm Sherman Tank Casualties, Sheet 3.
10. TNA, WO 205/1165, Captain H.B. Wright, RAMC and Captain R.D. Harkness, RAMC, A Survey of Casualties Amongst Armoured Units in North West Europe,

Medical Research Council Team, No. 2 Operational Research Section (ORS), Main H.Q. 21 Army Group, January 1946, p.3.
11. TNA, WO 205/1165, Wright, RAMC and Harkness, RAMC, A Survey of Casualties, p.4.
12. TNA, WO 205/1165, Wright, RAMC and Harkness, RAMC, A Survey of Casualties, p.5.
13. TNA, WO 205/1165, Wright, RAMC and Harkness, RAMC, A Survey of Casualties, pp.3-6.
14. WGA, Box File: Training, 1944-1945, Extracts from a letter written by Lieutenant N. Kearsley, 2nd (Armoured Recce) Battalion, Welsh Guards, 9 August 1944. Subject: Experiences of Combat and Lessons Learned. The letter was circulated to Regimental Headquarters, Welsh Guards, London, and the Guards Armoured Training Wing, Stanley Barracks, Dorset, and Training Battalion, Barnard Castle.
15. TNA, WO 205/1165, Wright, RAMC and Harkness, RAMC, A Survey of Casualties, pp.6-7.
16. TNA, WO 205/1165, Wright, RAMC and Harkness, RAMC, A Survey of Casualties, p.58.
17. John Ellis, *The Sharp End: The Fighting Man in World War II* (Newton Abbot: David & Charles, 1980), p.158.
18. Forbes, *6th Guards Tank Brigade*, p.26.
19. Buckley, *British Armour in the Normandy Campaign 1944*, pp.120-121.
20. IWM Archive, Private Papers of Lieutenant General Sir Giffard Martel KCB, Box No: Con Shelf (Volume 14), 8/3 Miscellaneous Correspondence Files, 1936-1955, Letter from B. Liddell Hart to Martel, 11 March 1952, Tanks in Normandy – As seen from the German side.
21. County Offaly, Ireland, Birr Castle Archives (BCA), The Rosse Papers, T45, Trunk, Box 1, 1st (Motor) Battalion, Grenadier Guards, Draft Regimental History, April 1944 to June 1945, Anonymous, Partial Account: an introduction and chapters 1 to 6, pp.6-7.
22. IWM, Interview with Christopher Corby Isham Schofield, 4th Tank Battalion, Coldstream Guards, 6th Guards Tank Brigade, Catalogue No. 22121, REEL 1, Recorded 2001.
23. IWM, Interview with Reg Sollitt, 4th Tank Battalion, Grenadier Guards, 6th Guards Tank Brigade, Catalogue No. 30006, REEL 3, Recorded 2007.
24. TNA, WO 166/12466, War Diary, 4th (Tank) Battalion, Grenadier Guards, Churchill tank, April 1943.
25. Patrick Forbes, *6th Guards Tank Brigade: The Story of Guardsmen in Churchhill Tanks*, The Naval (London: Sampson, Low, Marston & Co., 1946), pp.2-5.
26. TNA, WO 205/1165, A Survey of Casualties Amongst Armoured Units in North West Europe, Captain H.B. Wright, R.A.M.C. and Captain R.D. Harkness, R.A.M.C. Medical Research Council Team, No. 2 Operational Research Section (ORS), Main H.Q. 21 Army Group, January 1946, pp.3-7.
27. TNA, WO 205/1165, A Survey of Casualties Amongst Armoured Units in North West Europe, Captain H.B. Wright, R.A.M.C. and Captain R.D. Harkness, R.A.M.C. Medical Research Council Team, No. 2 Operational Research Section (ORS), Main H.Q. 21 Army Group, January 1946, pp.101-102.
28. Robert Kershaw, *Tank Men: The Human Story of Tanks at War* (London: Hodder & Stoughton, 2008), pp.367-368.
29. Fletcher, *Churchill Tank*, p.20.
30. Erskine, *The Scots Guards*, pp.329-330.

Chapter Thirteen

1. Verney, *The Guards Armoured Division*, p.74.
2. TNA, WO 171/376, War Diary, HQ Guards Armoured Division, 1 September 1944.
3. TNA, WO 171/1252, War Diary, 5th Battalion, Coldstream Guards, 2 to 3 September 1944.
4. TNA, WO 171/638, War Diary, HQ 32 Guards Brigade, 3 September 1944.
5. TNA, WO 171/1256, War Diary, 2nd (Armoured) Battalion, Irish Guards, 3 September 1944.
6. TNA, WO 171/638, War Diary, HQ 32 Guards Brigade, 3 September 1944.
7. TNA, WO 171/376, War Diary, HQ Guards Armoured Division, 3 September 1944.
8. Rosse and Hill, *The Story of the Guards Armoured Division*, p.123.
9. Rosse and Hill, *The Story of the Guards Armoured Division*, pp.123–124.
10. Verney, *The Guards Armoured Division*, p.101.
11. Buckley and Preston-Hough, *Operation Market-Garden*, pp.58–73.
12. Buckingham, *Arnhem 1944*, pp.119–120.
13. Beevor, *Arnhem*, pp.67–68.
14. Buckingham, *Arnhem*, p.233.
15. Beevor, *Arnhem*, pp.219–220.
16. Robert Kershaw, *It Never Snows in September: The German View of MARKET-GARDEN and the Battle of Arnhem, September 1944* (Marlborough: The Crowood Press, 1990, repr. 2008), p.274.
17. Max Hastings, *All Hell Let Loose: The World at War 1939–1945* (London: HarperPress, 2011), p.581.
18. Richard Mead, *General 'BOY', The Life of Lieutenant General Sir Frederick Browning* (Barnsley: Pen & Sword Military, 2010, repr. 2017), p.62.
19. Richard Mead, *General 'BOY'*, pp.133–142.
20. Aaron Bates, *The Last German Victory: Operation Market Garden 1944* (Yorkshire: Pen & Sword Military, 2021), p.81.
21. Bates, *The Last German Victory*, p.33.
22. Bates, *The Last German Victory*, pp.88–89.
23. BCA, The Rosse Papers, T45, Trunk, Box 1, Summary of Actions and Lessons Learned, 2nd Household Cavalry Regiment, Document Undated, Author Unknown, Document Incomplete (Starting Page 16), p.25.
24. Bates, *The Last German Victory*, p.92.
25. Roberts, *From the Desert to the Baltic*, p.213.
26. Doherty, *British Armoured Divisions*, p.187.
27. TNA, WO 171/1256, War Diary, 2nd (Armoured) Battalion, Irish Guards, 28 to 30 September 1944.
28. Howard and Sparrow, *The Coldstream Guards*, pp.293–297.
29. Elliott, *Esprit de Corps*, p.110.
30. Carrington, *Reflect on Things Past*, p.51.
31. Fraser, *Wars and Shadows*, p.230.
32. TNA, WO 171/390, War Diary, Provost Company, Guards Armoured Division, September 1944.
33. G.D. Sheffield, *The Redcaps: A History of the Royal Military Police and Its Antecedents from the Middle Ages to the Gulf War* (London: Brassey's (UK) Ltd, 1994), pp.159–160.
34. Verney, *The Guards Armoured Division*, pp.115–116.
35. Alan Allport, *Browned Off and Bloody-Minded*, p.217.
36. Fraser, *Wars and Shadows*, pp.231–232.

37. Fitzgerald, *A History of the Irish Guards*, p.486.
38. Stephen Ashley Hart, *Colossal Cracks*, pp.31–32.
39. Buckley, *Monty's Men*, p.219.
40. Cornelius Ryan Collection of World War II Papers, Mahn Centre for Archives and Special Collections, Ohio University Libraries, Box 115, Folder 37, Transcript Brigadier J.O.E. Vandeleur (Lt Col), Irish Guards, April 1967.
41. John Sliz, *Bridging the Club Route: Guards Armoured Division's Engineers During Operation Market Garden* (Toronto, Canada: Travelogue 219, 2015), p.45.
42. Lieutenant Colonel Sir Julian Paget, 'The Capture of the Nijmegen Road Bridge', *The Guards Magazine*, spring edition, 1978, pp.2–9.
43. TNA, WO 171/638, 32 Guards Brigade, War Diaries, July to September 1944, Brigade Intelligence Summary No. 47, up to 1600hrs, 21 September 1944, pp.1–2.
44. Verney, *The Guards Armoured Division*, p.109.
45. Gorman, *Times of My Life*, Kindle eBook, Location 1197.
46. BCA, The Rosse Papers, T45, Story of Armour in NW Europe, 2nd Armoured Battalion, Irish Guards, July 1944–May 1945, Descriptive Stories of Actions and Successes, Written Account by 2I/C of Leading Sqn, pp.10–12.
47. BCA, The Rosse Papers, T45, Trunk, Box 1, Summary of Actions and Lessons Learned, 2nd Household Cavalry Regiment, pp.22–23.
48. Cornelius Ryan Collection of World War II Papers, Box 130, Folder 13, Colonel Hans-Peter Knaust, attached 10th SS Panzer, Transcript November 1967.
49. Lieutenant Colonel Elizabeth Ann Coble, 'Operation Market Garden: Case Study for Analysing Senior Leader Responsibilities' (partial fulfillment of Master of Strategic Studies, U.S. Army War College, 2009), p.25.
50. Cornelius Ryan Collection of World War II Papers, Box 114, Folder 38, Sir Allan Adair (General), Guards Armoured Division (Commander), Transcript April 1967.
51. Murrell, *Dunkirk to the Rhineland*, pp.162–166.
52. Lieutenant Colonel Coble, 'Operation Market Garden', p.27.
53. Cornelius Ryan Collection of World War II Papers, Box 115, Folder 36, Transcript Giles Vandeleur (Lt Col), Irish Guards, April 1967.

Chapter Fourteen
1. Forbes, *6th Guards Tank Brigade*, p.50.
2. Robin McNish, *The Iron Division: The History of the 3rd Division 1809–1989* (London: 3rd Armoured Division, HM Stationery Office, 1978; repr. 1990), pp.120–122.
3. Patrick Delaforce, *Monty's Iron Sides: From the Normandy Beaches to Bremen with the 3rd Division* (London: Chancellor Press, 1995 repr. 1999), p.132.
4. Forbes, *6th Guards Tank Brigade*, pp.54–55.
5. TNA, WO 171/607, War Diary, 6th Guards (Tank) Brigade HQ, 12–19 October 1944.
6. TNA, WO 171/1255, War Diary, 4th (Tank) Battalion, Grenadier Guards, Entry 20 October 1944 and Appendix A, Special Order of the Day, Brigadier Greenacre, October 1944.
7. IWM, Interview with Robert Charles Dare, Guardsman, 4th (Tank) Battalion, Coldstream Guards, Catalogue No. 18268, REELS 1–3, Produced 1999.
8. TNA, WO 171/1251, War Diary, 4th (Tank) Battalion, Coldstream Guards, 1 December 1944.
9. Forbes, *6th Guards Tank Brigade*, p.85.

Chapter Fifteen
1. Military Library Research Service (MLRS), Headquarters 21 Army Group, 10 May 1946, Report on Operation 'VERITABLE', pp.30–31.
2. TNA, WO 171/4321, War Diary, HQ 6th Guards (Tank) Brigade, 1 February–27 March 1945.
3. Delaforce, *Monty's Iron Sides*, pp.157–167.
4. MLRS, Headquarters 21st Army Group, 10 May 1946, Report on Operation 'VERITABLE' 8 February to 10 March 1945, pp.45–86.
5. Whitaker, *Rhineland*, p.268.
6. R.W. Thompson, *The Battle for the Rhineland* (London: Hutchinson & Co. (Publishers) Ltd, 1958), pp.225–229.
7. Verney, *The Guards Armoured Division*, p.135.
8. TNA, WO 171/5149, War Diary, 2nd Battalion, Scots Guards, 3 February 1945.
9. TNA, WO 171/5149, War Diary, 2nd Battalion, Scots Guards, February 1945, Appendix C, Drills for Operations and Training Based on Lessons Recently Learned; Appendix D, Demonstration Sqn/Coy GP Tactics.
10. TNA, WO 171/5144, War Diary, 1st (Motor) Battalion, Grenadier Guards, 26 to 27 January 1945.
11. TNA, WO 171/5144, War Diary, 1st (Motor) Battalion Grenadier Guards, 17 to 20 March 1945.
12. TNA, WO 171/5147, War Diary, 2nd (Armoured) Battalion, Irish Guards, March 1945, Training Instructions No. 3, 11 March 1945, Lt Col G. Vandeleur.
13. TNA, WO 171/372, War Diary, HQ Guards Armoured Division, 25 November 1944, Counter Mortar Policy.
14. TNA, WO 171/4357, War Diary, HQ 32 Guards Brigade, 10 February 1945.
15. TNA, WO 171/4318, War Diary, HQ 5 Guards Armoured Brigade, February 1945.

Chapter Sixteen
1. Adair, *A Guards' General*, p.136.
2. Theo Farrell, 'Improving in War: Military Adaptation and the British in Helmand Province, Afghanistan, 2006–2009', *The Journal of Strategic Studies*, 33.4, 567–94.
3. TNA, WO 171/1256, War Diary, 2nd (Armoured) Battalion, Irish Guards, 28 July 1944.
4. TNA, WO 171/5141, War Diary, 1st (Armoured) Battalion, Coldstream Guards, 28 March 1944.
5. Hanning, *The British Grenadiers*, p.197.
6. Robert T. Foley, Stuart Griffin, and Helen McCartney, '"Transformation in Contact": Learning the Lessons of Modern War', *International Affairs (Royal Institute of International Affairs 1944)*, 87.2, 253–70, (p.266).
7. Foley, Griffin, and McCartney, 'Transformation in Contact', p.266.
8. Max Visser, 'Organisational Learning Capability and Battlefield Performance', *International Journal of Organizational Analysis*, 24.4 (2016), 573–90, (p.580).
9. Buckley, *British Armour in the Normandy Campaign 1944*, pp.108–109.
10. Cambridge University: Churchill Archives Centre, Archive of Sir Percy James Grigg, PJGG 9/8-9, Correspondence with Field-Marshal Montgomery 1943–1945, Personal letter, dated 25 June 1944 and accompanying 2-page directive (21 A Gp/1088/C-in-C) forbidding criticism of British operations and equipment.
11. Fraser, *Wars and Shadows*, pp.205–206.
12. TNA, WO 171/1256, War Diary, 2nd (Armoured) Battalion, Irish Guards, 2 September 1944.

13. Erskine, *The Scots Guards*, pp.432–433.
14. TBNA, Great Work by Guards Division: Armoured Charge on Modern Lines, *The Aberdeen Evening Express*, Saturday, 7 April 1945, p.8.
15. TBNA, Guards' Night Dash, *The Scotsman*, Saturday, 7 April 1945, p.7.
16. TBNA, Guards' Armour Open the Way, *The Nottingham Journal*, Nottingham, Saturday, 7 April 1945, p.1.
17. TNA, WO 171/5149, War Diary, 2nd Battalion, Scots Guards, February 1945, Appendix C, Drills for Operations and Training Based on Lessons Recently Learned.
18. WGA, 2nd Battalion, Welsh Guards, Box File: Training, 1944–1945, Tactical Employment of Armour, Lt Col J.C. Lewis, 10 October 1944, p.3.
19. TNA, WO 171/4103, War Diary, HQ 'G' Branch, Guards Armoured Division, Appendix 30, Tactical Investigation Directorate, Use of Sherman Tks in Arty Role, 30 January 1945.
20. The Regimental Archivist, Regimental Headquarters, Coldstream Guards, Wellington Barracks, London, War Diary, 1st (Armoured) Battalion Coldstream Guards, 28 March 1945.
21. Boscawen, *Armoured Guardsmen*, p.195.
22. David Fletcher and Steven J. Zaloga, 'Staghound Armoured Car', in *British Battle Tanks: US Made Tanks of World War II* (Oxford: Osprey Publishing, 2018), Kindle eBook, Location 4702.
23. Boscawen, *Armoured Guardsmen*, pp.198–199.
24. David Fletcher, *Sherman Firefly* (Oxford: Osprey Publishing, 2008), Kindle eBook, p.8.
25. TNA, WO 171/5141, War Diary, 1st (Armoured) Battalion, Coldstream Guards, 3 to 4 April 1945.
26. TNA, WO 171/5143, War Diary, 5 Battalion, Coldstream Guards, 3 April 1945.
27. TBNA, More about the Rocket Barrage, *The Sphere Illustrated Newspaper*, 24 March 1945, p.372.
28. TNA, WO 171/5141, War Diary, 1st (Armoured) Battalion, Coldstream Guards, 3 April 1945.

Chapter Seventeen
1. TBNA, The Sixth Guards Tank Brigade's Capture of Munster, Capital of Westphalia: British Guardsmen and Infantry of the U.S. 17th Airborne Division Conferring in the Heart of the City During Patrol, *The Illustrated London News*, Saturday 14 April 1945.
2. TNA, WO 171/4321, War Diary, HQ 6th Guards (Tank) Brigade, 27 March 1945.
3. TNA, WO 171/5142, War Diary, 4th Battalion, Coldstream Guards, 27 March 1945.
4. TNA, WO 171/5142, War Diaries, 4th Battalion Coldstream Guards, 27 March–7 April 1945, and WO 171/5150, 3rd Battalion, Scots Guards, 27 March–31 March 1945.
5. TNA, WO 171/4321, War Diary, HQ 6th Guards (Tank) Brigade, 3 April 1945.
6. TNA, WO 171/5142, War Diary, 4th Battalion, Coldstream Guards, 5 April 1945.
7. IWM, Interview with Major Charles Farrell, 3rd Battalion, Scots Guards, 6th Guards (Tank) Brigade, Catalogue No. 17835, REELS 12 and 13, Produced 1998.
8. Forbes, *6th Guards Tank Brigade*, p.194.
9. Forbes, *The Grenadier Guards in the War of 1939–1945*, pp.211–225.
10. Forbes, *6th Guards Tank Brigade: The Story of Guardsmen in Churchhill Tanks*.
11. Lieutenant General Sir Arthur Smith, Major General Commanding the Brigade of Guards and General Officer Commanding London District.
12. TNA, WO 32/10395, Brigade of Guards, Manpower Ceiling, 14 August 1943, the Secretary of State for War, Sir James Grigg, a note to Sir Alan 'Tommy' Lascelles, Private Secretary to King George VI.

13. Verney, *The Guards Armoured Division: A Short History*, p.162.
14. TNA, WO 32/10395, Brigade of Guards, Manpower Ceiling, Ref No. S/466, 19 May 1945, Letter from Lieutenant General Sir H. Charles Loyd, Major General Commanding the Brigade of Guards, to Major General J.S. Steele, Director of Staff Duties (DSD).
15. TNA, WO 32/10395, Brigade of Guards, Manpower Ceiling, DO/SDI/9876(SDI), 21 May, Letter from Major General J.S. Steele, Director of Staff Duties (DSD), Responding to Letter S/466 from Lieutenant General Sir H. Charles Loyd, Major General Commanding the Brigade of Guards.
16. TNA, WO 32/10395, Brigade of Guards, Manpower Ceiling, 25 May 1945, The Organisation of the Brigade of Guards in the Second Stage of the War, Deputy Chief of the Imperial General Staff (DCIGS).
17. TNA, WO 32/11542, Brigade of Guards Organisation, 1945–1949, File No. GOC. 4/86543, Letter from Lieutenant General Sir H. Charles Loyd, Major General Commanding the Brigade of Guards, to Major General J.S. Steele, Director of Staff Duties (DSD).
18. TNA, WO 32/11542, Brigade of Guards Organisation, 1945–1949, 28 May 1945, Letter from Major General J.S. Steele, Director of Staff Duties (DSD) to Lieutenant General Sir H. Charles Loyd, Major General Commanding the Brigade of Guards.
19. TNA, WO 32/10395, Brigade of Guards, Manpower Ceiling, 9 June 1945, Memorandum, 20/Misc/2638 (SDI), Subject: Organisation of the Brigade of Guards, Major General J.S. Steele, Director of Staff Duties (DSD).
20. TNA, WO 32/10395, Brigade of Guards, Manpower Ceiling, 10 June 1945, Prime Minister, Winston Churchill, Personal Minute, Serial No M.588/5 to the Secretary of State for War, Sir James Grigg.
21. TNA, WO 32/10395, Brigade of Guards, Manpower Ceiling, 11 June 1945, Note from Secretary of State for War, Sir James Grigg, in Response to Minute M.588/5, Prime Minister, Winston Churchill.
22. TNA, WO 32/10395, Brigade of Guards, Manpower Ceiling, Undated, Anonymous, Draft Note, Headed Prime Minister, 6A. Subject: Guards Armoured Units to Revert to Infantry.
23. Farewell to Armour: The Guards Lose Their Tanks, *The Guards Museum YouTube Channel*, 8 June 2020, www.youtube.com/watch?v=5jzYdBheYgg [accessed 7 August 2022].
24. TNA, WO 171/5143, War Diary, 5 Battalion, Coldstream Guards, June 1945, Farewell to Armour Parade Programme.
25. TNA, WO 171/5149, War Diary, 2nd Battalion, Scots Guards, 1 May 1945, Appendix A, Subject: Personal Message to Commander, GAD from Commander, 12 Corps.
26. H. Essame, *The Battle for Germany* (New York: Bonanza Books, 1969), p.213.
27. Fraser, *Wars and Shadows*, p.263.

Conclusions

1. *Military Effectiveness, Volume 1, The First World War, New Edition*, ed. by Allan R. Millett and Williamson Murray, (Cambridge: Cambridge University Press, 1988; repr. 2010), pp.1–4.
2. Harris, *Men, Ideas and Tanks*, pp.195–278.
3. TNA, CAB 106/220, Final Report of the Bartholomew Committee on lessons to be learnt from the operations in Flanders, July 1940.
4. TNA, 'PREM 3/55/10, Prime Minister's Office: Operational Correspondence and Papers, Army Manpower Requirements and Distribution, 1944–1945.

5. TNA, WO 205/1165, Wright, RAMC and Harkness, RAMC, A Survey of Casualties, pp.3–4.
6. TNA, WO 32/10395, Brigade of Guards, Manpower Ceiling, 9 June 1945, Memorandum, 20/Misc/2638 (SDI), Subject: Organisation of the Brigade of Guards, Major General J.S. Steele, Director of Staff Duties (DSD).
7. Buckley, *British Armour in the Normandy Campaign 1944*, p.29.
8. Martin, *The Fifteenth Scottish Division 1939–1945*, pp.29–57.
9. TNA, CAB 106/1061 N.W. Europe Campaign, OPERATION 'GOODWOOD', 18 July 1944, Notes of Conversation between General Dempsey Commander Second British Army and (a) Lt Col G.S. Jackson, 8 March 1951 (b) Capt. B.H. Liddell-Hart, 28 March 1952.'
10. Harrison Place, *Military Training in the British Army*, pp.111–114.
11. Murray, 'British Military Effectiveness in the Second World War', p.112.
12. TNA, WO 166/879, Guards Armoured Division, Training Directive No. 1. 21 August 1941.
13. Doherty, *British Armoured Divisions*, pp.118–121.
14. Farrell, *Reflections 1939–1945*, pp.59–75.
15. TNA, WO 171/1256, War Diary, 2nd (Armoured) Battalion, Irish Guards, 2 September 1944.
16. Lieutenant Colonel Coble, 'Operation Market Garden', p.27.
17. TNA, CAB 106/1060, Notes by Brigadier J. Hargest, Normandy Landing, June 1944.
18. Max Hastings, *Overlord: D-Day and the Battle for Normandy 1944* (London: Michael Joseph Ltd, 1984), pp.178–180.
19. Farrell, *Reflections 1939–1945*, pp.49–130.
20. TNA, WO 171/5142, War Diaries, 4th Battalion Coldstream Guards, 27 March–7 April 1945.
21. Buckley, *British Armour in the Normandy Campaign 1944*, p.120.
22. TNA, WO 205/1165, Wright, RAMC and Harkness, RAMC, A Survey of Casualties, p.4.
23. TNA, CAB 106/1060, Notes by Brigadier J. Hargest, Normandy Landing, June 1944, Notes, 30 June 1944, Tanks, p.30.
24. Jonathan Trigg, *D-Day Through German Eyes: How the Wehrmacht Lost France*. (Stroud: Amberley Publishing, 2019; repr. 2020), p.204.
25. Trigg, *D-Day Through German Eyes*, p.204.
26. Forbes, *The Grenadier Guards in the War of 1939–1945*, p.57.
27. Adair, *A Guards' General*, p.136.
28. Forty, *Companion to the British Army*, pp.328–329.
29. Doherty, *British Armoured Divisions*, p.122.
30. Howard and Sparrow, *The Coldstream Guards*, p.55.
31. Peaty, 'British Manpower Crisis, 1944', pp.143–145.
32. Verney, *The Guards Armoured Division*, p.15.
33. Erskine, *The Scots Guards*, p.396.

Postscript
1. S.P. Mackenzie, *British War Films 1939–1945* (London: Hambledon and London Ltd, 2001), pp.129–131.
2. Sue Harper and Vincent Porter, *British Cinema of the 1950s: The Decline of Deference* (Oxford: Oxford University Press, 2003; repr. 2007), p.281.
3. TBNA, C.A. LeJeune, 'They Were Not Divided', *The Sketch*, The Cinema, Wednesday 26 April 1950, p.386.

4. TBNA, Peter Burdett, 'The First Week of a Thrilling New Serial "They Were Not Divided"', *The Leven Mail*, Wednesday, 23 August 1950, p.6.
5. TBNA, Peter Burdett, 'They Were Not Divided', *Coatbridge Leader*, Saturday, 10 June 1950, p.4.
6. TBNA, 'They Were Not Divided', *The Brechin Advertiser*, Tuesday, 31 October 1950, p.7.
7. Mackenzie, *British War Films*, pp.130–131.
8. Trevor Popple, 'They Were Not Divided', *After the Battle*, Issue No. 133, 2006, pp.38–45.
9. Mackenzie, *British War Films*, p.131.
10. *They Were Not Divided*, dir. by Terence Young, (Two Cities, 1950), on DVD.
11. BCA, The Rosse Papers, T45, Envelopes 1–2, Letter, 5 January 1946, HQ Guards Division, Koln, Germany to Lord Rosse, Subject – Proposal to Write a History of the Guards Armoured Division.
12. BCA, The Rosse Papers, Box 2, T47, 1945–1957, Letter, 3 June 1946, Major General J.C.O. Marriott, Guards Division, BAOR, to Lord Rosse, asking if he will consider writing the History of the Guards Armoured Division.
13. Doherty, *British Armoured Divisions*, p.244.
14. Buckley, *British Armour in the Normandy*, pp.203–204.
15. Major Peter Verney, 'An Armoured Guardsman at War – Major General G.L. Verney, DSO, MVO, Genadier and Irish Guards (Part Three)', *The Guards Magazine*, Autumn edition, 2011, p.29.
16. History of the Guards Armoured Division, *The Guards Magazine*, autumn edition, 1951, p.141.
17. Frank Field, 'Obituary: Lord Bonham-Carter', *Independent*, Tuesday, 6 September 1994, www.independent.co.uk/news/people/obituary-lord-bonhamcarter-1447274.html [accessed 20 August 2022].
18. BCA, The Rosse Papers, Box 2, T47, 1945–1957, 4 April 1952, Letter from Major General J.A. Gascoigne, Headquarters, London District, Brigade of Guards to Lord Rosse copy of a letter he had written to G.L. Verney.
19. Adrian Bullock, Chris Jennings, and Nicola Timbrell, 'Net Book Agreement (NBA)', *A Dictionary of Publishing*, Oxford University Press, 2019, www.oxfordreference.com/view/10.1093/acref/9780191863592.001.0001/acref-9780191863592-e-159 [accessed 20 August 2022].
20. BCA, The Rosse Papers, Box 2, T47, 1945–1957, 24 April 1952, Letter from Major General G.L. Verney to Lord Rosse on subject of book dedication.
21. BCA, The Rosse Papers, Box 2, T47, 1945–1957, 9 December 1954, Letter, Lord Rosse to G.L. Verney about publication of their book.
22. BCA, The Rosse Papers, Box 2, T47, 1945–1957, 18 December 1954, Letter from Lord Rosse expressing disappointment with G.L. Verney's previous letter.
23. BCA, The Rosse Papers, Box 2, T47, 1945–1957, 30 December 1954, a note from G.L. Verney to Lord Rosse.
24. BCA, The Rosse Papers, Box 2, T47, 1945–1957, 9 February 1955, a detailed list of claims mainly against the Brigade of Guards by G.L. Verney to Lord Rosse.
25. BCA, The Rosse Papers, Box 2, T47, 1945–1957, 25 February 1955, Letter from Corbould Rigby & Co., Solicitors, to Lord Rosse including copy of commissioning letter for the Rosse and Hill book.
26. BCA, The Rosse Papers, Box 2, T47, 1945–1957, 9 June 1955, Letter from G.L. Verney to Major General Johnson regarding the book on the Guards Armoured Division.
27. BCA, The Rosse Papers, Box 2, T47, 1945–1957, 23 June 1955, Letter from G.L. Verney to Lord Rosse regarding the book project and dispute.

28. BCA, The Rosse Papers, Box 2, T47, 1945–1957, 12–13 July 1955, an exchange of letters between Collins publishers and Lord Rosse re. the book.
29. BCA, The Rosse Papers, Box 4, T46, 3 January 1956, Letter from Major Erskine Crum to Lord Rosse including Memorandum of Agreement dated 14 November 1955.
30. BCA, The Rosse Papers, Box 4, T46, 14 August 1956, Letter from G.L. Verney to Brigade Major, Household Brigade regarding copyright.
31. BCA, The Rosse Papers, Box 4, T46, 15 August 1956, Colonel Hill's response to G.L. Verney's letter of 14 August 1956.
32. BCA, The Rosse Papers, Box 4, T46, 21 August 1956, Major Vernon Erskine Crum, Brigade Headquarters, Horse Guards to Lord Rosse Re situation of dispute with G.L. Verney as of 21 August 1956.
33. BCA, The Rosse Papers, Box 4, T46, 21 August 1956 and 29 August 1956, Situation reports on the book dispute with G.L. Verney from Erskine Crum, Major, Brigade Major, Household Brigade.
34. The Story of the Guards Armoured Division by Captain the Earl of Rosse, MBE, and Colonel E.R. Hill, DSO., *The Guards Magazine*, summer edition, 1956, p.4.
35. BCA, The Rosse Papers, Box 4, T46, 17 September 1956, Letter from Mr. Gibb, Geoffrey Bles Ltd, Publishers, to Lord Rosse on the successful launch of the book, *The History of the Guards Armoured Division*.
36. BCA, The Rosse Papers, Box 4, T46, 28 September 1956, Note written by Major Erskine Crum on behalf of the Major General attaching a copy of a review of *The Story of the Guards Armoured Division* by G.L. Verney that appeared in *The Irish Times*, 22 September 1956.
37. BCA, The Rosse Papers, Box 4, T46, 20 November 1956, Letter from Lieutenant-Colonel V.F. Erskine Crum, Scots Guards, to Lord Rosse Re. G.L. Verney.
38. Verney, *The Guards Armoured Division: A Short History*, p.165.
39. Major General J.C. Haydon, 'Obituary Major General G.L. Verney, DSO, MVO, Lately Irish Guards.', *The Guards Magazine*, Summer edition 1957, pp.92–93.
40. Richard Attenborough, *A Bridge Too Far* (UK/US: Joseph E. Levine Presents, 1977).
41. A.T. McKenna, 'Joseph E. Levine and A Bridge Too Far (1977): A Producer's Labor of Love', *Historical Journal of Film, Radio and Television*, 31.2 (2011), pp.212–217.
42. Mead, *General 'BOY'*, pp.227–229.
43. Mead, *General 'BOY'*, pp.230–231.
44. Lieutenant Colonel Sir Julian Paget, 'The Capture of the Nijmegen Road Bridge', *The Guards Magazine*, spring 1978, pp.2–3.
45. Attenborough, *A Bridge Too Far*, on DVD.
46. A.T. McKenna, 'Joseph E. Levine and A Bridge Too Far (1977): A Producer's Labor of Love', *Historical Journal of Film, Radio and Television*, 31.2 (2011), p.218.
47. The Editor, 'The Film 'A Bridge Too Far'', *The Guards Magazine*, spring 1978, p.2.
48. Lieutenant Colonel Sir Julian Paget, 'The Capture of the Nijmegen Road Bridge', *The Guards Magazine*, spring 1978, pp.3–6.
49. Lieutenant Colonel Sir Julian Paget, 'The Capture of the Nijmegen Road Bridge', *The Guards Magazine*, spring 1978, p.9.
50. A.T. McKenna, 'Joseph E. Levine and A Bridge Too Far (1977): A Producer's Labor of Love', *Historical Journal of Film, Radio and Television*, 31.2 (2011), p.220.
51. Mead, *General 'BOY'*, p.231.
52. 'A Bridge Too Far (1977)', *Box Office Mojo* www.boxofficemojo.com/title/tt0075784/?ref_=bo_rl_ti [accessed 12 September 2022].

53. Roger Ebert, 'A Bridge Too Far', *Chicago Sun-Times*, 17 June 1977, www.rogerebert.com/reviews/a-bridge-too-far–1977 [accessed 12 September 2022].
54. A.T. McKenna, 'Joseph E. Levine and A Bridge Too Far (1977): A Producer's Labor of Love', *Historical Journal of Film, Radio and Television*, 31.2 (2011), pp.221–222.

Bibliography

Primary sources, unpublished
Birr Castle Archive (BCA), Rosse Papers
The Rosse Papers, T45, Trunk, Box 1, 1st (Motor) Battalion, Grenadier Guards, April 1944 to June 1945, Anonymous, Partial Account.
The Rosse Papers, T45, Story of Armour in NW Europe, 2nd Armoured Battalion, Irish Guards, July 1944–May 1945, Descriptive Stories of Actions and Successes, Written Account by 2I/C of Leading Sqn.
The Rosse Papers, T45, Trunk, Box 1, Summary of Actions and Lessons Learned, 2nd Household Cavalry Regiment, Document Undated, Author Unknown, Document Incomplete (Starting Page 16).
The Rosse Papers, T45, Envelopes 1–2, Letter, 5 January 1946, HQ Guards Division, Koln, Germany to Lord Rosse, Subject – Proposal to Write a History of the Guards Armoured Division, 1946.
The Rosse Papers, Box 2, T47, 1945–1957, Letter, 3 June 1946, Major General J.C.O. Marriott, Guards Division, BAOR, to Lord Rosse Asking If He Will Consider Writing the History of the Guards Armoured Division.
The Rosse Papers, Box 2, T47, 1945–1957, 4 April 1952, Letter from Major General J.A. Gascoigne, Headquarters, London District, Brigade of Guards to Lord Rosse Copy of a Letter He Had Written to G.L. Verney.
The Rosse Papers, Box 2, T47, 1945–1957, 24 April 1952, G.L. Verney, Letter.
The Rosse Papers, Box 2, T47, 1945–1957, 9 December 1954, Letter, Lord Rosse to G.L. Verney about Publication of Their Book.
The Rosse Papers, Box 2, T47, 1945–1957, 18 December 1954, Letter from Lord Rosse Expressing Disappointment with G.L. Verney's Previous Letter.
The Rosse Papers, Box 2, T47, 1945–1957, 30 December 1954, a Note from G.L. Verney to Lord Rosse.
The Rosse Papers, Box 2, T47, 1945–1957, 9 February 1955, a Detailed List of Claims Mainly against the Brigade of Guards by G.L. Verney to Lord Rosse.
The Rosse Papers, Box 2, T47, 1945–1957, 25 February 1955, Letter from Corbould Rigby & Co., Solicitors, to Lord Rosse.
The Rosse Papers, Box 2, T47, 1945–1957, 9 June 1955, Letter from G.L. Verney to Major General Johnson Regarding the History of the Guards Armoured Division Book.
The Rosse Papers, Box 2, T47, 1945–1957, 23 June 1955, Letter from G.L. Verney to Lord Rosse Regarding the Book Project.
The Rosse Papers, Box 2, T47, 1945–1957, 12–13 July 1955, an Exchange of Letters between Collins Publishers and Lord Rosse Re the Book.
The Rosse Papers, Box 4, T46, 3 January 1956, Letter from Major Erskine Crum to Lord Rosse Including Memorandum of Agreement Dated 14 November 1955.
The Rosse Papers, Box 4, T46, 14 August 1956, Letter from G.L. Verney to Brigade Major, Household Brigade Regarding Copyright.

The Rosse Papers, Box 4, T46, 15 August 1956, Colonel Hill's Response to G.L. Verney's Letter of 14 August 1956.
The Rosse Papers, Box 4, T46, 21 August 1956 and 29 August 1956, Situation Reports on the Book Dispute with G.L. Verney from Erskine Crum, Major, Brigade Major, Household Brigade.
The Rosse Papers, Box 4, T46, 17 September 1956, a Letter from Mr. Gibb, Geoffrey Bles Ltd, Publishers, to Lord Rosse on the Successful Launch of the Book, The History of the Guards Armoured Division.
The Rosse Papers, Box 4, T46, 28 September 1956, Note Written by Major Erskine Crum on Behalf of the Major General Attaching a Copy of a Review of The Story of the Guards Armoured Division by G.L. Verney That Appeared in The Irish Times, 22 September.
The Rosse Papers, Box 4, T46, 20 November 1956, Letter from Lieutenant Colonel V.F. Erskine Crum, Scots Guards, to Lord Rosse Re. G.L. Verney.

Churchill Archives Centre, Cambridge
Cambridge University: Churchill Archives Centre, Archive of Sir Percy James Grigg, PJGG 9/8-9, Correspondence with Field-Marshal Montgomery 1943–1945.

Cornelius Ryan Collection of World War II Papers
Box 115, Folder 37, Transcript Brigadier J.O.E. Vandeleur (Lt Col), Irish Guards, April 1967.
Box 114, Folder 38, Transcript Sir Allan Adair (General), Guards Armoured Division (Commander), April 1967.
Box 115, Folder 36, Transcript Giles Vandeleur (Lt Col), Irish Guards, April 1967.
Box 130, Folder 13, Colonel Hans-Peter Knaust, attached 10th SS Panzer, Transcript November 1967.

Imperial War Museum (IWM), London
IWM Archive, Private Papers of Lieutenant General Sir Giffard Martel KCB, Box No: Con Shelf (Volume 14), 8/3 Miscellaneous Correspondence Files, 1936–1955, B. Liddell Hart, Lessons from Normandy, February 1953, pp.1–3.
IWM (Oral History), Interview with Christopher Corby Isham Schofield, 4th Tank Battalion, Coldstream Guards, 6th Guards Tank Brigade, Catalogue No. 22121, REEL 1, Recorded 2001.
IWM (Oral History), Interview with George Ernest Teal, 1st (Armoured) Battalion, Coldstream Guards, Catalogue No. 18698, REEL 3, Recorded March 1999.
IWM (Oral History), Interview with Gordon Thomas Calthrop Campbell, 131st Field Regt, Royal Artillery, 15th (Scottish) Infantry Division, 1943, Catalogue No. 11955, REEL 4, Recorded 1991.
IWM (Oral History), Interview with Kenneth Banks Ohlson, 531st Battery, 190 Field Regiment, Royal Artillery, 15th (Scottish) Division, 1943–1944, Catalogue No. 33890, REEL 4, Recorded 2013.
IWM (Oral History), Interview with Major Charles Farrell, 3rd Battalion, Scots Guards, 6th Guards (Tank) Brigade, Catalogue No. 17835, REELS 12 and 13, Recorded 1998.
IWM (Oral History), Interview with Reg Sollitt, 4th Tank Battalion, Grenadier Guards, 6th Guards Tank Brigade, Catalogue No. 30006, REEL 3, Recorded 2007.
IWM (Oral History), Interview with Robert Charles Dare, Guardsman, 4th (Tank) Battalion, Coldstream Guards, Catalogue No. 18268, REELS 1–3, Recorded 1999.
IWM (Oral History), Interview with Ronald Buckland, Intelligence Officer, 4th (Tank) Battalion, Coldstream Guards, Catalogue No. 22369, REEL 1, Recorded 2002.

IWM (Oral History), Interview with William Gordon Cantlay, 14 Field Squadron, Royal Engineers, Guards Armoured Division, Catalogue No. 22100, REELS 1–6, Recorded 2001.

IWM (Oral History), Interview with William Hugh Griffiths, 2nd Battalion, Welsh Guards, Guards Armoured Division, Catalogue No.17506, REEL 1, Recorded 1997.

Regimental Archive, Coldstream Guards, Wellington Barracks, London

The Regimental Archivist, Regimental Headquarters, Coldstream Guards, Wellington Barracks, London, War Diary, 1st (Armoured) Battalion Coldstream Guards, 1944–1945.

Second World War Experience Centre (SWWEC)

Sound archive, Tapes 627 and 650, Interview with General Peter R. Leuchars, Recorded October 2000.

The Liddell Hart Centre for Military Archives, King's College London

O'CONNOR, Gen Sir Richard, (1889–1981), OCONNOR: 8, Appraisal of the Careers of Selected Senior Military Personnel, 1971, Major J.K. Nairne Recollections of Major General Sir Allan Adair. (London).

O'CONNOR, Gen Sir Richard, (1889–1981), OCONNOR: 8, Appraisal of the Careers of Selected Senior Military Personnel, 1971, Subject Major General Sir Allan Adair (London, 1971).

The National Archives (TNA), Kew, London

CAB 106/1060, Notes by Brigadier J. Hargest, Normandy Landing, June 1944.

CAB 106/1061, N.W. Europe Campaign, OPERATION 'GOODWOOD', 18 July 1944, Notes of Conversation between General Dempsey Commander Second British Army and (a) Lt Col G.S. Jackson, 8 March 1951 (b) Capt. B.H. Liddell-Hart, 28 March 1952.

CAB 106/220, Final Report of the Bartholomew Committee on Lessons to Be Learnt from the Operations in Flanders, July 1940.

PREM 3/55/10, Prime Minister's Office: Operational Correspondence and Papers, Army Manpower Requirements and Distribution, 1944–1945.

WO 32/10395, Brigade of Guards, Manpower Ceiling, Prime Minister, Winston Churchill, Personal Minute, Serial No M.588/5 to the Secretary of State for War, Sir James Grigg, 10 June 1945.

WO 32/10395, Brigade of Guards, Manpower Ceiling, Note from Secretary of State for War, Sir James Grigg, in Response to Minute M.588/5, Prime Minister, Winston Churchill, 11 June 1945.

WO 32/10395, Brigade of Guards, Manpower Ceiling, the Secretary of State for War, Sir James Grigg, a Note to Sir Alan 'Tommy' Lascelles, Private Secretary to King George VI, 14 August 1943.

WO 32/10395, Brigade of Guards, Manpower Ceiling, The Organisation of the Brigade of Guards in the Second Stage of the War, Deputy Chief of the Imperial General Staff (DCIGS), 25 May 1945.

WO 32/10395, Brigade of Guards, Manpower Ceiling, Memorandum, 20/Misc/2638 (SDI), Subject: Organisation of the Brigade of Guards, Major General J.S. Steele, Director of Staff Duties (DSD), 9 June 1945.

WO 32/10395, Brigade of Guards, Manpower Ceiling, DO/SDI/9876(SDI), Letter from Major General J.S. Steele, Director of Staff Duties (DSD), Responding to Letter S/466 from Lieutenant General Sir H. Charles Loyd, Major General Commanding the Brigade of Guards, 21 May 1945.

Bibliography 193

WO 32/10395, Brigade of Guards, Manpower Ceiling, Ref. No. S/466, Letter from Lieutenant General Sir H. Charles Loyd, Major General Commanding the Brigade of Guards, to Major General J.S. Steele, Director of Staff Duties (DSD), 19 May 1945.

WO 32/10395, Brigade of Guards, Manpower Ceiling, Undated, Anonymous, Draft Note, Headed Prime Minister, 6A. Subject: Guards Armoured Units to Revert to Infantry.

WO 32/11542, Brigade of Guards Organisation, 1945–1949, Letter from Major General J.S. Steele, Director of Staff Duties (DSD) to Lieutenant General Sir H. Charles Loyd, Major General Commanding the Brigade of Guards, 28 May 1945.

WO 32/11542, Brigade of Guards Organisation, 1945–1949, File No. GOC. 4/86543, Letter from Lieutenant General Sir H. Charles Loyd, Major General Commanding the Brigade of Guards, to Major General J.S. Steele, Director of Staff Duties (DSD).

WO 166/10733, War Diary, H.Q. 5th Guards Armoured Brigade, 5 May 1943.

WO 166/12461, War Diary, 4th (Tank) Battalion, Coldstream Guards, 6–26 March 1943.

WO 166/12466, War Diary, 4th (Tank) Battalion, Grenadier Guards, Brigade Exercise ALEXANDER, 23–26 July 1943.

WO 166/12468, War Diary, 2nd (Armoured) Battalion, Irish Guards, 16 March 1943.

WO 166/12469, War Diary, 3rd (Infantry) Battalion, Irish Guards, Northwood, 1–4 February 1943.

WO 166/12470, War Diary, 3rd (Tank) Battalion, Scots Guards, 14–15 June 1943.

WO 166/12470, War Diary, 3rd (Tank) Battalion, Scots Guards, Exercise BLACKCOCK, August–October 1943.

WO 166/12473, War Diary, 2nd Battalion, Welsh Guards, March 1943.

WO 166/12546, War Diary, 2nd Battalion, Glasgow Highlanders, Appendix A, Training Programme, 15 June–2 July 1943. Appendix H, Training Instructions No. 4 with 4th (Tank) Battalion, Coldstream Guards, 1943.

WO 166/12597, War Diary, 6th Battalion, King's Own Scottish Borderers, May–July 1943.

WO 166/4091, War Diary, 1st (Armoured) Battalion, Coldstream Guards, Appendix C, Battalion Reorganisation, Instruction No. 2., September 1941.

WO 166/4091, War Diary, 1st Battalion, Coldstream Guards, Appendix 2, Reorganisation, General Instructions, 19 June 1941.

WO 166/6656, War Diary, Headquarters, 6th Guards (Armoured) Brigade, Appendix B, Exercise CRUISER, 5–6 June 1942.

WO 166/6656, War Diary, HQ 6th Guards (Armoured) Brigade, 23 September 1942.

WO 166/8566, War Diary, 4th Battalion, Coldstream Guards, 6th Brigade, Guards Armoured Division, 12 November 1942.

WO 166/8569, Letter from Sergison-Brooke to Brigade of Guards.

WO 166/8576 War Diary, 2nd (Armoured) Battalion, Irish Guards, 22 June 1942.

WO 166/8576, War Diary, 2nd (Armoured) Battalion, Irish Guards, 12 June 1942.

WO 166/8576, War Diary, 2nd (Armoured) Battalion, Irish Guards, 19 October 1942.

WO 166/8576, War Diary, 2nd (Armoured) Battalion, Irish Guards, Exercise on Salisbury Plain, 22 May 1942.

WO 166/879, Schreiber, D., Guards Armoured Division, Training Directive No. 1. Detailed Notes on Individual and Crew Training for Armoured Brigades, 1941.

WO 166/879, Training Directive No. 10: Amendment of Training for Armoured Brigades and Bns.

WO 171/1251, War Diary, 4th (Tank) Battalion, Coldstream Guards, 1 December 1944.

WO 171/1253, 1st (Motor) Battalion, Grenadier Guards, Appendix A, Account of the Clearing of DROUET WOODS and Battle of DROUET HILL, 2–4 August 1944, pp.3–5.

WO 171/1255, War Diary, 4th (Tank) Battalion, Grenadier Guards, Entry 20 October 1944 and Appendix A, Special Order of the Day, Brigadier Greenacre, October 1944.
WO 171/1256, War Diary, 2nd (Armoured) Battalion, Irish Guards, 2 September 1944.
WO 171/1256, War Diary, 2nd (Armoured) Battalion, Irish Guards, 28 July 1944.
WO 171/1256, War Diary, 2nd (Armoured) Battalion, Irish Guards, September 1944.
WO 171/1258, War Diary, 3rd (Tank) Battalion, Scots Guards, Appendix K1, Account of 3rd (Tank) Battalion, Scots Guards Action at CAUMONT, Sheet Six, 30 July 1944.
WO 171/1258, War Diary, 3rd (Tank) Battalion, Scots Guards, Appendix K3, Account of Action Fought by 32nd Guards Brigade and 3rd (Tank) Battalion, Scots Guards at Chenedolle, Sheet 7 (p.13), 1944.
WO 171/377, HQ Guards Armoured Division, October to November 1944, GDS ARMD DIV REVISED COMPOSITION OF BRIGADES, 30 November 1944.
WO 171/377, War Diary, Headquarters, Guards Armoured Division, November 1944, Appendix HH, Intelligence Summary, 18 October 1944.
WO 171/390, War Diary, Provost Company, Guards Armoured Division, September 1944.
WO 171/4321, War Diary, HQ 6th Guards (Armoured) Brigade, 27 March 1945.
WO 171/4321, War Diary, HQ 6th Guards (Tank) Brigade, 1 February–27 March 1945.
WO 171/4321, War Diary, HQ 6th Guards (Tank) Brigade, 3 April 1945. 1945.
WO 171/5141, War Diary, 1st (Armoured) Battalion, Coldstream Guards, 28 March 1944.
WO 171/5142, War Diaries, 4th Battalion Coldstream Guards, 27 March–7 April 1945.
WO 171/5142, War Diary, 4th Battalion, Coldstream Guards, 27 March 1945.
WO 171/5142, War Diary, 4th Battalion, Coldstream Guards, 5 April 1945.
WO 171/5144 War Diary 1st (Motor) Battalion Grenadier Guards 1945.
WO 171/5147, War Diary, 2nd (Armoured) Battalion, Irish Guards, March 1945, Training Instructions No. 3, Lt Col G. Vandeleur, 11 March 1945.
WO 171/5149, War Diary, 2nd Battalion, Scots Guards, 3 February 1945.
WO 171/5149, War Diary, 2nd Battalion, Scots Guards, Appendix C, Drills for Operations and Training Based on Lessons Recently Learned, February 1945.
WO 171/5150, 3rd Battalion, Scots Guards, 27 March – 31 March 1945.
WO 171/607, War Diary, 6th Guards (Tank) Brigade HQ, 12–19 October 1944.
WO 171/638, 32nd Guards Brigade, War Diaries, Brigade Intelligence Summary No. 47, up to 1600hrs 21 September 1944.
WO171/1252, War Diary, 5th Battalion, Coldstream Guards, 13 July 1944.
WO171/1253, War Diary, 1st (Motor) Battalion, Grenadier Guards, Appendix A, Account of Clearing DROUET WOODS and Battle of DROUET HILL, p.3, August 1944.
WO171/1253, War Diary, 1st (Motor) Battalion, Grenadier Guards, 13 July 1944.
WO171/1256, War Diary, 2nd (Armoured) Battalion, Irish Guards, 10 July 1944.
WO171/372, War Diary, HQ Guards Armoured Division, Counter Mortar Policy, 25 November 1944.
WO171/376, War Diary, HQ Guards Armoured Division, 1 September 1944.
WO171/4103, War Diary, HQ 'G' Branch, Guards Armoured Division, Appendix 30, Tactical Investigation Directorate, Use of Sherman Tks in Arty Role, 30 January 1945.
WO171/4318, War Diary, HQ 5th Guards Armoured Brigade, February 1945.
WO171/4357, War Diary, HQ 32nd Guards Brigade, 10 February 1945.
WO171/5141, War Diary, 1st (Armoured) Battalion, Coldstream Guards, 3 to 4 April 1945.
WO171/5143, War Diary, 5th Battalion, Coldstream Guards, 3 April 1945.
WO171/5143, War Diary, 5th Battalion, Coldstream Guards, Farewell to Armour Parade Programme, June 1945.

WO 171/5149, War Diary, 2nd Battalion, Scots Guards, 1 May 1945, Appendix A, Subject: Personal Message to Commander, GAD from Commander, 12 Corps.
WO171/605, 5th Guards Armoured Brigade, War Diaries, Appendix J., Memorandum Entitled Fighting in Bocage Country, 15 August 1944.
WO171/638, War Diary, HQ 32nd Guards Brigade, July 1944, Entry for 13 July 1944.
WO 194/845, Fighting Vehicle Proving Establishment, F.T. 1553, Field Trials Report on Comparative Trials of Various A.F.V.s in Soft Ground Conditions, December 1944.
WO 205/1165, A Survey of Casualties Amongst Armoured Units in North West Europe, Captain H.B. Wright, R.A.M.C. and Captain R.D. Harkness, R.A.M.C. Medical Research Council Team, No. 2 Operational Research Section (ORS), Main H.Q. 21 Army Group.
WO 291/2385, Analysis of 75mm Sherman Tank Casualties between 6 June and 10 July 1944. No. 2 Operational Research Section, 3 April 1945.
WO 291/399, Army Operational Research Group, A.O.R.G. Memorandum No. 45, Casualties to Churchill Tanks in 25 PDR H.E. Concentrations, Appendix C – Short Account of the Trials at Larkhill, 5 June 1943.
WO 291/399, Army Operational Research Group, A.O.R.G. Memorandum No. 45, Casualties to Churchill Tanks in 25 PDR H.E. Concentrations, 9 July 1943.

War Office Publications
Military Training Pamphlet No. 41, Part 2, The Armoured Regiment: The Tactical Handling of the Armoured Division and Its Components, 1943.
Military Training Pamphlet No. 63, The Co-Operation of Tanks and Infantry Divisions, 1944.

Welsh Guards Archive (WGA), Wellington Barracks, London
WGA, 2nd Battalion, Welsh Guards, Box File: Training, 1944–1945, five-page assessment of the organisation and training of 2nd Battalion, Welsh Guards, the author is anonymous.
WGA, 2nd Battalion, Welsh Guards, Box File: Training, 1944–1945, Tactical Employment of Armour, Lt Col J.C. Lewis, 10 October 1944, p.3.
WGA, Box File: Training, 1944–1945, Extracts from a Letter Written by Lieutenant N. Kearsley, 2nd (Armoured Recce) Battalion, Welsh Guards, 9 August 1944. Subject: Experiences of Combat and Lessons Learned. The Letter Was Circulated to Regimental Headquarters.
WGA, Sergeant Charles Murrell, Box-Folder 123, Hand-Written Diaries, Volume 11, Guards Armoured Division (Ii), 1942–1944, Thursday 10 June 1943, p.119.
WGA, Sergeant Charles Murrell, Box-Folder 123, Hand-Written Diaries, Volume 11, Guards Armoured Division (Ii), 1942–1944, Thursday 19 November 1942, p.56.
WGA, Sergeant Charles Murrell, Box-Folder 123, Hand-Written Diaries, Volume 11, Guards Armoured Division (ii), 1942–1944, Thursday 25 May 1944, Visit by General Eisenhower and Speech, pp.245–246.

Primary sources, published
Adair, Allan, *A Guards' General: The Memoirs of Major General Sir Allan Adair* (London: Hamish Hamilton, 1986).
Boscawen, Robert, *Armoured Guardsmen: A War Diary, June 1944–April 1945* (Pen & Sword, 2001).
Bulteel, Christopher, *Something About a Soldier: The Wartime Memoirs of Christopher Bulteel, MC* (Shrewsbury: Airlife Publishing Ltd, 2000).
Carrington, Peter Alexander Rupert, *Reflect on Things Past: The Memoirs of Lord Carrington* (London: Collins, 1988).

Carver, Michael, *Out of Step: Memoirs of a Field Marshal* (London: Hutchinson, 1989).
Eager, William Arthur, *Beyond the Rhine – The Sacrificial Lamb* (Amazon, 1995).
Elliott, W.A., *Esprit de Corps: A Scots Guards Officer on Active Service 1943–1945* (Norwich: Michael Russell (Publishing) Ltd, 1996).
Farrell, Charles, *Reflections 1939–1945: A Scots Guards Officer in Training and War* (Bishop Auckland: Pentland Press, 2000).
Fraser, David, *Wars and Shadows: Memoirs of General Sir David Fraser* (London: Allen Lane, Penguin Press, 2002).
Gorman, Sir John, *Times of My Life: An Autobiography* (Leo Cooper, 2002).
Hills, Stuart, *By Tank into Normandy* (2nd ed.; Orion Books Ltd: London, 2003).
Horrocks, Lieutenant General Sir Brian, *A Full Life* (London: Collins, 1960).
Howard, Michael Eliot, *Captain Professor: A Life in War and Peace* (Continuum UK: London, 2006).
Montgomery, Field Marshal Viscount of Alamein, *21 Army Group: Normandy to the Baltic* (Pickle Partners Publishing, 1946).
Murrell, Charles, *Dunkirk to the RhineLand: Diaries and Sketches of Sergeant C.S. Murrell, Welsh Guards*, ed. by Nick Murrell (Barnsley: Pen & Sword Military, 2011).
Pereira, Jocelyn, *A Distant Drum: War Memories of the Intelligence Officer of the 5th Bn Coldstream Guards: 1944–45* (Gale & Polden, 1948).
Render, David; Tootal, Stuart, *Tank Action: An Armoured Troop Commander's War 1944–45* (Hachette UK, 2016).
Roberts, Major General G.P.B., *From the Desert to the Baltic* (London: William Kimber and Co. Ltd, 1987).
Robson, Margaret, *Dig or Die: The Memoirs of Guardsman John Elliott, The Second Battalion Coldstream Guards in Tunisia and Italy 1943–1944* (Adam Robson, 2016).
Tout, Ken, *By Tank: D to VE Days* (Robert Hale Limited, 2007).
Vandeleur, J.O.E, *A Soldier's Story* (privately printed for the author by Gale & Polden, 1967).
Whitelaw, William, *The Whitelaw Memoirs* (Aurum Press Ltd: London, 1989).
Wilson, B.D., *The Ever Open Eye* (Cambridge: Melrose Books, 2014).

Secondary sources
Books
Adams, John A., *The Battle for Western Europe, Fall 1944: An Operational Assessment* (Indiana University Press, 2010).
Allport, Alan, *Browned Off and Bloody-Minded: The British Soldier Goes to War, 1939–1945* (New Haven and London: Yale University Press, 2015).
Anonymous, *Taurus Pursuant: A History of 11th Armoured Division* (Headquarters 11th Armoured Division, 1945).
Bates, Aaron, *The Last German Victory: Operation Market Garden 1944* (Yorkshire: Pen & Sword Military, 2021).
Baynes, John Christopher Malcolm, *The Forgotten Victor: General Sir Richard O'Connor, KT, GCB, DSO, MC* (London: Brassey's (UK) Ltd, 1989).
Beevor, Antony, *Arnhem: The Battle for the Bridges, 1944* (London: Penguin Random House UK, 2018).
Bennett, David, *A Magnificent Disaster: The Failure of Market Garden, the Arnhem Operation, September 1944* (Casemate, 2008).
Black, Jeremy, *Tank Warfare* (Indiana: Indiana University Press, 2020).
Blaxland, Gregory, *Destination Dunkirk: The Story of Gort's Army* (London: William Kimber and Co. Ltd, 1973).

Briant, Keith, *Fighting with the Guards* (Evans Bros., 1958).
Buckingham, William F., *Arnhem 1944* (Stroud: Tempus Publishing Ltd).
Buckley, John, *Monty's Men: The British Army and the Liberation of Europe* (New Haven and London: Yale University Press, 2013).
——, *British Armour in the Normandy Campaign 1944* (London: Routledge, 2004).
Buckley, John, and Peter Preston-Hough, *Operation Market-Garden: The Campaign for the Low Countries, Autumn 1944: Seventy Years On*, ed. by Peter Buckley, John, Preston-Hough (Solihull: Helion and Company Ltd, 2016).
Bullock, Adrian, Chris Jennings, and Nicola Timbrell, 'Net Book Agreement (NBA)', *A Dictionary of Publishing.: Oxford University Press.*, 2019, www.oxfordreference.com/view/10.1093/acref/9780191863592.001.0001/acref-9780191863592-e-159 [accessed 20 August 2022].
Caravaggio, Angelo, *21 Days in Normandy: Maj. Gen. George Kitching & the 4th Canadian Armoured Division*; 1st ed. (Pen & Sword, 2016).
Coble, Lt Col Elizabeth A., *Operation Market Garden: Case Study for Analyzing Senior Leader Responsibilities* (Pickle Partners Publishing, 2015).
Collier, Richard, *The Sands of Dunkirk* (Glasgow: William Collins Sons & Co. Ltd., 1961).
Cooper, Belton Y., *Death Traps: The Survival of an American Armoured Division in World War II* (New York: The Random House Publishing Group, 1998).
Copp, Terry, *Cinderella Army: The Canadians in North-west Europe, 1944–1945* (University of Toronto Press, 2007).
Daglish, I., *Operation Bluecoat (Battleground Europe)* (Pen & Sword: South Yorkshire, 2003).
——, *Operation Goodwood: Attack by Three British Armoured Divisions* (Barnsley: Pen & Sword Books Limited, 2004).
Danchev, Alex, and Daniel Todman, eds., *War Diaries, 1939–1945: Field Marshal Lord Alanbrooke* (London: Weidenfeld & Nicolson, 2001).
Darby, Hugh, and Marcus Cunliffe, *A Short Story of 21 Army Group: The British and Canadian Armies in the Campaigns in North-West Europe, 1944–1945* (Aldershot: Gale & Polden Limited, 1949).
Delaforce, Patrick, *Monty's Rhine Adventure: War and Peace September 1944 NW Europe* (Fonthill Media, 2014).
——, *Churchill's Desert Rats: From Normandy to Berlin with the 7th Armoured Division* (2nd ed.; Pen & Sword: South Yorkshire, 2010).
——, *Monty's Iron Sides: From the Normandy Beaches to Bremen with the 3rd Division* (Chancellor Press: London, 1995).
——, *The Black Bull: From Normandy to the Baltic with the 11th Armoured Division*, repr. 2002 (Stroud: Sutton Publishing Ltd, 1993).
Doherty, Richard, *British Armoured Divisions and Their Commanders, 1939–1945* (Barnsley: Pen & Sword, 2013).
Dunphie, Christopher, *The Pendulum of Battle: Operation GOODWOOD – July 1944* (Barnsley: Pen & Sword Books Limited, 2004).
Ellis, John, *The Sharp End: The Fighting Man in World War II* (Newton Abbot: David & Charles, 1980).
Ellis, Major Lionel Frederic., *Victory in the West, Volume I, The Battle of Normandy* (H.M. Stationery Office, 1962).
——, and Warhurst, Lt Colonel A.E., *Victory in the West, Volume II, The Defeat of Germany* (Her Majesty's Stationery Office: London, 1962).
——, *Welsh Guards at War* (Aldershot: Gale and Polden, 1946).

Erskine, David, *The Scots Guards, 1919–1955* (London: William Clowes and Sons Ltd, 1956).
Essame, H., *The Battle for Germany* (New York: Bonanza Books, 1969).
Fennell, Jonathan, *Fighting the People's War: The British and Commonwealth Armies and the Second World War* (Cambridge: Cambridge University Press, 2019).
Fitzgerald, Desmond J.L., *History of the Irish Guards in the Second World War* (Aldershot: Gale and Polden, 1949).
Fletcher, David, and Steven J Zaloga, 'Staghound Armoured Car', in *British Battle Tanks: US Made Tanks of World War II* (Oxford: Osprey Publishing, 2018).
——, *British Battle Tanks: British-Made Tanks of World War II* (Oxford: Osprey Publishing, 2017).
——, *Sherman Firefly* (Oxford: Osprey Publishing, 2008).
——, *The Great Tank Scandal: British Armour in the Second World War* (London: Stationery Office Books, 1989).
——, *The Universal Tank: British Armour in the Second World War* (London: Stationery Office Books, 1989).
——, *Churchill Tank: Vehicle History and Specification* (HMSO: London, 1983).
Forbes, Patrick, *The Grenadier Guards in the War of 1939–1945: The Campaigns in North-West Europe* (Aldershot: Gale and Polden Limited, 1949).
——, *6th Guards Tank Brigade: The Story of Guardsmen in Churchhill Tanks*, The Naval (London: Sampson, Low, Marston & Co., 1946).
Ford, Ken, *Caen 1944: Montgomery's Break-out Attempt* (Bloomsbury Publishing, 2011).
Ford, Roger, *The Sherman Tank* (Staplehurst: Brown Packaging Books Ltd, 1999).
Forrester, Charles, *Monty's Functional Doctrine: Combined Arms Doctrine in British 21st Army Group in North-west Europe, 1944–45* (Helion and Company, 2015).
Forty, George, *Companion to the British Army 1939–1945* (Port Stroud: The History Press, 1998).
French, David, *Military Identities: The Regimental System, the British Army, and the British People c. 1870–2000* (Oxford University Press, 2005).
——, *Raising Churchill's Army: The British Army and the War against Germany, 1919–1945* (New York: Oxford University Press, 2000).
Gat, Azar, *British Armour Theory and the Rise of the Panzer Arm: Revising the Revisionists* (St Antony's Series, Palgrave Macmillan, 2000).
Genesis, Employment, Aftermath: First World War Tanks and the New Warfare, 1900–1945, Ed. Searle, Alaric, (Helion and Company Ltd: Solihull, 2015).
Gill, Ronald and Groves, John, *Club Route in Europe: The Story of 30 Corps in the European Campaign* (Werner Degener: Hanover, 1945).
Grant, Neil, *British Tank Crewman 1939–45* (Yale University Press, New Haven and London, 2017).
Hanning, H., *The British Grenadiers: Three Hundred and Fifty Years of the First Regiment of Foot Guards 1656–2006* (Pen & Sword Military, 2006).
Harper, Sue, and Vincent Porter, *British Cinema of the 1950s: The Decline of Deference* (Oxford: Oxford University Press, 2003).
Harris, J.P., *Men, Ideas and Tanks: British Military Thought and Armoured Forces, 1903–1939* (Manchester: Manchester University Press, 1995).
Hart, Russell A., *Clash of Arms: How the Allies Won in Normandy* (Boulder, USA: Lynne Rienner Publishers, 2001).
Hart, Stephen Ashley, *Colossal Cracks: Montgomery's 21st Army Group in North-west Europe, 1944–45* (Stackpole Books, 2007).

Hastings, Max, *Armageddon: The Battle for Germany 1944–45* (Pan Macmillan, 2012).
——, *All Hell Let Loose: The World at War 1939–1945* (London: HarperPress, 2011).
——, *Overlord: D-Day and the Battle for Normandy 1944* (Michael Joseph Ltd: London, 1984).
Holland, James, *Brothers in Arms: One Legendary Tank Regiment's Bloody War from D-Day to VE-Day* (London: Bantam Press, 2021).
——, *Normandy '44: D-Day and the Battle for France* (Transworld Publishers: London, 2019).
How, Major J.J., *Normandy: The British Breakout* (London: William Kimber and Co. Ltd, 1981).
Howard, Michael Eliot, and John Hanbury Angus Sparrow, *The Coldstream Guards: 1920–1946* (London: Oxford University Press, 1951).
Jackson, G.S., *Operations of Eighth Corps: Account of Operations from Normandy to the River Rhine* (St. Clements Press, 1948).
Keegan, John, ed., *Churchill's Generals* (London: George Weidenfeld & Nicolson Ltd, 1991).
——, *Six Armies in Normandy: From D-Day to the Liberation of Paris* (Jonathan Cape Ltd: London, 1982).
Kersh, Gerald, *They Die with Their Boots Clean* (London: William Heinemann Ltd, 1941).
Kershaw, Robert, *Tank Men: The Human Story of Tanks at War* (Hodder & Stoughton: London, 2008).
——, *It Never Snows in September: The German View of MARKET-GARDEN and the Battle of Arnhem, September 1944* (Marlborough: The Crowood Press, 1990).
Liddell Hart, Basil H., *The Tanks: The History of the Royal Tank Regiment. Vol. II* (London, 1959).
Mackenzie, S.P., *British War Films 1939–1945* (London: Hambledon and London Ltd, 2001).
Martel, Lieutenant General Sir Giffard Le Q., *Our Armoured Forces* (London: Faber and Faber Limited, 1945).
Martin, Lieutenant General H.G., *The Fifteenth Scottish Division 1939–1945* (2022 ed.; William Blackwood and Sons Ltd, 1948).
McKee, Alexander, *The Race for the Rhine Bridges, 1940, 1944, 1945* (Souvenir Press, 2012).
——, *Caen: Anvil of Victory* (London: Souvenir Press, 1964).
McNish, Robin, *The Iron Division: The History of the 3rd Division 1809–1989* (3rd Armoured Division, HM Stationery Office: London, 1978).
Mead, Richard, *General 'BOY', The Life of Lieutenant General Sir Frederick Browning* (Barnsley: Pen & Sword Military, 2010).
Melvin, Ronald, *The Guards and Caterham: The Soldier's Story* (Old Coulsdon: Guardroom Publications, 1999).
Messenger, Charles, *For Love of Regiment: A History of British Infantry, Volume 2, 1915–1994* (Pen & Sword, 1994).
Millett, Allan R., and Williamson Murray, eds., *Military Effectiveness, Volume 1, The First World War, New Edition*, New Editio (Cambridge: Cambridge University Press, 2010).
Murray, Williamson, 'British Military Effectiveness in the Second World War', in *Military Effectiveness: Volume 3 The Second World War New Edition*, ed. by Allan R. Millett and Williamson Murray (Cambridge: Cambridge University Press, 2010).
Napier, Stephen, *The Armoured Campaign in Normandy: June–August 1944* (The History Press, 2015).
Neillands, Robin, *The Battle of Normandy 1944* (London: Cassell Military Paperbacks, 2002).
Orde, Roden, *The Household Cavalry at War: Second Household Cavalry Regiment* (Aldershot: Gale and Polden, 1953).
Paget, Julian, *The Crusading General: The Life of General Sir Bernard Paget, GCB, DSO, MC* (Barnsley: Pen & Sword Books Limited, 2008).

——, *Second to None: The History of the Coldstream Guards 1650–2000* (Pen & Sword, 2000).
Place, Timothy Harrison, *Military Training in the British Army, 1940–1944: From Dunkirk to D-Day* (London: Frank Cass Publishers, 2000).
Plant, John, *British Tank Warfare* (New Generation Publishing: London, 2015).
Report on Operation 'Veritable' 8 February to 10 March 1945, 1946.
Rosse, Captain the Earl of, and Colonel E.R. Hill, *The Story of the Guards Armoured Division 1941–1945* (London: Geoffrey Bles Ltd, 1956).
Rostron, Peter, *The Life and Times of General Sir Miles Dempsey: Monty's Army Commander* (Pen & Sword Military, 2010).
Ryan, Cornelius, *A Bridge Too Far* (Wordsworth Editions Ltd: Ware, 1999).
Ryder, Rowland, *Oliver Leese* (London: Hamish Hamilton Ltd, 1987).
Salmon, Andrew, *To the Last Round: The Epic British Stand on the Imjin River, Korea 1951* (London: Aurum Press Ltd, 2009).
Samuels, Martin, *Piercing the Fog of War: The Theory and Practice of Command in the British and German Armies, 1918–1940* (Warwick: Helion and Company Ltd, 2019).
Sandars, John, and Michael Chappell, *British Guards Armoured Division 1941–45* (Oxford: Osprey Publishing, 1979).
Saunders, Tim, *Hell's Highway: US 101st Airborne – 1944* (Pen & Sword, 2009).
——, *Nijmegen: US 82nd Airborne Division–1944* (Pen & Sword, 2008.)
Searle, Alaric, *Armoured Warfare: A Military, Political and Global History* (London: Bloomsbury Publishing, 2017).
——, ed., *The Military Papers and Correspondence of Major General J.F.C. Fuller, 1916–1933* (Stroud: The History Press for the Army Records Society, 2017).
Sheffield, G.D., *The Redcaps: A History of the Royal Military Police and Its Antecedents from the Middle Ages to the Gulf War* (London: Brassey's (UK) Ltd, 1994).
Sliz, John, *Bridging the Club Route: Guards Armoured Division's Engineers During Operation Market Garden* (Toronto, Canada: Travelogue 219, 2015).
Thompson, R.W., *The Battle for the Rhineland* (London: Hutchinson & Co. (Publishers) Ltd, 1958).
Trigg, Jonathan, *D-Day Through German Eyes: How the Wehrmacht Lost France* (Stroud: Amberley Publishing, 2019).
Urban, Mark, *The Tank War: The Men, the Machines and the Long Road to Victory* (Hachette UK, 2013).
Urquhart, Robert Elliott, *Arnhem* (Pen & Sword, 2011).
Verney, Major General G.L., *The Desert Rats: The History of the 7th Armoured Division, 1938 to 1945* (With a Foreword by Sir John Harding; 2nd ed.; Arrow Books: London, 1957).
——, *The Guards Armoured Division: A Short History* (London: Hutchinson & Co. (Publishers) Ltd, 1955).
Verney, Peter, *The Micks: The Story of the Irish Guards*, Abridged (London: Pan Books Ltd, 1970).
Warner, Philip, *Horrocks: The General Who Led from the Front* (Hamish Hamilton Ltd: London, 1984).
Whitaker, W.D. & S., *Rhineland: The Battle to End the War* (London: Mandarin Paperbacks, 1989).
Whitworth, Reginald Henry; Whitworth, Rex, *The Grenadier Guards (the First or Grenadier Regiment of Foot Guards)* (Leo Cooper Books, 1974).
Williams, Philip Hamlyn, *War on Wheels: The Mechanisation of the British Army in the Second World War* (The History Press, 2016).

Winton, Harold R., *To Change an Army: General Sir John Burnett-Stuart and British Armored Doctrine, 1927–1938* (Lawrence: University Press of Kansas, 1988).
Zaloga, Steven J., *Operation Market-Garden 1944: The American Airborne Missions* (Bloomsbury Publishing, 2014).
——, *Armored Thunderbolt: The U.S. Army Sherman in World War II* (Merchanicsburg: Stackpole Books, 2008).
——, *Sherman Medium Tank 1942–1945* (Oxford: Osprey Publishing, 1993).

Journals and newspapers
'14 Killed on War Exercise', *Daily Mirror*, Tuesday 14 April 1942.
'An Irish Guardsman tells how the Army's No. 1 fighting man is made. To the Telegraph's military correspondent he reveals that Guardsmen are human under the bearskin', *Ballymena Weekly Telegraph*, April 1941, p.6.
Adair, Major General A.H.S., 'The Guards Armoured Division', *The Household Brigade Magazine*, Winter, 1945, pp.141–146.
'Army Manoeuvres – M.P.s to Ask About Casualties', *The Daily Mail*, Thursday 16 April 1942.
Austin, A.B., 'THE GUARDS SNAP INTO TANKS', *Daily Herald*, 1942.
Bennett, David, 'A Bridge Too Far: The Canadian Role in the Evacuation of the British 1st Airborne Division from Arnhem-Oosterbeek, September 1944', *Canadian Military Journal*, Winter 2005–2006, 95–102.
Breitmeyer, Brigadier A.N., 'Operation Market Garden – The Bigger Picture', *The Guards Magazine*, Winter 1997, pp.225–228.
Buckley, John, 'Tackling the Tiger: The Development of British Armoured Doctrine for Normandy 1944', *The Journal of Military History*, 2010, 74, 1161–1184.
——, 'Victory and Defeat? Perceptions of the British Army in North-west Europe, 1944–1945', *Global War Studies*, 2013, 10, 76–97.
Burdett, Peter, "They Were Not Divided', *Coatbridge Leader*, 10 June 1950.
——, 'The First Week of a Thrilling New Serial "They Were Not Divided"', *The Leven Mail*, 23 August 1950.
'Casualties in Manoeuvres – M.P.s Questions', *The Coventry Evening Telegraph*, 16 April 1942.
Clark, Major Frank, 'Sixty-Five Years On: Operation Market Garden Revisited', *The Guards Magazine*, 2010, pp.16–18.
Copp, Terry (1992) 'Fifth Brigade at Verrieres Ridge', Canadian Military History: Vol. 1: Iss. 1, Article 5. Available at: http://scholars.wlu.ca/cmh/vol1/iss1/5.
Dick, Charles J, 'The Goodwood Concept – Situating the Appreciation', *The RUSI Journal*, 127.1 (1982), 22–28.
Ebert, Roger, 'A Bridge Too Far', *Chicago Sun-Times*, 1977, www.rogerebert.com/reviews/a-bridge-too-far–1977 [accessed 12 September 2022].
Editor, The, 'The Film "A Bridge Too Far"', *The Guards Magazine*, 1978, p.2.
——, The, 'The Liberation of Brussels 1944', *The Guards Magazine*, Summer, 1984, pp.52–56.
Farrell, Theo, 'Improving in War: Military Adaptation and the British in Helmand Province, Afghanistan, 2006–2009', *The Journal of Strategic Studies*, 33.4, 567–94.
Field, Frank, 'Obituary: Lord Bonham-Carter', *Independent*, 1994, www.independent.co.uk/news/people/obituary-lord-bonhamcarter-1447274.html [accessed 20 August 2022].
Foley, Robert T., Stuart Griffin, and Helen McCartney, '"Transformation in Contact": Learning the Lessons of Modern War', *International Affairs (Royal Institute of International Affairs 1944)*, 87.2, 253–70.
French, David, 'Colonel Blimp and the British Army: British Divisional Commanders in the War against Germany, 1939--1945', *The English Historical Review*, 111.444 (1996), 1182–1201.

Gorman, Sir John, 'The Times of my Life: Cagny and the Tiger Royal', *The Guards Magazine*, Spring, 2004, pp.4–6.
Gow, General Sir Michael, 'Churchill and the Foot Guards in World War Two', *The Guards Magazine*, 1984, pp.2–5.
'Great Work by Guards Division: Armoured Charge on Modern Lines.', *The Aberdeen Evening Express* (Aberdeen, April 1945), p.8.
'Guards' Night Dash: Scots Rode on Top of Welsh Tanks', *The Scotsman*, 7 April 1945, p.7.
Haydon, Major General J.C., 'Obituary Major General G.L. Verney, DSO, MVO, Lately Irish Guards.', *The Guards Magazine*, 1957.
Head, Major. A., 'The Guards Armoured Division', *The Household Brigade Magazine*, Spring 1942, pp.13–14.
Heywood, Lieutenant A.G., "GOODWOOD", *The Household Brigade Magazine*, Winter 1956, pp.171–177.
Heywood, Brigadier A.G., 'A Duel with a Tiger', *The Guards Magazine*, Spring 1995, pp.8–9.
'History of the Guards Armoured Division', *The Guards Magazine*, 1951.
Jackson, Ashley, 'The Evolution of the Division in British Military History', *The RUSI Journal*, 2007, 152, 76–81.
Jarymowycz, R.J., 'Der Gegenangriff Vor Verrieres: German Counterattacks during Operation 'Spring,' 25–26 July 1944', *Canadian Military History*, 1993, 2, 6.
Kayss, Sarah Katharina, 'Competent, Assertive, Athletic and Privileged? Britain's Future Army Officers', *Wavell Room: Contemporary British Military Thought*, https://wavellroom.com/2018/09/11/competent-assertive-athletic-and-privileged-britains-future-army-officers [accessed 31 May 2022].
LeJeune, C.A., 'They Were Not Divided', *The Sketch*, 26 April 1950.
Marsland Gander, L., '8th Battling Ahead in 'Quagmire' More Minefields and Demolitions, 1000 Prisoners Taken, Germans Rush Reinforcements from North Italy', *The Scotsman*, December 1943, p.5.
McKenna, A.T., 'Joseph E. Levine and A Bridge Too Far (1977): A Producer's Labor of Love', *Historical Journal of Film, Radio and Television*, 31.2 (2011), 211–27.
'More about the Rocket Barrage', *The Sphere Illustrated Newspaper*, March 1945, p.372.
Musketeer, 'The Campaign in North-West Europe – I: June–September 1944', *Royal United Services Institution. Journal*, 1957, 102, 197–210.
Musketeer, 'The Campaign in North-West Europe – II.', *Royal United Services Institution. Journal*, 1957, 102, 339–353.
Musketeer, 'The Campaign in North-West Europe – III: June, 1944–February, 1945 Some Aspects of Administration', *Royal United Services Institution. Journal*, 1958, 103, 72–81.
Otley, Desmond, 'The German Surrender to the Guards Armoured Division', *The Guards Magazine*, 2005, pp.157–160.
Paget, Lieutenant Colonel Sir Julian, 'The Capture of the Nijmegen Road Bridge', *The Guards Magazine*, 1978, pp.2–9.
Popple, Trevor, 'They Were Not Divided', *After the Battle* (Essex, 2006).
Rickard, John Nelson, 'The Test of Command: McNaughton and Exercise 'Spartan,' 4–12 March 1943', *Canadian Military History*, 8.3/3 (2012).
Samuels, Martin, 'Operation GOODWOOD – "The Caen Carve-Up"', *British Army Review*, 1990, 96, 4–13.
Scotter, General Sir William, 'A Role for Non-Mechanised Infantry', *The RUSI Journal*, 125.4 (1980), 59–62.
Stone, Duncan, 'Deconstructing the Gentleman Amateur', *Cultural and Social History*, 2019, 1–22.

Bibliography

The Grand Duke of Luxembourg, His Royal Highness, 'A Colonel's Story', *Guards Magazine*, 1999, pp.6–8.
'The New Army', *The Scotsman*, Wednesday 1 April 1942, p.4.
'The Sixth Guards Tank Brigade's Capture of Munster, Capital of Westphalia: British Guardsmen and Infantry of the U.S. 17th Airborne Division Conferring in the Heart of the City During Patrol', *The Illustrated London News*, 14 April 1945.
"They Were Not Divided", *The Brechin Advertiser*, Tuesday 31 October 1950.
Trefusis, Major R.J.R, 'The First Days of the Guards Armoured Division', *The Guards Magazine* summer edition, 1996, pp.76–77.
Verney, Major Peter, 'An Armoured Guardsman at War – Major General G.L. Verney, DSO, MVO, Grenadier and Irish Guards (Part Three)', *The Guards Magazine*, 2011.
Visser, Max, 'Organisational Learning Capability and Battlefield Performance', *International Journal of Organizational Analysis*, 24.4 (2016), 573–90.

Published Thesis

Cates, Major Sam, 'Why Was General Richard O'Connor's Command in North-west Europe Less Effective Than Expected?', (School of Advanced Military Studies United States Army Command and General Staff College Fort Leavenworth, Kansas, 2011).
Denny, Major Bryan E., 'The Evolution and Demise of U.S. Tank Destroyer Doctrine in the Second World War', (Faculty of the U.S. Army Command and General Staff College, 1990).
Hahn, Daniel A., 'The Process of Change: The British Armoured Division; Its Development and Employment in North Africa During World War II', (Master of Military Art and Science, U.S. Army Command and General Staff College, 1985).
Hart, Russell Allan, 'Learning Lessons: Military Adaptation and Innovation in the American, British, Canadian and German Armies during the 1944 Normandy Campaign', (Ohio State University, 1997).
Heginbotham, Eric, 'The British and American armies in World War II: Explaining Variations in Organizational Learning Patterns', (Defense and Arms Control Studies Program, Center for International Studies, Massachusetts Institute of Technology, 1996).
Jarymowycz, Roman J., 'The Quest for Operational Manoeuvre in the Normandy Campaign: Simonds and Montgomery Attempt the Armoured Breakout' (McGill University, 1997).

Unpublished Thesis

Beer, Mark Anthony, 'The Evolution of Operational Doctrine of U.S. Armored Forces, 1917–1942' (Kansas State University, 1988).
Denny, Major Bryan E., 'The Evolution and Demise of U.S. Tank Destroyer Doctrine in the Second World War' (Faculty of the U.S. Army Command and General Staff College, 1990).
Peaty, J.R., 'British Army Manpower Crisis, 1944' (London: University of London, 2000).

Online/websites

'A Bridge Too Far (1977)', *Box Office Mojo*, www.boxofficemojo.com/title/tt0075784/?ref_=bo_rl_ti [accessed 12 September 2022].
'Farewell to Armour: The Guards Lose Their Tanks', *The Guards Museum YouTube Channel*, www.youtube.com/watch?v=5jzYdBheYgg [accessed 7 August 2022].
Hicks, B. 'Memories of World War II (Part 2): With the Guards Armoured Division', *BBC WW2 People's War*.
www.bbc.co.uk/history/ww2peopleswar/stories/17/a2162017.shtml [accessed 28 July 2020].